[illegible] the Court in the [illegible] Mexican [illegible] this work is a [illegible] analysis that permits us to understand the [illegible] changes in the Supreme Court and [illegible] point [illegible] [illegible] Sánchez [illegible] and [illegible] Mexico and [illegible] in the field of [illegible] [illegible] analysis.

— [illegible] Sánchez, [illegible]

[illegible] the [illegible] by which the court has [illegible] the [illegible] phase as well as the court's decision-making [illegible] Mexican democracy. It [illegible] and [illegible] The results are compelling and [illegible] with practical implications for [illegible]

— [illegible] Chávez, [illegible]

JUDICIAL POLITICS IN MEXICO

After more than seventy years of uninterrupted authoritarian government headed by the Partido Revolucionario Institucional (PRI), Mexico formally began the transition to democracy in 2000. Unlike most other new democracies in Latin America, no special Constitutional Court was set up, nor was there any designated bench of the Supreme Court for constitutional adjudication. Instead, the judiciary saw its powers expand incrementally. Under this new context inevitable questions emerged: How have the justices interpreted the constitution? What is the relation of the court with the other political institutions? How much autonomy do justices display in their decisions? Has the court considered the necessary adjustments to face the challenges of democracy?

It has become essential in studying the new role of the Supreme Court to obtain a more accurate and detailed diagnosis of the performances of its justices in this new political environment. Through critical review of relevant debates and using original data sets to empirically analyze the way justices voted on the three main means of constitutional control from 2000 through 2011, leading legal scholars provide a thoughtful and much needed new interpretation of the role the judiciary plays in a country's transition to democracy.

This book is designed for graduate courses in law and courts, judicial politics, comparative judicial politics, Latin American institutions, and transitions to democracy. This book will equip scholars and students with the knowledge required to understand the importance of the independence of the judiciary in the transition to democracy.

Andrea Castagnola is a Post-Doctoral Fellow in the Comparative Politics Department at the University of Bergen and is Assistant Professor at FLACSO-Mexico. Her research focuses on judicial politics in Latin America and comparative politics.

Saúl López Noriega is Associate Professor at the Centro de Investigación y Docencia Económica (CIDE). He teaches courses on constitutional law and democracy, power, and media. His research focuses on issues of constitutional justice, democracy and constitutional courts, and media concentration.

LAW, COURTS AND POLITICS

Edited by Robert M. Howard, Georgia State University

In *Democracy in America*, Alexis de Tocqueville famously noted that "scarcely any political question arises in the United States that is not resolved, sooner or later, into a judicial question." The importance of courts in settling political questions in areas ranging from health care to immigration shows the continuing astuteness of de Tocqueville's observation. To understand how courts resolve these important questions, empirical analyses of law, courts and judges, and the politics and policy influence of law and courts have never been more salient or more essential.

Law, Courts and Politics was developed to analyze these critically important questions. This series presents empirically driven manuscripts in the broad field of judicial politics and public law by scholars in law and social science. It uses the most up to date scholarship and seeks an audience of students, academics, upper division undergraduate and graduate courses in law, political science and sociology as well as anyone interested in learning more about law, courts and politics.

1. The Dual System of Privacy Rights in the United States
Mary McThomas

2. Making Law and Courts Research Relevant
Brandon L. Bartels and Chris W. Bonneau

3. The Europeanization of Judicial Review
Nicola Corkin

4. The New Myth of the Court
The media, the court, and the misrepresentation
Rorie Spill Solberg and Eric N. Waltenburg

5. EU Treaties and the Judicial Politics of National Courts
A law and politics approach
Pablo José Castillo Ortiz

6. Judicial Politics in Mexico
The Supreme Court and the transition to democracy
Edited by Andrea Castagnola and Saúl López Noriega

7. Judicial Elections in the 21st Century
Edited by Chris W. Bonneau and Melinda Gann Hall

JUDICIAL POLITICS IN MEXICO

The Supreme Court and the transition to democracy

Edited by Andrea Castagnola and Saúl López Noriega

Routledge
Taylor & Francis Group
NEW YORK AND LONDON

First published 2017
by Routledge
605 Third Avenue, New York, NY 10017

and by Routledge
4 Park Square, Milton Park, Abingdon, Oxon OX14 4RN

Routledge is an imprint of the Taylor & Francis Group, an informa business

Library of Congress Cataloging in Publication Data
Names: Castagnola, Andrea, editor, author. | Lâopez Noriega, Saâul, editor, author.
Title: Judicial politics in Mexico : the Supreme Court and the transition to democracy / edited by Andrea Castagnola and Saâul Lâopez Noriega.
Description: Milton Park, Abingdon, Oxon ; New York, NY : Routledge, 2017. |
Series: Law, courts and politics | Includes bibliographical references and index.
Identifiers: LCCN 2016018325| ISBN 9781138697812 (hbk) | ISBN 9781138697829 (pbk)
Subjects: LCSH: Mexico. Suprema Corte de Justicia. | Political questions and judicial power–Mexico. | Judicial process–Mexico. | Democracy–Mexico.
Classification: LCC KGF2530 .J83 2017 | DDC 347.72/035–dc23
LC record available at https://lccn.loc.gov/2016018325

ISBN: 978-1-138-69781-2 (hbk)
ISBN: 978-1-138-69782-9 (pbk)
ISBN: 978-1-315-52061-2 (ebk)

Typeset in Bembo
by Taylor & Francis Books

CONTENTS

LIST OF ILLUSTRATIONS

Figures

Tables

ACKNOWLEDGMENTS

This book is the result of many years of work and collaborative research. The first version of the book was discussed in early 2013 at a special workshop organized at the Instituto Tecnológico Autónomo de México (ITAM). We are indebted for academic and financial support from the members of ITAM and from the Facultad Latinoamericana de Ciencias Sociales-México (FLACSO), who believed in the importance of this collective work and had given us their unconditional support during the first stages of this endeavor. We would also like to thank the students who joined us: Gustavo Marín Hernández, Daniel Murillo, and Franz Oberarzbacher, with Gustavo being the most loyal and long-lasting member of this team. We are also grateful for support from our current institution affiliations: Estudios Jurídicos at Centro de Investigación y Docencia Económica (Mexico), the Department of Comparative Politics at the University of Bergen, and the UiB-CMI Center for Law & Social Transformation (Norway), who since 2014 have been committed to this project. Finally, we have been extremely fortunate in having: Andrea, Francisca, Julio, Matt, Pedro, and Tom joining us in the enterprise for all this time.

CONTRIBUTORS

Andrea Castagnola holds a Post-Doctoral Fellowship in the Comparative Politics Department at the University of Bergen and is Assistant Professor at Facultad Latinoamericana de Ciencias Sociales (FLACSO) in Mexico. She holds a Ph.D. in Political Science from the University of Pittsburgh. Her research focuses on judicial politics in Latin America and comparative politics. Her work has been published in journals such as *Journal of Politics*, *Journal of Politics in Latin America*, and *Política y Gobierno*.

Tom Ginsburg is the Leo Spitz Professor of International Law at the University of Chicago, where he also holds an appointment in the Political Science Department. He holds B.A., J.D., and Ph.D. degrees from the University of California at Berkeley. He currently co-directs the Comparative Constitutions Project, a National Science Foundation (NSF)-funded data set cataloging the world's constitutions since 1789. His recent co-authored book, *The Endurance of National Constitutions* (Cambridge University Press, 2009), won the best book award from the Comparative Democratization Section of the American Political Science Association. His other books include *Judicial Review in New Democracies* (Cambridge University Press, 2003); *Administrative Law and Governance in Asia* (Routledge, 2008); *Rule By Law: The Politics of Courts in Authoritarian Regimes* (with Tamir Moustafa) (Cambridge University Press, 2008); and *Comparative Constitutional Law* (with Rosalind Dixon) (Edward Elgar, 2011). Before entering law teaching, he served as a legal advisor on the Iran–U.S. Claims Tribunal, The Hague, Netherlands, and has consulted with numerous international development agencies and governments on legal and constitutional reform.

Matthew C. Ingram Matthew C. Ingram is currently an Assistant Professor of Political Science, University at Albany, State University of New York. His research focuses on the justice sector and violence in Latin America and the Caribbean, primarily in Brazil and Mexico. He holds a law degree and a Ph.D. in Political Science, both from the University of New Mexico. Prior to joining the faculty at the University at Albany, he was a post-doctoral fellow at the Center for U.S.–Mexican Studies at the University of California, San Diego, and at the Kellogg Institute for International Studies at the University of Notre Dame. His book, *Crafting Courts in New Democracies* (Cambridge University Press, 2016) presents his work on the politics of subnational court reform in Brazil and Mexico. Other academic work has appeared in several peer-reviewed journals (e.g., *Comparative Politics, Latin American Politics & Society*, and the *Journal of Law, Economics, and Organization*) and in edited volumes.

Saúl López Noriega is Associate Professor at the Centro de Investigación y Docencia Económica (CIDE). He holds a Ph.D. in Political Philosophy and Constitutional Law at the Universidad Autónoma de Madrid (UAM). He teaches courses on constitutional law and democracy, power, and media. His research focuses on issues of constitutional justice, democracy and constitutional courts, and media concentration. His publications include: *Democracia, poder y medios de comunicación* (Fontamara-Konrad Adenauer, 2009); *El IFE frente a los medios de comunicación* (TEPJF, 2011); and *Libertades individuales y usos y costumbres: la tensión constitucional. Análisis de la sentencia Shilubana vs. Nwamitwa de la Corte Constitucional de Sudáfrica* (TEPJF, 2014).

Francisca Pou Giménez is Associate Professor at the Instituto Tecnológico Autónomo de México (ITAM) Department of Law in Mexico City. She holds a Ph.D. from the Yale Law School and teaches Constitutional Law and Comparative Constitutional Law. She was a law clerk to Justice Cossío Díaz at the Mexican Supreme Court from 2004 to 2011. She has written articles and book chapters on constitutional adjudication, fundamental rights protection, linguistic pluralism, and Latin American constitutionalism. Her current work focuses on constitutional change in contemporary Mexico including the study of: constitutional amendment dynamics; the judiciary institutional and procedural architectures; the transformation of judicial reviews; and the relations between internal and external sources of law.

Andrea Pozas-Loyo is an Assistant Professor at the Instituto de Investigaciones Jurídicas (IIJ)–UNAM (Universidad Nacional Autónoma de México). She holds a Ph.D. and an M.A. in Politics from New York University (NYU), and an M.A. in Philosophy from the New School for Social Research (NSSR). She teaches Legal and Political Theory both in law schools and in political science departments. Her current research interests are constitutional efficacy and change, both theoretically and empirically (in particular in Latin America). She has published on these topics in American journals, such as *Comparative Politics* and *Texas Law Review*), and Latin American and European journals and edited volumes.

Julio Ríos-Figueroa is Associate Professor of Political Science at the Centro de Investigación y Docencia Económica (CIDE), in Mexico City. He received his Ph.D. in Politics from New York University (NYU). His research on comparative institutions, constitutionalism, law and courts, and Latin American politics has been published in journals such as *Comparative Political Studies, Journal of Law, Economics & Organization*, and *Latin American Politics & Society*. He is author of the book *Constitutional Courts as Mediators: Armed Conflict, Civil-Military Relations, and the Rule of Law in Latin America* (Cambridge University Press, 2016), as well as co-editor with Gretchen Helmke of the volume *Courts in Latin America* (Cambridge University Press, 2011). He has been a Hauser Research Scholar at the NYU School of Law, Visiting Professor at the Juan March Institute in Madrid, and O'Gorman Fellow at Columbia University.

Pedro Salazar Ugarte is a Researcher and Professor at the Instituto de Investigaciones Jurídicas (IIJ)–UNAM (Universidad Nacional Autónoma de México). He obtained his Ph.D. in Political Philosophy from the University of Turin, Italy, and gained a B.A. in Law from the Instituto Tecnológico Autónomo de México (ITAM). His research topics are constitutional law, human rights, and democracy. He is a member of the editorial boards of *Isonomía* and *Teoria Política* and a frequent contributor to *Nexos* magazine. He has published *La democracia constitucional. Una radiografía teórica* (FCE/UNAM, 2006) and *Crítica de la mano dura* (Océano, 2012).

INTRODUCTION

Tom Ginsburg

Mexico's process of democratic reform since the early 1990s has been remarkable in many ways, and the increasing prominence of law and courts is certainly one of the most important. In the transition from a dominant-party authoritarian regime to a vigorous democracy, it is perhaps not surprising that the Mexican Supreme Court has become a much more important actor. Starting with the judicial reform which had been implemented at the beginning of 1995, and accelerating after the 2000 election that led to the first change in power in several decades, the court has emerged as an important actor in the Mexican political scene.

There has been a set of important interdisciplinary studies accompanying these reforms, integrating legal and political analysis, by Mexican and other academics (see, e.g., Ríos-Figueroa 2007; Magaloni 2003, 2006; Sánchez et al. 2011; Inclán 2009). This work is among the most varied and interesting anywhere in the field of comparative judicial studies, and the present volume is no exception. Using a wide array of methodologies, the authors here help elucidate the evolving role of the court in Mexico's democracy. The chapters deserve close scrutiny, not only by scholars of Mexico, but by others interested in understanding the role of courts and the dynamics of democratization. In this introduction, I briefly place the Mexican case in comparative perspective and then make some comments on the chapters that follow. Together, they make a major contribution to the literature on comparative judicial politics.

I

Let me begin by considering a paradigmatic democratic transition from authoritarian rule in recent decades. Such a transition, whether fast or slow, by definition involves the introduction of genuine political competition; it typically will also involve constitutional reform or even replacement. It may or may not involve some effort to come to grips with the past. And it will also be accompanied, almost certainly, by an increasing role for law and courts. Relative to the authoritarian period, courts are likely to play a more prominent role in the protection of rights in democratization; they may also occupy a more prominent role in resolving political disputes.

The expansion of rights and democracy is natural. Democracy, as we now understand it, requires the boundaries of a secure constitutional order to be effective. These bounds include defining the rules of the game and also providing for certain zones—embodied in constitutional rights—that the political process cannot touch. Democratization nowadays involves the articulation of rights, along with a machinery to protect them.

The creation of a constitutional court designed to serve as the institutional locus of constitutional review has been a major trend in many countries. Such a court will have the ultimate word on interpreting the constitution, and will naturally become deeply enmeshed in political life in the countries in which they have been set up. There are, however, many other kinds of institutions that have been set up to enhance rights protection, including human rights commissions, ombudsmen, and special chambers in the ordinary judiciary.

Besides the protection of rights, the general phenomenon of judicialization has meant that other courts are playing more central roles in resolving political disputes. Political conflicts, which in former days may have been resolved within the confines of a single party or junta, now spill out into the open and take legal form. Naturally, this means courts are confronted with various questions related to political transition, involving distributive questions, administrative justice, and the resolution of electoral disputes. It seems that many new democracies find themselves in the position of the U.S. as noted by Tocqueville in the early nineteenth century: scarcely any political or social dispute arises that does not find its way into the courts.

Courts have reacted to their new demands with a range of responses. One way to think about this is in term of the judicial role (Kapiszewski et al. 2013). Roles are constrained by institutional structure, but courts also have some power to articulate their own position in the democratic order, by virtue of the cases they choose to decide, their view of their own jurisdiction as expansive or limited, and the substantive decisions they take. In some countries courts have played a major role in the reform process itself. Other courts have been much more passive, waiting until deep into the consolidation process before exercising more authority. And a small number of courts have played a major role in defending the prerogatives of the ancient regime, defending the past against the future.

In short, democratization is generally accompanied by an expansion in the scope and level of judicial power. But that broad statement hides a good deal of variation, and so it behooves us to examine the dynamics in particular contexts.

In examining the role of any particular high court, we must take into account the institutional environment, the socialization and attitudes of the judges, and the responses to judicial power of other actors in the political system. For example, in Chile, as Lisa Hilbink (2007) has demonstrated, judges were very reluctant to expand their role, drawing on a long tradition of apoliticism. In South Africa, in contrast, both a tradition of judicial autonomy and the need for an effective commitment device led political actors to be quite willing to give the constitutional court a prominent place in democratic transition (Meierhenrich 2008). Political actors not only delegate powers to courts, they also react to it, and increasing political fragmentation can give the courts more room for maneuver. In this sense, democracy by definition provides more room for courts to shape their roles.

Time is another important dimension of analysis, as the comparative literature has helped us to understand that roles can change over time. There is some indication that, with democratic consolidation, Chilean courts are changing their ideas about their proper role (Couso et al. 2011). The Hungarian Constitutional Court, in contrast, played a major role in the early years of constitutional transformation but has since become much less active, as other political institutions have actively sought to constrain it. Taking into account the dimensions of role, institutional and political environment, and time can help us to understand why the courts act the way they do in any particular time and place.

II

Turning to Mexico, it is clear that, as in any democratic transition, the legacy of the past and the particular dynamics of reform have been especially important in shaping the present. During the authoritarian period, judges and justices, like other high officials in the country, were integrated into a system dominated by the Institutional Revolutionary Party (PRI). As is typical of dominant-party systems, courts were not particularly important in governance, though they were formally autonomous in the authoritarian pluralist regime. While formally endowed with the power of constitutional review, the Mexican Supreme Court decided only 55 constitutional controversies between 1917 and 1994, as Castagnola and Noriega point out in Chapter 3 in this volume. Courts relied on a kind of civil law formalism to keep within a circumscribed zone.

The late 1980s saw a period of reforms that gradually led to democratization (Magaloni 2006; Ríos-Figueroa 2007). As in many other democratizing situations, political reform was accompanied by judicial empowerment. However, the gradual nature of Mexico's political transition meant that institutional reforms to the court system did not come all at once, but instead were pursued episodically. Unlike most other new democracies in Latin America, no special constitutional court was set up, nor was there any designated bench of the Supreme Court for constitutional adjudication. Instead, the judiciary has seen its power expand incrementally. A major judicial reform in 1995 expanded constitutional jurisdiction and introduced a judicial council to insulate judicial appointments and administration from the political process; it also modified the structure of the Supreme Court itself. Further reforms in 1999 and 2011 along with several important decisions by the Supreme Court helped to develop the institutional framework. The 2011 reforms, reinforced in 2013, removed the longstanding limitation on the writ of *amparo* to having only legal effect on the parties to the case itself (so-called *inter partes* effect). This had posed a major limit on the policy-making power of Mexican courts, but the judiciary now has many of the basic tools necessary to play the paradigmatic role described above. Furthermore, the possibility of directly applying international treaties gives the judiciary a significant new arsenal.

Naturally judicial behavior has changed with democratization, and the contributions in this volume help us to understand the changes. Chapter 1, by Andrea Pozas-Loyo and Julio Ríos-Figueroa, shows how the transition has affected one very important but understudied area. As part of a broader comparative research project, they trace the evolution of the jurisdictional relationships between military and civilian courts, demonstrating how the recent period has witnessed a significant court-led reduction in military jurisdiction. This provides one example of what we might describe as a paradigmatic democratizing move by courts. The chapter uses this area of law to develop the idea of the judicial role beyond the earlier comparative literature, and thus makes a helpful theoretical contribution.

Still, despite major expansions in its role and power, there is an overall sense among the other authors in this volume that the capacity of the Mexican Supreme Court lags behind the greater role demanded of it, and that it reflects the growing pains one might observe in a much younger court. There seem to be many missed opportunities, and indeed, some risks for the court, should it be unable to meet the greater demands that accompany democratization. The analyses are thus worth paying close attention to.

Francisca Pou Gimenez's chapter (Chapter 5) is a powerful indictment of certain institutional deficiencies. In her lucid analysis, she first demonstrates that democratization led to the expansion of roles of the court and the tasks demanded of it. In addition to serving as the supreme court of appeal over a large federal judicial system, the Supreme Court plays a major role in judicial administration. This means that it has very limited time for *any* of its tasks. In this regard, she notes that the decision to retain a single Supreme Court rather than to set up a designated constitutional court on the Keslenian model turned out to be fateful. The court must be concerned with its own constitutional jurisprudence, with the management of a complex judiciary, and with deciding appeals from around the country. All this makes the docket somewhat unmanageable. In the transition to democracy, Mexico's court has been accumulating tasks without discarding any.

As if this were not enough, Pou's analysis describes many features of the court's operations that seem pre-modern. The continuing popularity among litigants of *ex parte* informal meetings with judges, and the practice of judges publicly announcing their decisions well before the decisions are formulated in writing are two central examples that will be of great interest to comparativists because they seem so unusual, and somewhat at odds with a paradigmatic rule of law system. The problems are not simply formal, though. Pou focuses on what she calls the "decisional fuzziness" that results: the lack of clarity as to what the court has actually decided.

In some contexts, of course, ambiguity can be strategic and advantageous. For example, Cass Sunstein (1995) has celebrated the merits of judicial decisions that are "incompletely theorized" because they may allow for evolution in the law. But the Mexican Court seems to have taken this a step further to make what we might call "incompletely formulated" decisions, in which commentators analyze the public announcements of individual judges rather than the final written *tesis* that only appears months later. While incompletely formulated decisions have the same political virtue of allowing different actors to read different things into the court decision, they have the vice of failing to produce any real jurisprudence, as Pou's recounting of the court's abortion decisions between 2008 and 2011 demonstrates.

These institutional inadequacies have consequences in terms of the court being able to develop a reputation among the legal community. Reputation is a central resource for the exercise of judicial power, and courts can make some choices about which audiences they want to focus on (Garoupa and Ginsburg 2011). Institutional factors matter too. The ordinary judiciaries in civil law jurisdictions tend to focus on the collective reputation of the court, leaving individual judges anonymous. In contrast, common law judiciaries, and constitutional courts generally, emphasize individual reputation. By moving to a system of individually announced opinions, the Mexican Supreme Court seems to be shifting its mechanism for producing reputation, and moving toward a greater reliance on the public. This shift is however incomplete. And there is a tension between the court's newfound ability to "go public" (Staton 2010), which allows it to appeal over the heads of professionals, and its core function of managing a coherent legal system that has a good reputation in the eyes of legal professionals. In the long run, the institutional weaknesses could limit the court's impact. Public popularity, the argument implies, will not be enough if the court does not have a solid reputation among core actors in the legal system.

Andrea Castagnola and Saul Noriega have two careful studies in this volume analyzing decisions by individual judges in over 1,000 cases between 2000 and 2011. In their first, Chapter 3, they grapple with the question of whether the Mexican Supreme Court is an effective mediator among powers, and answer in the negative. In their second, Chapter 4, they examine judicial behavior in rights cases, both in *amparo* cases and in those involving so-called constitutional actions.

As in the best empirical work, they discover some surprising facts about the pattern of judicial decision-making, which will come as a surprise even to seasoned observers of the Supreme Court. For example, they show that, in recent years, PRI-appointed justices are much more likely than are National Action Party (PAN)-appointed justices to uphold *amparo* claims. Overall, though, they find the court to be fairly conservative, and not particularly counter-majoritarian. Again, this seems consistent with the view of a court still trying to find its role, an ongoing task that is still incomplete.

The 2011 constitutional reforms focused heavily on human rights, re-articulating many of the fundamental guarantees in the constitution using this language. This suggests that there is social demand for the court to become known as a human rights body, rather than one focused on managing federalism. It is too early to say more than that any such change is still ongoing. Pedro Salazar Ugarte's study (Chapter 2) of strategic litigation lays out a theoretical account of the role of rights litigation. Rights litigation, he shows, goes to the core of the mission of courts in a constitutional democracy, especially in an era of internationalization of rights. He includes several fascinating case studies of litigation, but overall, thinks that the Mexican Supreme Court could do more. Again, one is left wondering whether the continued accumulation of tasks and roles—with all the expectations that accompany them—has simply stretched the court too thinly.

III

Judicial power is too contingent to make specific predictions about the particular directions the court might take or the timing of any shifts that might occur. One of the nice features of the chapters in this volume is that each takes a dynamic perspective, and the overall picture is of a court in transition. Much has changed in the last 20 years, and there are some signs that the court could continue to enhance its role, as one might expect from the experience of other courts in democratization.

One way to illustrate the issues at stake in Mexico today is to contrast two alternative visions for what the court might look like in, say, 2030. One vision is that of the 2011 human rights reforms coming to full fruition, and the court emerging as a major player in protecting citizens from the various threats to their rights from both government and private actors. In this view, a rich set of support structures, including lawyers, non-governmental organizations (NGOs) and the media, will work together with the court to form a kind of ecology for rights. Both court and social actors will play mutually reinforcing roles. Mexican society will emerge as a more just one.

There is, however, another less transformative vision. This is of a court that does not choose to seize the opportunity provided by the new jurisdictional and legal tools. Pressed by the weight of all its accumulated workload, the court will muddle through. In this view, the court would retain its focus as an appellate body in ordinary legal matters, perhaps with a specialty in adjudicating issues related to constitutional federalism. The political life of the country may remain much as it is today, albeit with some new challenges.

Which vision will prevail? What will the role of the court be in a decade or two? Implicit in some of the critique in this volume is the hope that the former vision will prevail, but one has the overall sense that the wheel is still in spin. Clearly, development of the maximalist, rights-oriented direction will require greater attention to the challenges of caseload and capacity identified above. It may also require further generational change among the justices, so that individuals with different role expectations take the bench. And it will require an academic community that continues to challenge the courts with rigorous studies of their performance, serving as a monitor on behalf of society. This volume is a fine example of such work.

References

Couso, Javier, Alexandra Huneeus, and Rachel Sieder (eds) (2011) *Cultures of Legality: Judicialization and Political Activism in Latin America.* New York: Cambridge University Press.

Garoupa, Nuno and Tom Ginsburg (2011) "Reputation, Information and the Organization of the Judiciary" *Journal of Comparative Law* 4(2): 226–254.

Hilbink, Lisa (2007) *Judges beyond Politics in Democracy and Dictatorship: Lessons from Chile.* New York: Cambridge University Press.

Inclan, Silvia (2009) "Judicial Reform in Mexico: Political Insurance or the Search for Political Legitimacy?" *Political Research Quarterly* 62(4):753–766.

Kapiszewski, Diana, Robert Kagan, and Gordon Silverstein (eds) (2013) *Consequential Courts.* New York: Cambridge University Press.

Magaloni, Beatriz (2003) "Authoritarianism, Democracy and the Supreme Court: Horizontal Exchange and the Rule of Law in Mexico." In Scott Mainwaring and Christopher Welna (eds) *Democratic Accountability in Latin America.* New York: Oxford University Press, pp. 206–305.

Magaloni, Beatriz (2006) *Voting for Autocracy: Hegemonic Party Survival and its Demise in Mexico.* New York: Cambridge University Press.

Meierhenrich, Jens (2008) *The Legacies of Law: Long-Run Consequences of Legal Development in South Africa, 1652–2000.* New York: Cambridge University Press.

Ríos-Figueroa, Julio (2007) "The Emergence of an Effective Judiciary in Mexico, 1994–2002." *Latin American Politics & Society* 49(1): 31–57.

Sánchez, Arianna, Beatriz Magaloni, and Eric Magar (2011) "Legalist vs. interpretivist: The Supreme Court and the Democratic Transition in Mexico." In Gretchen Helmke and Julio Ríos-Figueroa (eds) *Courts in Latin America.* New York: Cambridge University Press, pp. 187–218.

Staton, Jeffrey (2010) *Judicial Power and Strategic Communication in Mexico.* New York: Cambridge University Press.

Sunstein, Cass (1995) "Incompletely Theorized Agreements." *Harvard Law Review* 108(7): 1733–1772.

1

THE TRANSFORMATIONS OF THE ROLE OF THE MEXICAN SUPREME COURT

Andrea Pozas-Loyo and Julio Ríos-Figueroa

I Introduction

The objective of this chapter is to give a broad but systematic introduction to the roles the Mexican Supreme Court has played in almost one hundred years of functioning, from 1917 to 2013. We aim at presenting an account that incorporates the political *and* the legal perspectives on the work of the court, establishing a dialogue within the current literature on this high tribunal. We hope it will be of interest to both students and specialists, and that it will contribute to building bridges among scholars who study the Mexican Supreme Court from different fields of knowledge.

The last decade has seen an important increase in the number of studies devoted to analyzing different aspects of the Mexican Supreme Court.[1] In contrast to a not very distant past, these studies come from diverse disciplines in the social sciences and not almost exclusively from legal scholarship. For starters, there is now a series of richly descriptive empirical studies that unveil important issues and processes, such as how the justices are elected and how they decide cases (Elizondo and Magaloni 2010); how many and what type of cases the Supreme Court decides either in general (Bustillos 2009) or through specific instruments of constitutional review, such as the action of constitutionality (López Ayllón and Valladares 2009) and the constitutional controversy (Hernández 2011).[2] These studies have provided fundamental information on the Supreme Court and have called attention to the basic data we still lack on central issues.

There is also a series of political science studies aimed at explaining the behavior of the Supreme Court Judges emphasizing the effects of different kinds of non-legal constraints on the justices' decisions. In this vein, for instance, it has been shown that Supreme Court Judges began leveling the electoral playing field soon after the 1994 reform (e.g. Finkel 2003), which divided government in 1997 and increased the likelihood of decisions against the Partido Revolucionario Institucional (PRI) (e.g. Ríos-Figueroa 2007), and in which party turnover in executive power in 2000 also increased the likelihood of decisions of unconstitutionality (e.g. Magaloni et al. 2011). It has also been shown that since 1995 the Supreme Court has actively sought the support of public opinion in order to build its power and authority (e.g. Staton 2004, 2010). One of the central lessons of this political science scholarship is that the Supreme Court is a strategic political actor that has concentrated its efforts on arbitrating political conflicts, downplaying its role as protector of fundamental rights (e.g. Ansolabehere 2010; Helmke and Ríos-Figueroa 2011; Magaloni et al. 2011).

In part as a response to the shortcomings of political science work on the Supreme Court, and in part because of the increasing importance of the court's jurisprudence for policies and politics, legal scholars have begun to produce systematic jurisprudential lines on specific topics. This novel work (in Mexico) has produced specialized jurisprudential knowledge in areas such as criminal due process rights (e.g. Magaloni Kerpel and Ibarra Olguín 2008); the taxing capacity of the state and the just imposition of fiscal burdens (e.g. Elizondo and Pérez de Acha 2006); federalism (e.g. Caballero 2010); separation of powers and political representation (e.g. Carbonell and Salazar Ugarte 2006; Ibarra Cárdenas 2014); the scope and limits of sexual and reproductive freedom (e.g. Madrazo and Vela 2011; Pou Giménez 2010); and freedom of speech (e.g. Cossío, Hernández, and Mejía 2014). In terms of judicial behavior, of the central lessons of these studies is that the court is building—quite slowly, and in disparate and not always consistent ways—its understanding of the basic rules of the political game, and of the effective protection of fundamental rights.[3]

In sum, scholarship on the Mexican Supreme Court has made considerable progress in the last two decades. However, while we now have social science and legal analyses on the court these two perspectives remain isolated; they don't talk to each other. Because the Supreme Court is a key legal and political actor, we believe that it is much more fruitful to analyze its work from these two perspectives simultaneously. Moreover, we believe that each of these perspectives tends to embrace a misleading assumption that needs to be abandoned to account for the evolution and the determinants of judicial behavior in Mexico.

On the one hand, while most social science studies on the Supreme Court focus on the last two decades it is important to recognize that the court has been a key actor in Mexico's political life for a long time, though its role has changed across time and across issues.[4] Moreover, to understand the changing roles of the court it is crucial to analyze in detail its decisions on specific political problems, something that social science studies that focus on general patterns do not usually do in depth. On the other hand, contrary to what an important part of the legal scholarship implies, it is important to recognize that the decisions of the Supreme Court are often influenced by extra-legal factors and that these can be systematically accounted for. Justices are motivated both by their constitutional and by their political constraints and incentives. Because they are neither the Montesquieuan "mouths of the law," nor purely Machiavellian power seekers, we need a theoretical framework that enables an account that combines the political and legal perspectives.

In this chapter, we use a notion of "role" that enables an analysis of judicial behavior from these two perspectives simultaneously. In turn our empirical research has a diachronic structure and focuses on a single but highly relevant area of issue that we analyze in depth. We believe this structure, which is characteristic of jurisprudential lines (López Medina 2009), is particularly fruitful in showing the interaction of political and legal aspects of judicial behavior.

Specifically, we focus on the Supreme Court's jurisprudence from 1917 to 2013 on military autonomy, defined as the "military's decision making authority that ranges from education to intelligence gathering to human rights" (Pion-Berlin 1992: 84). We look at cases reaching court where some aspect of the military's decision-making authority is challenged, and then zoom in on the subset of those cases that deal with the scope of military jurisdiction.[5] This is a relatively small but privileged window from which to observe the dual legal/political nature of the Supreme Court because it captures the legal responses that the Supreme Court has given to a highly political question, as well as the ways in which the constitutional design of judicial institutions has affected the court's jurisprudence. Moreover, the trajectory of the Supreme Court's jurisprudence on military autonomy and the scope of military jurisdiction broadly also reflect its jurisprudence in other areas, such as rights protection and the arbitration of political conflicts. But, of course, a more specific analysis on particular issues will show variations in the timing, type, and direction of jurisprudential trajectories.

Our account is divided into three broad periods marked by important changes in the justices' roles that lead to three different responses to the legal question regarding military autonomy and the scope of the military jurisdiction. The three periods are:

1. From 1917 to 1940: In this period the Supreme Court Justices' role was largely that of *adjudicators*, therefore, their jurisprudence regarding military jurisdiction basically applied the quite restrictive scope established in Article 13 of the Mexican Constitution.
2. From 1941 to 1997: In this period the justices' role was that of *regime supporters* and their jurisprudence regarding military jurisdiction gave prevalence to an expansive Code of Military Justice over the constitution overlooking the explicit content of Article 13, and in this way protecting the interests of the military and the regime elite.
3. From 1998 to 2013: In this period the justices' role has had important transformations enabling them to function at times as *constitutional interpreters*. On military jurisdiction, this role has been played inconsistently but it is

possible to say that it became clearer with the jurisprudence produced from *ca.* 2009 onward.

Section II of the chapter is sub-divided into five parts. In the first, we briefly discuss different notions of "roles" and clarify the one we use here.[6] We also give a broad introduction to the military–civic relations in Mexico and to the issue of military autonomy and military jurisdiction in particular over the long period analyzed in this chapter. The second, third, and fourth parts deal with each one of the three periods we have just described. In particular in each part, we first present the roles of the Supreme Court Justices in that period in order to then discuss its jurisprudence on the scope of the military jurisdiction. Section III briefly concludes.

II Roles and military jurisdiction

II.I "Role": A definition

"Judicial roles" has been used in legal and social science studies on courts in different ways. Broadly speaking, we can identify two different conceptualizations of "judicial role." The first one, mainly used in social science studies, refers to the court's function or task in a particular political system or in a particular time such as a democratic transition (see Ginsburg 2012; Kapiszewski et al. 2013). Under this notion the collective agent who plays the "role" is the court. This notion is helpful to describe how the court, as an institutional agent, interacts with other institutional agents such as the executive and the legislative powers, or with other political actors such as the authoritarian and democratic forces, in a critical juncture. This notion is therefore often used as the dependent variable in studies that aim to explain why a given court played such and such a function in a certain period. While very helpful, this conceptualization is often loosely used, and not always explicitly and clearly defined.

The second notion of judicial role refers to the self-conception of individual judges' own task, i.e. the beliefs judges have over their function. This notion is often used as an independent variable to give account of judicial decisions (e.g. Hilbink 2007). This notion can of course also be used as a dependent variable in historical studies that ask: "Why do judges conceive their function the way they do?", or simply "How do specific justices conceive of their own task?" (Pozas-Loyo 2012b). This notion is also helpful, but it faces the challenge of capturing in a systematic way the often elusive judges' self-conceptions.

The conceptualization of "role" we use here shares the usefulness of the other two notions, while it evades the problems we have mentioned. In particular, it has an explicit and analytically clear definition the former lacks. And, unlike the latter, the full description of roles is provided by norms (legal and political) that are known in the political context analyzed (for more details on this notion see

Pozas-Loyo, 2012a).[7] In a nutshell, a role is an abstract description of an agent's or an object's expected function (Zambonelli et al. 2003; see Masolo et al. 2004) due to its position in a set of relations (see Davis and Barret 2002 and Pozas-Loyo 2012a). Examples of roles in this sense are: professor, wife, and president.

Political and constitutional roles are part of a subtype of roles called "statuses." A status is a role that carries powers, prohibitions, rights, requirements, and permissions (Knoke and Kuklinski 1982: 19). Hence, the complete description of an individual's political or constitutional role is the set of powers, prohibitions, rights, requirements, and permissions the specific role has in that political or constitutional system (Searle 2010: 102). For instance, the *constitutional role* of the Supreme Court Justice in Mexico can be fully described by listing all the powers, prohibitions, rights, requirements, and permissions the Mexican Constitution grants to justices. In this way we address the concerns regarding the fuzziness of the first notion of role and the elusiveness of the second.

In order to clarify our narrative we divide the Supreme Court Justices' roles into two parts: the constitutional role on the one hand, and the political role on the other. This analytic separation makes sense since the set of powers, prohibitions, rights, requirements, and permissions contained in the constitutional and the political norms can oppose or reinforce each other, and therefore separating them would enable us to account for the *de jure/de facto* interaction and its consequences for constitutional efficacy (see Pozas-Loyo 2012b).[8]

We can now provide clear definitions of constitutional and political roles:

1. A constitutional role is a status function whose complete description can be obtained in a written constitution. In the instance that concerns us here, it is the complete set of powers, prohibitions, rights, requirements, and permissions that the Mexican Constitution grants to the Supreme Court Justices.
2. A political role is the status function whose complete description can be obtained from the unwritten norms of the political system. So the powers, prohibitions, rights, requirements, and permissions present in the norms of the Mexican political system provide the full description of Supreme Court Justices' political role.

The usefulness of these definitions is that they provide the theoretical justification for focusing on the constitutional and political powers, prohibitions, rights, requirements, and permissions to give account of the roles the Supreme Court had in the three periods we identify.

II.II Civil–military relations and military jurisdiction in Mexico

Democratic civilian governments and their armed forces clash over how to subject the military to the democratic rule of law without jeopardizing its *esprit de corps* and its efficacy (cf. Agüero 1995; Barany 2012; Serra 2010). In other words, the construction of a "democratic army," an army that unconditionally supports democratic governance, involves striking a delicate balance between ensuring the loyalty of the military to the popularly elected politicians while simultaneously granting to the military sufficient autonomy and strength to successfully discharge its functions and execute its missions (Barany 2012). Conflict between civilian governments and the armed forces is thus inherent to democracy. Of course, these conflicts are more acute and more regular in countries undergoing regime transition and also where the armed forces are called upon to perform activities related to internal security, such as fighting against terrorism, drug trafficking, organized crime, and sometimes even regular street policing. As former Spanish Defense Minister puts it "striking a balance between controlling the military and maintaining discipline on the one hand, and inspiring motivation and necessary collaboration in order to construct and apply a new framework of relationships on the other, is one of the most difficult challenges in a period of consolidation of democracy" (Serra 2010: 153).

In the inherently tense relations between civilian governments and their military forces there can be a series of difficult outcomes. One extreme outcome is, to be sure, a military coup and the establishment of a military government. Another extreme outcome is a stable and workable military subordination to the civilian government. In between these two extremes, which in a pure form are rarely found, is where the tensions between these two actors need to be sorted out in a pacific way. In democracies, the peaceful solution of tensions is not enough and those solutions should also be compatible with certain principles, values, and laws. This is important because whereas a tense civil–military regime may not necessarily produce a coup or military intervention, they do have the potential to hollow out democracies. It is in this middle ground where the existence of institutions such as the Supreme Court can be helpful, or not, in accommodating the interests of both the military and the civilian government.

In the particular case of Mexico, within the time frame of this chapter the desire to build a working democracy as well as tense civil–military relations has been present since the revolution. The long period from 1917 to 2013 has witnessed interesting differences in regime types: a competitive but highly unstable democracy (from approximately 1917 to 1940), a hegemonic party authoritarian regime (from approximately 1941 to 1997), and a more stable democracy (from 1997 to date). To be sure, different ways to accommodate civil–military relations are intertwined with these three regime types. Interestingly, the roles of the Supreme Court, and in particular its jurisprudence on military autonomy and the scope of the military jurisdiction, also vary accordingly.

The military jurisdiction, *fuero militar* in Spanish, has traditionally been justified on the grounds that members of the armed forces require a separate body of law, prosecutors, and courts that take into account the specifics of their job in order to give institutional stability and legal security to its members. Even though this justification has merit, in places with a history of military interventions, military participation in public security within national borders, and executive dominance, military jurisdiction gave way to impunity and arbitrariness. In particular, a broad military jurisdiction became a blank check for members of the armed forces who had committed crimes that had nothing to do with their specialized mission, as well as a vehicle for repressing political opponents. In such places, members of the armed forces and executives got used to a very wide scope of military jurisdiction and usually resisted attempts to reduce it, judicially or otherwise. Mexico is not an exception.

What happened in Mexico when cases that challenged a decision made within the armed forces reached the Supreme Court? Figure 1.1 shows the so-called jurisprudential thesis (*tesis de jurisprudencia*)[9] by the Supreme Court (1917–2013) on military autonomy.[10] The constitutional organ can reject or amend a previous decision made by a military authority, which we code as "limiting autonomy," or rather uphold it, which we consider as "respecting autonomy." The most interesting finding in Figure 1.1 is that whereas during the limited democratic period of 1917–1940 there are more decisions restricting military autonomy, the opposite is true during the hegemonic party period (1941–1997). Figure 1.2 shows a similar pattern regarding so-called "conflicts of jurisdiction": whenever the

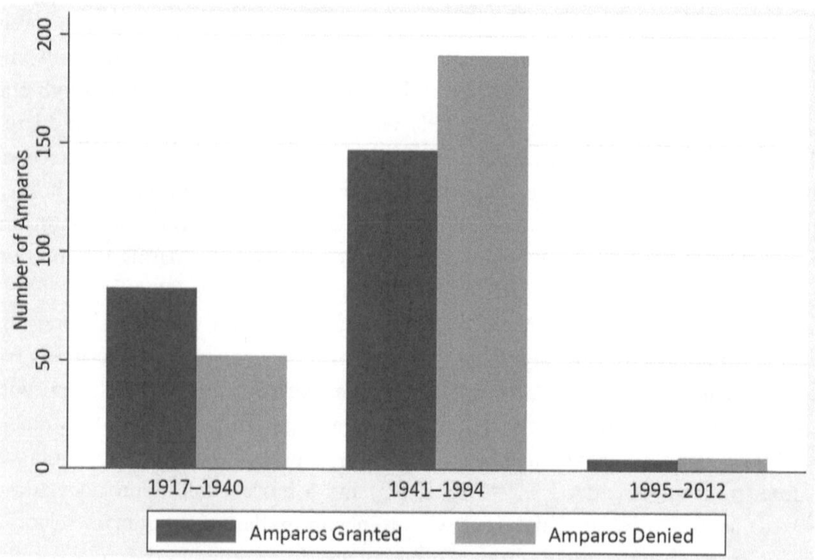

FIGURE 1.1 SCJN decisions on military autonomy, 1917–2012
Notes: The Supreme Court of Justice of the Nation (SCJN) can reject or amend a previous decision made by a military authority, which is coded as "limiting autonomy," or rather uphold it, which is coded as "respecting autonomy." The figure shows raw numbers. The percentage of "*amparos* granted"/"*amparos* denied" in the first, second, and third periods (respectively) are: 62 percent/38 percent; 43 percent/57 percent; and 48 percent/52 percent.

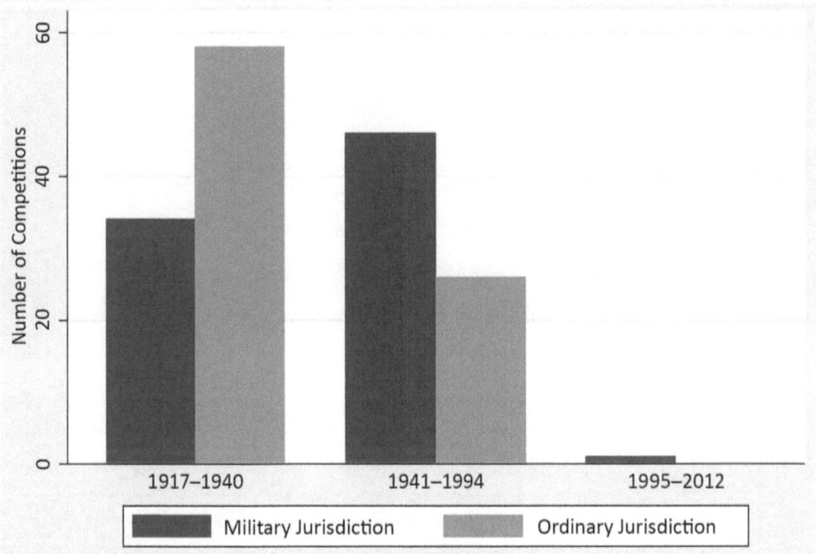

FIGURE 1.2 SCJN decisions on conflict of jurisdiction
Notes: The Supreme Court decides whether a given case should be sent to the military or to ordinary jurisdiction when such jurisdiction is contested. The total number of so-called *competencias* is 159. The figure shows raw numbers; the percentage of cases sent to military jurisdiction in period 1 is 37 percent, period 2 is 64 percent, period 3 is 100 percent; the corresponding percentages sent to civil jurisdiction are 63 percent, 36 percent, and 0 percent.

military jurisdiction was challenged as the appropriate forum for investigation and trial, the Supreme Court sent more cases to the ordinary jurisdiction in the first period, and more to the military jurisdiction in the hegemonic party period. In other words, in general Supreme Court's decisions follow the political context under which they were made.

Figure 1.3 shows the general trajectory of the Supreme Court's jurisprudence: from 1920 to roughly 1940, the court more often than not held a narrow scope of military jurisdiction but it progressively expanded its interpretation of Article 13 (see below); from around 1940 to roughly 2005, the court established a wider scope of military jurisdiction; and from 2005 to 2012, although there are relatively few *tesis*, apparently the court is moving toward narrowing the scope of military jurisdiction. Note the period from 1930 to 1960 when there were widely different interpretations of the proper scope of military jurisdiction which are reflected in inconsistent jurisprudence. Figure 1.3 also includes the constitutional response to the question on military jurisdiction that is the horizontal line situated at "AAFF for military crimes." Article 13 of the Mexican Constitution of 1917 establishes and delimits military jurisdiction. It clearly states that:

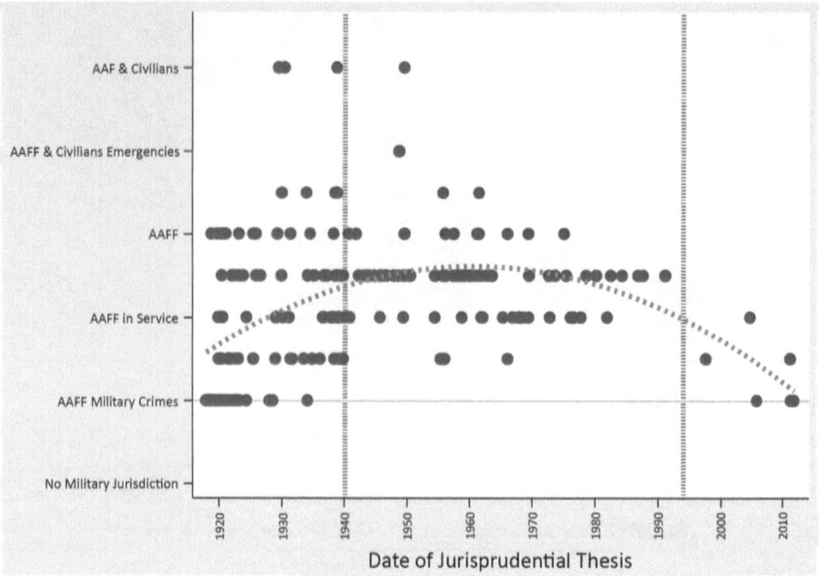

FIGURE 1.3 Scope of military jurisdiction, 1917–2012
Notes: Decisions by the Supreme Court on "Who can be judged in military courts, and under what circumstances?" For a better display, the vertical axis shows only even numbers. The red line displays a locally weighted regression on the data (lowest in STATA). The dotted blue line represents the answer to the question on the scope of military jurisdiction by the constitution of 1917.

> The military jurisdiction will deal with military crimes and offenses to the military discipline. The military tribunals never, and for no reason, will extend their jurisdiction to persons that do not belong to the armed forces. When a civilian is involved in a military crime or an offense to the military discipline, the case will be decided in the correspondent ordinary court (emphasis added).

It is apparent that the scope of military jurisdiction is defined very narrowly in the constitution. During the debates of the constituent assembly in 1916 some deputies even proposed to eliminate military jurisdiction altogether (González Oropeza 2006: 190). Article 13 is exactly the same today as it was in 1917, which makes it one of the few relevant articles that have not been changed in the more than five hundred amendments that the 1917 constitution has undergone. While Article 13 is quite clear and has remained constant, the Supreme Court's jurisprudence on the scope of military jurisdiction has fluctuated in important ways. This is one of the reasons why this issue is particularly fruitful for pinning down the extra-legal determinants of the Supreme Court's jurisprudential changes. In the remainder of the chapter, we present a diachronic analysis of the legal development of the scope of military jurisdiction, divided into three periods.

III Supreme Court Justices as adjudicators: 1917–1940

III.I Political context and civil–military relations

After years of armed conflict which started toward the end of 1910, the Constitutional Congress that convened in Querétaro produced the constitution that since February 5, 1917 is Mexico's fundamental law. Even though the enactment of the constitution signals the victory of one of the three main revolutionary factions, sealed with the appointment of Venustiano Carranza as president under the new rules of the game, the political scene until 1920 was marked by the successive elimination of the revolutionary leaders—Zapata, Villa, and Carranza himself who was assassinated in May of that year. The administrations of Generals Álvaro Obregón (December 1, 1920 to December 1, 1924), and Plutarco Elías Calles (1924–1928) are the ones that introduced relatively more regular politics after the so-called "armed phase" of the Mexican Revolution.

During the 1920s, however, the multiplicity of political forces continuously threatened to derail the already precarious post-revolutionary regime (Rath 2013: Ch. 1). In this context, the main threat to Obregón's administration came from within his own group, with General De La Huerta's rebellion which was successfully repressed in 1923. This paved the way in 1924 for the election of Obregón's favorite, General Plutarco Elías Calles, who presided over a period when other rebellions were crushed, and when the constitution was amended to allow for the re-election in 1928 of Obregón. Obregón won the election but was assassinated before assuming office.

To channel the diversity of political forces, and in the shadow of the assassination of the president elect, General Calles pushed for the creation of an umbrella political organization under the name of National Revolutionary Party (PNR, Partido Nacional Revolucionario, 1929) which would become the main vehicle for politics and governance for the following seventy years (see Garrido 2005). For a few years, Calles successfully led the party and became the "power behind the throne" who effectively selected and controlled successive presidents. But Calles's choice for presidential candidate for the PNR in the elections of 1934, General Lázaro Cárdenas, managed to sideline Calles forcing him into exile in 1936. During Cárdenas's presidency (1934–1940), the PNR (which became the *Partido de la Revolución Mexicana* (PRM) in 1936, and then the *Partido Revolucionario Institutional* (PRI) in 1946) was transformed and consolidated as a corporatist political hegemonic machine.

To the extent to which the revolution provided common ground for both civilian and military elites, it contributed indirectly to shaping and circumscribing the role of the armed forces (Serrano 1995: 428). Indeed, Obregón and Calles initiated a series of reforms intended to reduce the size and budget of the armed forces as well as to make them more professional. Both purged the armed forces of rivals, or perceived rivals, by retiring hundreds of generals, eliminating others, and bribing the rest. They cut the armed forces' budget almost in half. However,

Obregón and Calles also made progress in professionalizing the armed forces, creating the Commission of Military Studies (1926) and the Superior School of War (1929) (Díez and Nicholls 2006: 6–8).[12]

III.II The justices' role: Adjudicators

Let us start with the justices' *constitutional role* whose complete description, as we have said, is composed by the set of powers, prohibitions, rights, requirements, and permissions found in the original Constitution of 1917. According to this constitutional text, Supreme Court Justices were elected by a simple majority from the total members of both houses of Congress out of a list composed of one candidate submitted by each state legislature (Art. 96); they enjoyed life tenure (i.e. "during good behavior") (Art. 94),[13] and could be eventually removed only if a simple majority of the house of deputies initiated an impeachment process (Art. 109). The Supreme Court was at the top of judicial power, not only in jurisdictional terms through constitutional interpretation and court of cassation, but also because it was in charge of the appointment of lower court federal judges (Art. 97). Regarding the instruments for constitutional review, the Constitution of 1917 included the *amparo suit*, an instrument to protect constitutional rights from government violations with *inter partes* effects, and created the constitutional controversy, an instrument to adjudicate conflicts of constitutional competence between branches and levels of government (Arts. 103, 105–107). In sum, the constitution established independent Supreme Court Justices with powers to make decisions over governmental infringements of individual rights, as well as to become the arbiters of political conflicts.[14] In a nutshell, *de jure* judicial independence was quite considerable, and the *de jure* powers of the court allowed it to intervene at least moderately in the political system.

The *political role* of justices in this period was not clearly defined since the political system was extremely volatile and therefore there were no stable political norms defining the powers, rights, permissions, and prohibitions of justices. The crucial point in understanding judicial behavior in this period of a highly fractionalized political arena is that political roles in general were not consolidated and therefore the effectiveness of the justices' *constitutional* role was not threatened by competing incentives coming from their *political* role. In other words, the fact that the political arena was so unstable and fractionalized enhanced the efficacy of the justices' constitutional role for two reasons.

First, one of the main sources of constitutional inefficacy is what Robert K. Merton called intra-personal role conflict, which occurs when the mandates of a role conflict with those of another role (see Pozas-Loyo 2012b). As we will argue in Section III, to some extent intra-personal role conflict between Supreme Court Justices' political and constitutional roles accounts for judicial behavior between 1941 and 1997. But because the justices' political role between 1917 and 1940 had not by then been well defined, it did not challenge their constitutional role: constitutional incentives could motivate individual justices without being tampered with by informal political incentives (as happened in the PRI era). Second, the fact that the political arena was so fractionalized meant that the roles of other institutional actors were not stable either, inhibiting external political threats that could have blocked the efficacy of the justices' constitutional roles. In sum, given that the Supreme Court Justices' constitutional role made them independent arbiters of conflict, and given that they lacked a well-defined political role, we would expect their jurisprudence on military jurisdiction to follow the clear and explicit criterion established by Article 13.

Prima facie one could think that political fragmentation implies a greater degree of democratization, and that therefore this period was highly democratic.[15] However, it is important to note that the relation between fragmentation and democratization is not linear since extreme fragmentation can lead to political instability and actually damage the prospects of democracy. This arguably was the case in the volatile period that immediately followed the revolution, where the lack of consolidated parties and the rampant political violence rendered the possibility of consolidating democracy very slim.

III.III Jurisprudence on military jurisdiction

What did the Supreme Court do in cases related to the armed forces? When the armed phase of the Mexican Revolution ended in 1920 and some kind of regular politics started to operate under a vigorous multiparty system, cases on military jurisdiction began to arrive at the Mexican Supreme Court. And the court consistently upheld, in line with Article 13, a quite narrow scope of military jurisdiction. For instance, in a *tesis de jurisprudencia* of 1924, the court argued that "it is not enough that a crime has been committed by a member of the armed forces, because if it does not affect military discipline or the armed forces honor, or it was not committed during military service, it cannot fall under the jurisdiction of military tribunals" (Reg. No. 285 360).[16] This strict application of constitutional Article 13 was the norm during the period. The court does not usually provide further argumentation than simply restating the literal content of Art. 13 (e.g. Reg. No. 811 824; Reg. No. 290 730).

During those years, the court also clearly stated that civilians should not be tried in military courts. Again, the court more often than not simply restates Art. 13 without further argumentation: "military tribunals never, and for no reason, will extend their jurisdiction to persons that do not belong to the armed forces" (Reg. No. 290 340). The court again upheld a limited scope of military jurisdiction when facing the difficult case of military officers committing a crime with civilians as accomplices: presumably responding to the litigant's request that the military official should be judged in a military court and the civilian in a civilian court, the court decided that "the same civilian tribunal should decide the case, so that it is not split into two courts" (cited in Cossío 2010: 328).

The Supreme Court's narrow interpretation of the scope of military jurisdiction, in line with Article 13, was in general upheld until 1933–1934. During those years the Supreme Court also restricted, more often than not, military autonomy mostly in administrative matters. For instance, when an ordinary judge suspended a military court order to detain a soldier, the Supreme Court upheld the lower court's decision saying nothing more than simply "military discipline is not damaged simply by suspending a detention order" (Reg. No. 291 315).[17] These decisions were not welcomed by members of the government or by members of the armed forces. The governments of those years, led by Generals Obregón and Calles, were trying to discipline the armed forces while getting rid of rivals within them. For this political goal, a broad military jurisdiction comes in handy, in particular if the government has influence over the top echelons of the armed forces and, through them, over the military judges and prosecutors. But the Supreme Court consistently truncated these efforts upholding the spirit of the constitution regarding the narrow scope of military autonomy and of military jurisdiction.

Then the process of undermining the independence of the Supreme Court was launched, and its effects can be seen in the erratic, yet interesting, jurisprudence on military autonomy during the period 1934–1940. On the one hand, in an important thesis of February 12, 1934 (which is atypical because of its relative length, its argumentation, and the fact that it was a divided vote of 8–7), the Supreme Court sustained the criterion that when both military personnel and civilians are involved in a crime an ordinary court should decide the case (Reg. No. 279 328; see also Reg. No. 309 807, a thesis of August 30, 1939). But by the end of the period the court consolidated a striking criterion that had already appeared in 1933: when military officers and civilians are involved in a crime, the former should go to military courts and the latter to civilian courts (e.g. Reg. No. 815 803; Reg. No. 809 416), even though this was contrary to the basic rights of due process (i.e. of equality and unity of justice) and also created significant problems in practice. The court went further in expanding the scope of military jurisdiction when it held that civilians could be considered capable of committing military crimes (Reg. No. 310 173). It should be noted that despite the fact that the Supreme Court admitted the expansion of military jurisdiction from strictly military to service-related crimes, the court did establish some limits to what it meant to be "in service" excluding passionate crimes (Reg. No. 309 272), and those committed by drunk officers in a bar fight (Reg. No. 309 881).

To understand the erratic jurisprudence from 1934 to 1940 it is important to remember the political context. As Mónica Serrano puts it:

> while it is true that by 1940 the possibility of army officers securing control of the party was averted with the withdrawal of the military sector, it is also clear that between 1920 and the 1940s disagreements and differences

> regarding the selection of party candidates and institutional responsibilities continued to challenge the civilian-military pact.
>
> *(Serrano 1995: 433)*

The conflicts of competence between civilian and military courts, and the pressures that both sides exerted on the Supreme Court are nicely reflected in the jurisprudence produced during these years. At that time, the Supreme Court was in transit from being quite independent to becoming a functional institution of the hegemonic party system.

In conclusion, the period that immediately followed the Mexican Revolution was an unstable time when the political sphere was fractionalized into several groups all led by caudillos from the military. There were no consolidated political parties and the political system had not yet produced a set of informal political norms to stabilize expectations. These political conditions enabled a certain degree of constitutional efficacy, and justices' autonomy granted by the constitution was materialized in jurisprudence that upheld the constitutional limits of military jurisdiction creating discomfort among the armed forces. These decisions, which upset the "revolutionary forces" in government, were not isolated, since similar jurisprudential patterns can be found regarding challenges to the revolutionary labor and agrarian legislations produced by the regime (see, e.g., James 2006).

Toward the end of this period the need for an organization capable of coordinating all political–military groups was palpable. To that effect General Calles founded the National Revolutionary Party (PNR) in 1929. The PNR stabilized and centralized political power: heterogeneity of alliances within the military was no longer tolerated. This did not mean that the civil government and the armed forces were separate. In this period military power and political power were one and the same. This political transformation had negative consequences for the efficacy of the justices' constitutional role, in particular for their autonomy, as we will discuss in the Section II.III.

IV The Supreme Court Justices as *Regime Supporters*: 1941–1997

IV.I Political context and civil–military relations

From 1928 to 1934 Plutarco Elías Calles became the *Jefe Máximo de la Revolución*, the leader of the newly founded PNR who pulled the political strings behind the presidential seat. Things changed when General Lázaro Cárdenas, selected by Calles as the PNR candidate to the presidency and elected in 1934, managed to expatriate Calles and expel the *callistas* from his government. During General Lázaro Cárdenas's (1934–1940) administration, the party successfully integrated the army and the coordinated workers and peasants into its structure and changed its name in 1936 to *Partido de la Revolución Mexicana* (PRM). The PRM gradually became the single most important political machine in the country within which most decisions regarding "who gets what, when, and why" were made. A decade later, in 1946, the party became hegemonic and changed its name to *Partido Revolucionario Institucional* (PRI). That same year the first civilian president, Miguel Alemán, was elected (see Garrido 2005; Serrano 1995).

Cárdenas's incorporation of the organized peasants, workers, and the armed forces into the PRM secured stability for the nascent regime, simultaneously reducing the relative power of the army. Despite the resistance of the armed forces (Serrano 1995: 433), Cárdenas introduced further changes for disciplining and professionalizing them, such as dividing the Ministry of War and Navy into two autonomous defense ministries (the Ministry of Defense, which included the Army and the Air Force, and the Ministry of the Navy), enacting legislation barring serving officers from participating in any political activity, and expanding earlier efforts aimed at the progressive education and training of the forces.[18] By the end of Cárdenas's administration, "the Mexican armed forces had been weakened and brought under the control of the national party" (Díez and Nicholls 2006: 9).

In exchange for loyalty to the PRM, as well as to the revolution and to the "Revolutionary family," the armed forces were given an important degree of autonomy in both legal and real terms with regard to the military's internal functioning, training, and promotions, along with a high level of discretion in spending. The exchange of loyalty to the regime for military autonomy is, in essence, what scholars refer to as the "civilian-military pact" (e.g. Díez and Nicholls 2006: 10; Serrano 1995: 433). While the basis of the pact was established under Cárdenas, it was further developed and sustained in successive administrations. A cornerstone of this development was the election of Miguel Alemán (1946–1952) as the first civilian president of the PRI era.

Civilian supremacy, however, did not imply that the armed forces lost political influence, but rather that it was channeled through more subtle mechanisms, and often behind the scenes (Ronfeldt 1985). In fact, while the president of the republic has been a civilian since 1946, the president of the PRI was a member of the armed forces until 1964, when Carlos A. Madrazo was elected.[19] Moreover, from 1940 and until 1994 "the presence of at least one military officer serving as a Supreme Court justice was a constant" (Caballero 2010: 157–158).[20] Military officers have also held several seats in Congress since 1940, always elected under the PRI label (Díez 2008).

The armed forces were key actors in securing internal political order during the golden years of the PRI regime. Importantly, the armed forces intervened at the behest of civilian authorities and always on a temporary basis. This was the case in 1958 when they were asked to suppress a railroad workers' strike, in 1968 when they intervened to suppress a student movement, and indeed throughout the 1960s and 1970s when they were ordered to put down guerrilla uprisings, especially in the southern state of Guerrero (Díez and Nicholls 2006: 10). The basic exchange of loyalty for autonomy of the civilian–military pact remains to this day (February

2016), but with some important changes produced both by the transition to democracy and by the increase in non-traditional tasks performed by the military since the 1970s and especially since the 1980s (Díez 2008, 2012; Serrano 1995).

IV.II The Justices' Role: Regime Supporters

The constitutional and political roles of the Mexican Supreme Court drastically changed with the emergence of the hegemonic party because it was accompanied by changes that completely transformed the justices' powers, prohibitions, rights, requirements, and permissions. Let us start with transformation of the Supreme Court Justices' constitutional role.

From the aftermath of the Mexican Revolution, *ca.* 1920, until the consolidation of the hegemonic party regime, three important reforms—which took place in 1928, 1934, and 1944—altered the constitutional role of Mexican Justices. These amendments basically affected the appointment and tenure of Supreme Court Judges, and they had as one of their main goals curtailment of the autonomy of the Supreme Court to fit it into the political dynamic of the one-party system.

In 1928 a constitutional amendment augmented the number of Supreme Court Justices from eleven to sixteen and modified their method of appointment: instead of exclusive congressional appointment by a two-thirds vote, the reform gave the president the right to propose a candidate, subject to Senate ratification. In 1934 another amendment again increased the number of judges to twenty-one and transformed the original life tenure of justices into a six-year tenure coincident with the presidential administration. Ten years later, in 1944, life tenure was restored with an interesting caveat: the President of the Republic could initiate proceedings to remove a judge who exhibited "bad behavior." When the tenure was restored the justices' political role as key players of the hegemonic party equilibrium had already been established so that this increment in their *de jure* independence was no longer a threat to the interests of the party. In a nutshell, the creation and consolidation of the hegemonic system brought important changes in the constitutional role of justices that made them less independent, and therefore facilitated the consolidation of a new political role under which Supreme Court Judges were integrated to the one-party political machine (see: Magaloni 2003; Weldon 1997).

To understand the emergence and consolidation of the justices' new political role and the consequences it had for their decisions, let us first notice that the fragmentalization and instability of the political arena was one of the conditions that enabled the efficacy of the previous *Adjudicator* constitutional role. As political fragmentalization and instability disappeared and a new highly centralized political reality emerged, the government was able to respond to the independent judicial decisions that threatened its interests. In particular, the constitutional reforms described above were a reaction to the independent Supreme Court decisions during the 1920s that, according to the government, were delaying the implementation of the revolutionary program regarding, for instance, the expropriation and redistribution of land (see James 2006; Marván Laborde 2010). The Supreme Court decisions on military jurisdiction were also producing reactions from the armed forces, which were also being disciplined and weakened by president Cárdenas. Hence, the constitutional autonomy that the justices enjoyed in the previous period disappeared and they became another piece in the political board game of the hegemonic party.

However, the justices' constitutional role was changing, and by 1934 they had acquired the new political role of *Regime Supporters*. There are two central features to this new role. First, starting from 1933 and lasting until 1994 an important unwritten political norm was in place: to be part of the Supreme Court, justices needed to be affiliated to the hegemonic party (Cabrera Acevedo 1998: 145). Second, justices' tenure coincided with the presidential one. New presidents had the *de facto* prerogative to ask the justices to "move on." This was the case even with the restoration of *de jure* life tenure. From 1944 to 1994 most presidents appointed more than 50 percent of justices during their terms and almost 40 percent of the justices lasted fewer than five years, coming and going according to the presidential term (Magaloni 2003: 288–9; see also Caballero 2010).

Therefore, the political rule establishing a short length of tenure collided with the constitutional role establishing a longer one, making the latter ineffective. Note that this is a clear example of intra-personal role conflict (see previous section), where the political role undermined the efficacy of the constitutional one. To understand why justices accepted this political norm even after constitutional life tenure was restored is fundamental to understanding that the Supreme Court was only one of many offices through which the political elite continually circulated, so justices who left the bench often "moved on" to another institutional post, and the possibility for continuing in the "political circuit" required obedience to the norms of the system (see Magaloni 2003).

The description of Supreme Court Judges as *Regime Supporters* would be incomplete without a central element: the great power justices had (and to an important extent continue to have) within the judiciary (see Pozas-Loyo and Ríos-Figueroa 2011; see also Pou (Chapter 5 in this volume). This duplication of characteristics, the political role of the court being externally subordinated (i.e. vis-à-vis the president and the party) but internally dominant (i.e. vis-à-vis the judiciary), was typical of the way the hegemonic party operated. As we have seen it also applied to the armed forces and to many other corporations. While the heads of mayoral institutions were required to put up with the "stick" of external subordination, they could enjoy the "carrot" of internal domination that gave them great political and economic gains. Losing these gains increased the costs of breaking the system's rules.

Internal dominance was (and still is) a characteristic of the constitutional role of justices in Mexico. Since 1917 the Supreme Court has had control over the appointment and promotions of lower court judges, which has arguably promoted clientelist practices. It is noteworthy that in 1987 a constitutional amendment transferred power to the Supreme Court to control the material resources of the judiciary, including not only the budget, but also decisions over the number and jurisdiction of courts. These new capacities added to their already great administrative powers.[21]

Noting that the internal dominance/external subordination character of the Supreme Court was a consequence of the hegemonic party politics is important since it is the source of one of the central characteristics of the Mexican judiciary to this day: the Supreme Court's centralized administrative power. It is important to understand that even if democratization brought an end to external subordination it has not been able to break internal dominance. As we will discuss in Section II.III, such dominance has had negative effects on the judiciary's performance.

Finally, there was another series of reforms aimed at improving the administrative efficacy of the judiciary, by expanding the number of lower federal courts, to deal with the ever-increasing caseload. Two reforms are good examples of this trend. First, in 1951 a constitutional amendment approved the appointment of auxiliary judges to the Supreme Court and also created a new layer of circuit courts with the aim of reducing the highest court's caseload regarding *amparo* suits,[22] namely cases where an individual citizen challenges a state action based on the argument that a public authority had violated his/her constitutionally protected rights (see Caballero 2010: 149–152). In 1968, again to overcome the backlog, another reform decided to limit the Supreme Court's appellate jurisdiction and to transform the collegial circuit courts, which were doubled in number, into last courts of appeal for most cases (see Caballero 2010: 166–170).

IV.III Jurisprudence on military jurisdiction

The Supreme Court´s jurisprudence on military jurisdiction nicely reflects its loss of independence from the government. The place to start is the Code of Military Justice enacted in 1933, which in its Article 57 not only considerably expanded the list of crimes that could be decided in military courts (including, for instance, fraud, robbery, and assault) (González Oropeza 2006),[23] but also stated that service-related crimes committed by military personnel would be decided in military courts. Thus, the scope of military jurisdiction defined in Art. 57 of the Code of Military Justice is manifestly broader than that stipulated by Art. 13 of the constitution. What did the Mexican Supreme Court do? After resisting somewhat erratic jurisprudence from 1934 to 1940, the court interpreted the constitution in such a way that made the code constitutional. In other words, the court adapted the constitution to the code, instead of the other way around.

Regarding military autonomy, during this period there are several examples (actually the majority of *tesis*, as shown in Figure 1.1) where the Supreme Court upheld what had been done within the armed forces. This includes cases where the court relaxed some rights of due process, for instance regarding times of appeal or standards of evidence, for cases within military jurisdiction on the grounds of an ambiguous notion of military honor (e.g. Reg. No. 233 985; Reg. No. 235 275; Reg. No. 235 276; Reg. No. 304 493). There is also a thesis where the court defends the due obedience of a soldier even if he knows that obeying an order implies a crime (Reg. No. 295 749).[24] Of course, in the ambiguous nature of the authoritarian electoral regime of the PRI (Schedler 2013), there was room for the Supreme Court also to limit military autonomy, for instance, reversing a military court decision based exclusively on hearsay provided by an untrustworthy witness (Reg. No. 802 453), or a murder conviction made without an autopsy (Reg. No. 302 454). The court also sometimes granted the *amparo* against military courts whose composition violated some requirements (Reg. No. 300 502), and even granted one when the petitioner argued that his right of freedom of expression had been violated (Reg. No. 235 466).

Regarding the scope of military jurisdiction from 1940 onwards, the Mexican Supreme Court basically upheld a criterion based on the identity of the person involved in a crime: if the person belongs to the armed forces then the case comes under military jurisdiction. Some outrageous examples that were sent to military courts include a rape case based on the argument that it was a "crime against military honor" (Reg. No. 235 610); a case of a drunk officer "in service" who killed a civilian (Reg. No. 236 995); and a case where a military officer dressed as a civilian and while off duty killed another military officer for reasons unrelated to any kind of military service (Reg. No. 257 727). As with military autonomy, the "personal identity" criterion was sometimes attenuated by sensibly keeping some conducts and situations out of military courts, such as when the officer is on vacation (Reg. No. 235 143), or when a military officer killed the referee during a soccer game (Reg. No. 235 231). It is noteworthy that the court explicitly invoked the "personal identity" criterion as late as 1991 (Reg. No. 206 199).

In this electoral authoritarian regime it is not completely surprising that there are also many *tesis* in which when facing apparently identical situations the court reaches the opposite conclusion. For instance, sometimes being drunk is enough to consider that the military officer has abandoned his position (Reg. No. 234 522) but other times it is not (Reg. No. 245 676). Sometimes obedience to a superior officer is due even when the subordinate is off duty (Reg. No. 312 980) but not others (Reg. No. 313 404). Sometimes retired officers still enjoy the prerogatives of military jurisdiction (Reg. No. 315 464), but not others (Reg. No. 315 245). One possible explanation for these inconsistencies may be that the Supreme Court decided differently depending on the level and the political connections of the military official in question. For instance, in 1945 there was a case against the governor of Sinaloa, a military officer close to the then President Manuel Ávila Camacho, who was accused of murder. The National Secretary of Defense, none other than former president General Lázaro Cárdenas, who argued that the case should be tried in military courts, filed an *amparo* suit. In the end, the governor was granted the *amparo* and eventually set free (cited in Caballero 2010: 142).

V The Supreme Court Justices as *Constitutional Interpreters*: 1998–2013

V.I Political context and civil–military relations

One of the most interesting features of the PRI was its capacity to remain in power for more than seven decades (1929–2000). Through a series of gradual reforms PRI successfully adapted to changing conditions, both internal and external, while simultaneously holding on to power. These reforms touched on every issue of the political and social system. The electoral reforms since 1977 are the paradigmatic example of constant and hard bargaining between the PRI—which did not want to lose much—and opposition forces—which needed to gain enough—that made the PRI order possible during seventy-one years. There are three crucial dates in the gradual electoral decline of the PRI: 1988 when the PRI lost the two-thirds majority in the lower house and thus the capacity to unilaterally change the constitution; 1997 when the PRI lost the majority in the lower house of Congress; and 2000 when it lost the presidency.

The changing political circumstances since the 1960s, but especially those of the 1970s and 1980s, had an impact on civilian–military relations. In particular, several crises in Central America in the 1980s, the emergence of drug trafficking as a threat to national security, and the 1994 Chiapas rebellion changed the role of the Mexican military as they acquired responsibilities well beyond acting as guardians of the regime, and of the "revolutionary family." These new responsibilities were accompanied by a corresponding growth in the size of Mexico's standing army, influence on policymaking, especially regarding public security, distortions in the process of promotions, and the development of military industries (Díez and Nicholls 2006: 27; Serrano 1995: 439–442).

The military's involvement in combating drug trafficking has been particularly consequential. This involvement started in the 1970s, but accelerated in the late 1980s under Carlos Salinas's administration (1988–1994) when he declared drug trafficking to be an issue of national security, and involvement continued to grow under Presidents Zedillo (1994–2000) and Fox (2000–2006). Under the administration of Felipe Calderón (2006–2012) it acquired tragic proportions. It is possible to trace a parallel increment in the involvement of the armed forces in policymaking, in particular regarding public security: Since the Zedillo administration, for example:

> the Drug Control Planning Center (CENDRO), the Federal Preventative Police (PFP) and the National Institute to Combat Drugs have been

> headed by military officers, and the Center for National Security and Intelligence—Mexico's intelligence agency—increasingly has been run by the military.
>
> *(Díez and Nicholls 2006: 33)*

Perhaps the clearest example of increased penetration by the armed forces into civilian branches of government was the appointment in 2000 of Brigadier General Rafael Macedo de la Concha to be Attorney General, the first time in Mexico's history that a military officer has ever served in that office.

Increased involvement of the military in the anti-narcotics campaign also had a huge cost in terms of violation of human rights, especially under the Calderón administration. From 1999 until 2004 the National Human Rights Commission received 1,069 complaints of abuse perpetrated by the armed forces. In 2008 the number of complaints was 1,231 and during the first six months of 2009 the National Commission on Human Rights (CNDH) received more than two thousand complaints against the army (Díez 2012). The Inter American Court of Human Rights (IACHR) has also decided against Mexico in cases where the army is involved, most famously in the *Radilla* case.[25] In any event, the involvement of the armed forces in the "war on drugs" as well as in other non-traditional activities has been accompanied by increments in the military's size, budget, and influence on policymaking; but also by very mild reductions in terms of military autonomy.

The armed forces have continued to operate with significant autonomy and weak legislative oversight, especially in the area of promotions and of allocation of the internal military budget, both processes in which civilians are not involved despite the prerogatives of both houses of Congress to do so (Díez 2008, 2012). In this regard, it is noteworthy that a restriction on military autonomy, in particular on the scope of military jurisdiction, came from the IACHR in the *Radilla Pacheco* case in 2009, followed by the intervention of the Supreme Court in 2010 in response to *Radilla*, and especially with a series of decisions in related cases during the summer of 2012.

V.II The Justices' constitutional and political roles: Enabling constitutional interpretation

Let us start by accounting for the changes in the constitutional role. The key constitutional reform in this period took place in 1994 when the Supreme Court was delegated considerable powers of judicial review and its membership was reduced and renewed in order to increase its legitimacy and independence vis-à-vis the other branches of government (see, e.g., Fix-Fierro 2003). The 1994 reform substantially increased the judicial review powers of the Mexican Supreme Court Judges by creating instruments of both concrete and abstract control with the possibility of generating *erga omnes* effects, and granted justices an effective fifteen-year tenure. These changes transformed the constitutional role of Mexican

Justices, giving them new powers and, as we will see, the possibility of becoming *at times* constitutional interpreters.

These changes to the justices' constitutional role did increase their independence and their powers of constitutional interpretation. However, it is important to mention that access to the two new instruments of constitutional review created or strengthened in 1994 (the action of unconstitutionality and the constitutional controversy, respectively) was allowed only to political authorities such as political parties, representatives of the three branches of government, or a legislative minority. Ordinary citizens do not have the standing to use these instruments, and this is also true for most autonomous organs such as the Federal Electoral Institute (IFE) or the Federal Institute of Transparency and Information (IFAI).[26] Moreover, the other instrument for constitutional review, the *amparo* suit, was weak not only because of its limited, *inter partes,* effects, but also its *de facto* inaccessibility for ordinary citizens because throughout the years it had become technically complex and quite expensive (see Pou, Chapter 5 in this volume). This limited accessibility to the highest court has had important consequences. In particular it has filtered the type of cases that reach the justices and therefore has arguably limited the potential spectrum of their decisions, most importantly regarding rights.

By then the role of *Regime Supporters* was twofold. On the one hand, justices needed to respect the system's rules and withstand the "stick" of external subordination. The set of constitutional powers, prohibitions, rights, requirements, and permissions that supported this subordination disappeared with these constitutional reforms. On the other hand, *Regime Support* justices had another set of constitutional powers that increased the costs of insubordination: those that gave them dominance vis-à-vis the judiciary. These latter powers are largely still in place, and as we will argue have affected the efficacy of the former (see Pou, Chapter 5, in this volume).

Details of the evolution of the constitutional powers that granted the Supreme Court dominance within the judiciary are as follows. The reform of 1994 also created a judicial council to which was delegated the enormous administrative power formerly enjoyed by the Supreme Court, both in terms of the administration of the judiciary's budget and of the appointment of judges and the management of their careers. The political motives behind the creation of the council were, first, to make the constitutional jurisdiction the special focus of the Supreme Court, and second, to reduce the Supreme Court's corporatist management of judicial careers. According to former Justice Jorge Carpizo, Supreme Court Judges used to take turns to fill a vacancy at any level of the judiciary, and the new judge's career was overseen by his "mentor" on the court, so that after some time each Supreme Court Justice had his own loyal clientele within the judiciary (Carpizo 2000). Also, Supreme Court Judges protected unprofessional and dishonest judges whom they had mentored, reasoning that public scandals damaged the reputation of the entire judiciary.[27]

The judicial council was originally composed of a majority of judges selected by lottery, a method that effectively removed from the Supreme Court control over lower court judges and over the material resources of the judiciary. The Supreme Court did not like this and started to lobby strongly in order to regain control over the administration of the judiciary and of the judicial career (see Carpizo 2000; Fix-Fierro 2003). The pressure was successful: in 1999, after four years of interesting battling between the council and the Supreme Court, a constitutional amendment changed the mechanisms to appoint judicial council members (see Pozas-Loyo and Ríos-Figueroa 2011). In essence, the amendment transformed the selection by lot of judges from different levels into a direct designation by the Supreme Court of judges from the district and circuit courts. This effectively gave the Supreme Court control over the majority of seats in the council, which automatically gave back to it control over the material resources of the judiciary and the careers of lower court judges.[28]

In sum, during the PRI era, the Supreme Court's internal dominance and external subordination were two faces of the same coin. Transition to democracy brought an end to the court's external subordination but it has still been unable to break its internal dominance. This had, and still has, negative effects on judiciary performance for at least two reasons. First, it affects the Supreme Court's behavior because it takes up much time, focus, and energy from constitutional adjudication, which is its most important (still underdeveloped) task. Second, it arguably affects the performance of lower court judges because it enables and promotes clientelist relations, thus blocking meritocratic selection. Hence, the lack of change in the justices' dominance over the judiciary has maintained many of the clientelist political practices which characterized the judiciary in the PRI era (see Pozas-Loyo and Ríos-Figueroa 2011).

With changes in the justices' political role, the PRI lost its hegemony so that the justices' political role was obviously transformed. To start with, justices were no longer members of the party. Most of the judges proposed in 1995 by the president and confirmed by the Senate were the product of consensus between at least two political parties, the PRI and the right-leaning PAN (*Partido Acción Nacional*) (Magaloni et al. 2011). So, as opposed to what had happened previously, to be able to be part of the Supreme Court candidates to it should not be perceived as unconditional for the PRI.

The elite circulation system also became ineffective: when tenure of the Supreme Court finished, justices could no longer rely on "moving on" to other important political offices. This change arguably had very important effects on justices who arguably had started to become more concerned about their legacies. This and other political transformations of the party system changed the political role of justices: little by little many of the unwritten political norms of the PRI era became ineffective. Moreover, as political fragmentation increased, the political roles of all the institutional actors changed. The increasing political diversity in the legislative and executive branches, as well as in local governments, decreased the threat of retaliation to independent rulings.

In sum, since 1999 the justice system has concentrated much of its power on the Supreme Court, an institution that dominates the system combining functions of constitutional tribunal, last courts of appeal, court of cassation, and administrator. Nowadays the constitution gives justices the possibility of becoming true constitutional interpreters: their instruments of judicial review, their relatively high independence, their power to attract cases deemed "transcendent and important," and their capacity to oversee lower courts' jurisprudence and to resolve conflicts of interpretation open this door. However, as we have said, access to constitutional litigation is still very restrictive and justices are also the head of administration of material and human resources of the whole judiciary (indirectly, via its influence over the judicial council).

These features of the justices' constitutional role and the difficult and long-lasting process of shaping a new political role for a multiparty system have arguably delayed the efficacy of the role of constitutional interpreter. On the issue of the scope of military jurisdiction, constitutional interpretation began to crystalize in 2009.

V.III Jurisprudence on military jurisdiction

Since 1994 and until 2009, despite judicial reform, the Supreme Court mostly kept a deferential silence regarding military autonomy. During more than a decade after the reform of 1994, the most important decisions of the Mexican Supreme Court regarding military justice were a handful of *tesis* in which the court imposed some restrictions on what it considered military crimes for military jurisdiction (e.g. Reg. No. 195 107; Reg. No. 192 786); a few *tesis* respecting the autonomy of the military jurisdiction on procedural matters (e.g. Reg. No. 200 451; Reg. No. 200 540; Reg. No. 200 661; Reg. No. 198 706); and a highly consequential 1996 (Action of Unconstitutionality 1/96) decision where the court upheld the constitutionality of military participation in matters of internal public security (cf. Carbonell 2002; Pedroza de la Llave and Thalía 2011).

In the action of unconstitutionality 1/96 (which produced *tesis* Reg. No. 192 084; Reg. No. 192 083; and Reg. No. 192 082) the court established four conditions for the participation of the armed forces in internal public security: that a civilian authority ask for help, for a limited time, specifying the functions to be played by the armed forces, and without violating human rights. Whereas the conditions were sensitive and well-intended, the internal security crisis overwhelmed them. Cases of human rights violations by the armed forces piled up and increasingly made headlines (remember the figures of complaints filed before the National Commission of Human Rights: in 2008 only, more than a thousand). Meanwhile, for quite a long time the Supreme Court remained aloof. The most telling example of this is the "Reynalda Morales" case. The case is named after the woman who filed an *amparo* suit against a lower court that granted jurisdiction to a military tribunal over a case related to her husband's death by military officers. The Mexican Supreme Court dismissed the *amparo* arguing that Ms. Morales lacked the "juridical interest" in this case required to file an *amparo* suit, because she was not "directly affected" by the members of the armed forces.[29] This was in 2009.

The Reynalda Morales case also marks the beginning of a change regarding jurisprudence on military autonomy. Justice José Ramón Cossío wrote a dissenting opinion in which he basically argued for the unconstitutionality of Article 57 of the Code of Military Justice and proposed a radical jurisprudential change in military jurisdiction (Cossío 2010). The importance of this dissenting opinion lies in its close resemblance to a recent opinion by the Mexican Supreme Court, where the scope of military jurisdiction is interpreted in very narrow terms (the so-called "Radilla Case"). Interestingly, on the Radilla case the Mexican Supreme Court merely issued an opinion agreeing with the arguments of the IACHR that pointed to, among other things, the unconstitutionality of Article 57 of the Code of Military Justice (see Mejía Garza 2011).

During the summer of 2012 the Mexican Supreme Court issued a series of decisions upholding and even extending its holding in the Radilla case, arguing that cases of violations of human rights do not belong in military courts, and started to distinguish the types of cases that could properly be heard in them.[30] To illustrate the spirit of this jurisprudence, focus is on the case of Bonfilio Rubio (AR 133/2012). Bonfilio was killed by members of the armed forces at a military checkpoint in the state of Guerrero in June 2009. The military jurisdiction attracted the case but Bonfilio's relatives, his father and brother, with the assistance of some non-governmental organizations (NGOs) filed an *amparo* suit arguing that the case should be heard in an ordinary criminal court. The *amparo* was granted, the Ministry of Defense appealed this decision, and the case reached the Supreme Court.

The first interesting point is that, in contrast to the Reynalda Morales case, the Supreme Court did not argue that Bonfilio's relatives lacked "juridical interest" and thus did not dismiss the *amparo* (although a couple of justices argued that it should have been dismissed on those procedural grounds). Moreover, the court ruled that Bonfilio's case should be decided by a regular criminal court. But perhaps more importantly, in its decision the court declared parts of Article 57 of the Code of Military Justice unconstitutional, as it had already established in the Radilla opinion but this time in a decision with real jurisprudential value. The Bonfilio case, therefore, closes a long history that started during the 1930s when the Supreme Court disingenuously interpreted the constitution in light of the Code of Military Justice.[31] This jurisprudential change was clearly influenced by the so-called human rights and the *amparo* reforms.

During April and July of 2011, that is to say in between the Radilla and Bonfilio cases, yet another couple of important constitutional reforms that directly affect the Supreme Court were approved in Mexico. The first reform transforms the human rights regime in the country. First, it expands the catalogue of justiciable rights: the reform introduces into the constitution the term "human rights" instead of "individual guarantees," which is not merely a linguistic change because whereas "individual guarantees" are located in the first twenty-nine articles of the constitution, "human rights" can be found anywhere in the constitution or in international treaties.[32] Second, the reform changed Article 1 of the constitution, which now includes the wording that all Mexican citizens enjoy the rights established in the constitution and in international treaties ratified by Mexico, and that the interpretation of those rights should always be the most favorable for the individual.

While the reform of human rights is important in itself, its potential was considerably augmented by the simultaneous reform of the *amparo* suit: the individual instrument of constitutional complaints which is the main legal tool for the protection of rights in Mexico. This reform expands the accessibility, scope, and applicability of the *amparo*. Contrary to the old *amparo* which was accessible only for someone with a "juridical interest" in a case (someone directly affected by a public authority), the new *amparo* is accessible for anyone with a "legitimate interest," and it will be useful for filing so-called *acciones colectivas*, which are similar to class actions. Contrary to the old *amparo* which was only useful for challenging governmental acts allegedly violating one of the "constitutional guarantees" present in the first twenty-nine articles of the constitution, the new *amparo* will be useful for challenging government acts that violate any human right recognized by the constitution or by international treaties. Last but not least, effects of decisions with the new *amparo* are somewhat more easily generalizable to a set of people beyond the parties in the case. The Supreme Court in the Bonfilio case was clearly influenced by human rights and *amparo* reforms. Whether these recent reforms will actually produce a broader "rights revolution" in the country remains to be seen.

VI Conclusion

We argued that the dual legal/political nature of the Supreme Court should be analyzed, to the fullest extent possible, from the perspectives of legal scholarship and the social sciences simultaneously. We presented a clearly defined notion of role that enabled an analysis of judicial behavior from these two perspectives. Our empirical research had a diachronic structure, and we focused on a single issue: the Supreme Court's jurisprudence on the scope of military jurisdiction from 1917 to 2013. Our analysis identified three periods in which the justices' political and constitutional roles changed in an important way, as did their response to the military jurisdiction question.

We chose to focus on the jurisprudence of military jurisdiction because this is a relatively small but privileged window from which to observe the dual legal/political nature of the Supreme Court. We thus believe that our findings—in particular the three roles that the Supreme Court has played in Mexico's recent history—are generalizable to other areas. But the timing of the Supreme Court's reaction to changing circumstances varies depending on the specific issue. For instance, the court's jurisprudence limiting the government on labor and agrarian *amparos* during the first period (1917–1940) is very similar to that on military jurisdiction (see James 2006). But while the court's jurisprudential change on military jurisdiction started to take shape in 2007, the role of constitutional interpreter is apparent much earlier in its jurisprudence on criminal process rights (*ca.* 2001) or in electoral cases (*ca.* 1997).

Finally, it is noteworthy that considerations about human rights (of both military officers and victims) appear in a consistent, yet still timid, way in the third period analyzed in this chapter (see Ginsburg's Introduction to this volume). This is due, in important part, to the restricted access to constitutional justice, simply because many rights violations cases do not reach the Supreme Court. But there are other factors that contribute to the poor performance of the court regarding rights protection, for instance, the weakness of the "support structure"[33] (see Epp 1998 for rights litigation in Mexico or the ideological and pro-judicial-restraint attitudes of some Supreme Court Judges [Magaloni et al. 2011]). Moreover, the fact that the Supreme Court is still "internally dominant" implies that, with its huge administrative load, Supreme Court Judges cannot concentrate on interpreting the constitution, providing persuasive arguments for their decisions, writing clear and concise sentences, and disentangling the abstract meaning of the rights clauses present in the constitution.

Whether the recently inaugurated Décima Época is characterized by the full enforcement by the court of human rights and *amparo* reforms is still unclear. On the one hand, some studies have documented a prudent but consistent change since about 2005 in the jurisprudence of the Mexican Supreme Court favoring the protection of, for instance, the right to privacy, some criminal due process rights, and the right to health (e.g. Madrazo and Vela 2011; Pou 2011; Magaloni and Ibarra 2008). On the other hand, the effects of the reforms will depend on how creatively and extensively litigants use the new *amparo* and how expansively judges interpret the "legitimate interest" standing in these suits. What is clear so far is that the new role of the Supreme Court as *interpreter of the constitution* now appears to have taken root. Debates are now around whether the court is interpreting the constitution well or poorly, rather than on whether or not it is the actor in charge doing that.

Notes

1 For a detailed review of socio-legal scholarship on Mexico, including the Supreme Court, see (Pérez-Perdomo 2012; Ríos-Figueroa 2012).
2 The Mexican Supreme Court itself has produced a database of its decisions at http://www2.scjn.gob.mx/alex/(accessed July 11, 2016).
3 An underlying, and not always explicit, explanation for the unsteady and incoherent jurisprudential construction is the traditional legal training, and socially conservative

ideology of some of the justices. Magaloni et al. (2011) show some evidence of the existence of these two dimensions, traditional legal training and conservative ideology, based on the frequency of voting coalitions in non-unanimous Supreme Court decisions. For a rich account on the causes of this "decisional fuzziness" see Pou Giménez (Chapter 5 in this volume).

4 As several authors have argued, understanding the role the Supreme Court played during the PRI era is fundamental not only for historical reasons, but also because without it one can hardly understand the structure of such central judicial instruments as the *amparo* and the legal paradigm that still shapes the constitutional understanding of several justices (Pou Giménez 2012).

5 Our analysis on this specific issue is based on Chap. 5 of *Constitutional Courts as Mediators*, a recently published book by one of the authors of this chapter (see Ríos-Figueroa 2016). We are grateful to the publisher for permission to draw on this chapter of the book, a previous version of which can be found in the Spanish edition of this volume.

6 The theoretical framework we present in this chapter, based on the concept of *role* (as we explain below), is more general than the one offered in Chap. 5 of Ríos-Figueroa (2016). Specifically, in Ríos-Figueroa (2016) the proposed theory of constitutional courts as mediators instantiates the three roles of the Supreme Court as arbitrators, delegates, and mediators (which, in the case of Mexico, correspond to the first, second, and third periods analyzed in this chapter). But a different theory could arguably instantiate in different ways the three roles for the court that we identify in this chapter.

7 While this chapter is merely descriptive, it is important to note that this notion of role can be used as an independent variable in explanatory studies.

8 Note that usually constitutional and political roles are not fully consistent, since in most places constitutional and political norms are not free from tensions.

9 A *tesis de jurisprudencia* is an authoritative interpretation of the constitution emitted by the Mexican Supreme Court. Jurisprudential *tesis* are short, law-like paragraphs or sentences, free of the facts of the case. While the ideal *tesis* contains a summary of the main argument made in the decision, the *tesis* are generally simple statements that make it difficult (sometimes impossible) to capture the legal reasoning that led the judges to reach that interpretation. The *tesis* are extracted from decisions on specific cases, and they constitute the relevant and obligatory interpretative guidelines of the constitution, the laws, and even the general principles of the law. This admittedly weird system of jurisprudence has its roots in Mexico's hybrid legal system, in place since the nineteenth century, combining features from Anglo Saxon common law and the European civil law systems (see López Medina 2009, 2011).

10 The database consists of 680 jurisprudential *tesis*, of which 507 come from *amparos* (individual constitutional complaints), 159 from conflicts of jurisdiction (between the ordinary and the military) that the Supreme Court resolves, and 14 from cases in which the Supreme Court solves conflictive interpretations of the same constitutional article or principle among circuit courts. With the help of Javier Zúñiga Ramiro we systematically and thoroughly searched the Supreme Court's database (IUS) for all cases on military jurisdiction and military autonomy. The full list of cases is available at http://www.investigadores.cide.edu/julio.rios/. If there are *tesis* not included in this database, we believe they would not alter the tendencies shown in Figures 1.1 and 1.2. Finally, this is a database of *tesis,* not decisions and there is no one-to-one relation between them. Moreover, the *tesis* deliberately omit facts and argumentation. Thus the *tesis* are used to establish general jurisdictional patterns, but when necessary the analysis in some parts of the chapter resorts to actual decisions.

11 This question establishes the "constitutional scenario," a factual question in which the interests of actors clash and whose answer requires an interpretation of the constitution (López Medina 2009: 154).

12 Important measures to professionalize and discipline the army actually started under Carranza, such as the reopening the Military College, the practice of rotation, the reduction in the number of troops, and the reorganization of the cavalry and infantry corps (Serrano 1995: 428).
13 Article 94 explicitly mentions that tenure during good behavior applies to those judges appointed after 1923. Those appointed in 1917 had two-year tenures, and the second cohort had a tenure of four years.
14 However, the role of adjudicator of political conflicts between levels of government was shared with the Senate, which enjoyed the power to resolve "political questions between branches of state governments" (Article 76).
15 As well as more democratic than the period since 1997 in Mexico during which we also observe political fragmentation but channeled through more stable institutional routes.
16 *Reg. No.* is the number with which the jurisprudential thesis cited is registered in the Supreme Court's Jurisprudence Database (IUS). The cited thesis can be accessed simply by writing down the reference number on the Supreme Court's website: http://sjf.scjn.gob.mx/sjfsist/Paginas/tesis.aspx?Tesis=Tesis (accessed February 18, 2015).
17 Apparently, the court did not grant preferential treatment to generals either. Tobler tells a story of General Escobar who was accused of not paying for a ranch and lost his case before the Supreme Court (Tobler 1971: 69).
18 At the same time, Cárdenas passed the Law of National Military Service establishing compulsory basic military training for 18-year-old males.
19 The presidents of the PRI during that period were Generals Sánchez Taboada (1946–1952); Gabriel Leyva Velázquez (1952–1956); Agustín Olachea (1956–1958); and Alfonso Corona del Rosal (1958–1964). Carlos A. Madrazo (1964–1965) was the first civilian president of the PRI.
20 "The case of Agustín Mercado Alarcón who joined the SCJN in 1944 and was there until 1967 is noteworthy. In 1969 another military officer joined the SCJN, Alberto Jiménez Castro" (Caballero 2010: 159).
21 The reform of 1987, however, by limiting even further the jurisdiction of the Supreme Court to "important cases" also signals the beginning of a new series of reforms aimed at empowerment of the Supreme Court as a constitutional tribunal. There was another important reform in 1982 that takes away from the president the capacity to initiate a removal procedure of Supreme Court Judges because of "bad behavior."
22 Especially those *amparos* filed against decisions of local judges, the so-called *amparo directo*. *Amparo* is sometimes translated as *habeas corpus* but it encompasses more than what this term implies in English. *Amparo* is more broadly an instrument of individual constitutional complaints.
23 The Military Code of Justice was published on August 31, 1993 by then President Abelardo Rodríguez who made use of extraordinary legislative powers delegated to him by Congress. The constitutionality of this executive unilateral publication was challenged in 2011, but the Supreme Court said its publication had been constitutional (with a dissenting vote by Justice Cossío, see Reg. No. 161 045 and Reg. No. 161 046).
24 The topic of what constitutes "due obedience" is raised in many *tesis* but the court does not develop a doctrine or even some rules on the matter (e.g. Reg. No. 233 978; Reg. No. 233 979; Reg. No. 234 162; Reg. No. 234 316; Reg. No. 234 306; Reg. No. 234 305; Reg. No. 235 077; Reg. No. 235 193, and Reg. No. 235 271).
25 *Caso Radilla Pacheco vs. México*, November 23, 2009.
26 The exception is CNDH, but only since 2006.
27 The corporatist logic within the judiciary reached its summit in 1993 when a former Supreme Court Judge was convicted on corruption charges in a case where circuit judges had liberated a defendant charged with the rape and murder of a little girl after

their "mentor" on the court asked them to do so in exchange for a sum of money paid by the defendant.

28 There is not much systematic information on the performance of the judicial council. Scattered data published in some analyses and by the council itself suggest that subordination of the council to the Supreme Court in 1999 had immediate consequences; see Fix-Fierro (2003: 235, 288) and González Compeán y Bauer (2002: 235).

29 A similar "deciding without resolving" strategy can be found in a constitutional controversy filed by the Mexico City mayor against the restriction placed by Mexico when ratifying the international treaty on forced disappearances (see Reg. No. 180 652).

30 The Supreme Court itself created a webpage on the topic in which it displays all the relevant materials, and holdings, on these recent cases. See http://fueromilitar.scjn.gob.mx/fm_jurisprudencia.htm.

31 In the series of cases on military autonomy that the Supreme Court decided in the summer of 2012 the focus was on violations of the rights of civilians. However, the court ignored potential violations of the rights of soldiers either by their superiors or by other soldiers.

32 The human rights reform also gives new powers to the CNDH. Among the most important are the power to investigate cases of grave violations of human rights and to give the results of investigations to prosecutors; the power of subpoena; the power to call on public security forces; and the capacity to demand detailed explanations from actors that fail to act according to the CNDH's recommendations.

33 The "support structure" refers to the existence of a network of lawyers, NGOs, and individuals who either litigate or contribute to finance litigation in favor of rights (Epp 1998: 2–3).

References

Agüero, Felipe (1995) *Militares, Civiles Y Democracia. La España Postfranquista En Perspectiva Comparada*. Madrid: Alianza Editorial.

Ansolabehere, Karina (2010) "More Power, More Rights? The Supreme Court and Society in Mexico." In Javier Couso, Alexandra Hunneus, and Rachel Sieder (eds) *Cultures of Legality. Judicialization and Political Activism in Latin America*. New York: Cambridge University Press, pp. 78–111.

Barany, Zoltan (2012) *The Soldier and the Changing State: Building Democratic Armies in Africa, Asia, Europe and the Americas*. Princeton, NJ: Princeton University Press.

Bustillos, Julio (2009) *La Justicia Constitucional En México. Análisis Cuantitativo de Las Resoluciones Judiciales En Materia Constitucional*. México City: IIJ-UNAM.

Caballero, José Antonio (2010) "Amparos Y Abogánsters. La Justicia En México Entre 1940 Y 1968." In Elisa Servín (ed.) *Del Nacionalismo Al Neoliberalismo (1940–1994)*. Mexico City: CIDE-FCE, pp. 45–73.

Cabrera Acevedo, Lucio (1998) *La Suprema Corte de Justicia Durante Los Gobiernos de Portes Gil, Ortiz Rubio Y Abelardo L. Rodriguez (1929–1934)*. Mexico City: Suprema Corte de Justicia de la Nación.

Carbonell, Miguel (2002) "El Rol de Las Fuerzas Armadas En La Constitución Mexicana." *Ius et Praxis* 8(1): 35–51.

Carbonell, Miguel and Pedro Salazar Ugarte (2006) *División de Poderes Y Régimen Presidencial En México*. México City: IIJ-UNAM.

Carpizo, Jorge (2000) "Otra Reforma Constitucional: La Subordinación Del Consejo de La Judicatura Federal." *Cuestiones Constitucionales* 2(2): 209–218.

Cossío, José Ramón (2010) "El Fuero Militar: Alcances Y Limitaciones." *Cuestiones Constitucionales* 22(2): 321–362.

Cossío, José Ramón, Omar Hernández, and Raúl Mejía (2014) *La Libertad de Expresión en las Sentencias de la Suprema Corte de Justicia.* Mexico City: Tirant-lo-Blanch.

Davis, A. and L. Barrett (2002) "Relations among Roles", Proceedings of OntoLex 02,9–16. Las Palmas, Canary Islands, May 27.

Díez, Jordi (2008) "Legislative Oversight of the Armed Forces in Mexico." *Mexican Studies/ Estudios Mexicanos* 24(1): 113–145.

Díez, Jordi (2012) "Civic-Military Relations in Mexico: The Unfinished Transition." In Rodric Ai Camp (ed.) *The Oxford Handbook of Mexican Politics.* New York: Oxford University Press, pp. 265–285.

Díez, Jordi and Ian Nicholls (2006) *I Challenges The Mexican Armed Forces in Transition.* Carlisle, PA: Strategic Studies Institute, U.S. Army War College. http://www.carlisle.army.mil/ssi (accessed May 11, 2013).

Elizondo, Carlos and Ana Laura Magaloni (2010) "La Forma Es Fondo: Cómo Se Nombran Y Deciden Los Ministros de La Suprema Corte de Justicia." *Cuestiones Constitucionales* 23(1): 27–60.

Elizondo, Carlos and Luis Manuel Pérez de Acha (2006) "Separación de Poderes Y Garantías Individuales: La Suprema Corte Y Los Derechos de Los Contribuyentes." *Cuestiones Constitucionales* 14(1): 91–130.

Epp, Charles R. (1998) *The Rights Revolution: Lawyers, Activists, and Supreme Courts in Comparative Perspective.* Chicago, IL: University of Chicago Press.

Finkel, Jodi S. (2003) "Supreme Court Decisions on Electoral Rules after Mexico's 1994 Judicial Reform: An Empowered Court." *Journal of Latin American Studies* 35(4): 779–805.

Fix-Fierro, Héctor (2003) "Judicial Reform in Mexico: What Next?" In Erik G. Jensen and Thomas C. Heller (eds) *Beyond Common Knowledge. Empirical Approaches to the Rule of Law.* Stanford, CA: Stanford University Press, pp. 240–289.

Garrido, Luis Javier (2005) *El Partido de La Revolución Institucionalizada (1928–1945).* Mexico City: Siglo XXI.

Ginsburg, Tom (2012) "Courts and New Democracies: Recent Works." *Law & Social Inquiry* 37: 720–742.

González Compeán, Miguel and Peter Bauer (2002). *Jurisdicción y democracia. Los nuevos rumbos del Poder Judicial en México.* Mexico City: Cal y Arena.

González Oropeza, Manuel (2006) "El Fuero Militar En México. La Injusticia En Las Fuerzas Armadas." In *Estudios En Homenaje a Marcia Muñoz de Alba Medrano. Estudios de Derecho Público Y Política,* 177–195. Mexico City: Instituto de Investigaciones Jurídicas – UNAM.

Helmke, Gretchen and Julio Ríos-Figueroa (2011) "Introduction: Courts in Latin America." In Gretchen Helmke and Julio Ríos-Figueroa (eds) *Courts in Latin America.* New York: Cambridge University Press, pp. 1–26.

Hernández, María Amparo (2011) *Suprema Corte Y Controversias Constitucionales. Análisis de Comportamiento Judicial,* PhD thesis, Club Universidad Nacional (UNAM).

Hilbink, Lisa (2007) *Judges beyond Politics in Autocracy and Democracy: Lessons from Chile.* New York: Cambridge University Press.

Ibarra Cárdenas, Jesús (2014) *La Construcción Judicial de La Democracia En México. Elecciones Y Representación Política En La Argumentación Constitucional 1997–2014.* México City: Fontamara.

James, T.M. (2006) *Law and Revolution in Mexico. A Constitutional History of the Amparo Suit and Social Reform during the Mexican Revolution.* Chicago, IL: University of Chicago Press.

Kapiszewski, Diana, Robert A. Kagan, and Gordon Silverstein (2013) *Consequential Courts: Judicial Roles in Global Perspective*. New York: Cambridge University Press.

Knoke, David and James H. Kuklinski (1982) *Network Analysis Quantitative Applications in the Social Sciences*. Beverly Hills, CA: Sage Publications.

López Ayllón, Sergio and Florencio Valladares (2009) "Las Acciones de Inconstitucionalidad En La Constitución Mexicana: Análisis Empírico de 12 Años de Ejercicio." *Cuestiones Constitucionales* 21(2): 175–212.

López Medina, Diego Eduardo (2009) *El Derecho de Los Jueces*. Bogota: Legis.

Madrazo, Alejandro and Estefanía Vela (2011) "The Mexican Supreme Court's (Sexual) Revolution?" *Texas Law Review* 89(7): 1863–1894.

Magaloni, Beatriz (2003) "Authoritarianism, Democracy and the Supreme Court: Horizontal Exchange and the Rule of Law in Mexico." In Scott Mainwaring and Christopher Welna (eds) *Democratic Accountability in Latin America*. Oxford: Oxford University Press, pp. 266–306.

Magaloni Kerpel, Ana Laura, and Ana María Ibarra Olguín (2008) "La Configuración Jurisprudencial de Los Derechos Fundamentales. El Caso Del Derecho a Una Defensa Adecuada." *Cuestiones Constitucionales* 19(1): 107–147.

Magaloni, Beatriz, Arianna Sánchez, and Eric Magar (2011) "Legalists vs Interpretativists: The Supreme Court and the Democratic Transition in Mexico." In Gretchen Helmke and Julio Ríos-Figueroa (eds) *Courts in Latin America*. New York: Cambridge University Press, pp. 187–218.

Marván Laborde, Ignacio (2010) "La Revolución Mexicana, 1908–1932." In Clara García Ayluardo and Ignacio Marván Laborde (eds) *Historia Crítica de Las Modernizaciones En México*. Mexico City: CIDE-FCE, pp. 1–40.

Masolo, C., L. Vieu, E. Bottazzi, C. Catenacci, R. Ferrario, A. Gangemi, and N. Guarino (2004) "Social Roles and their Descriptions." Proceedings of Ninth International Conference on the Principles of Knowledge Representation and Reasoning. Whistler, Vancouver, BC, June 2–5. Palo Alto, CA: Association for the Advancement of Artificial Intelligence (AAAI) Press, pp. 267–277.

Mejía Garza, Raúl (2011) "Jurisdicción Militar: Leyes Y Tribunales Especiales." In Supreme Court (ed.) *Sentencias de La Suprema Corte de Justicia de La Nación Desde La Perspectiva de Los Derechos Humanos*. Mexico City: Suprema Corte de Justicia de la Nación, pp. 801–838.

Pedroza de la Llave, Susana Thalía (2011) "La Reinterpretación Constitucional Del Fuero de Guerra O Militar En El Marco Del Estado Democrático." *Cuestiones Constitucionales* 25(1): 152–198.

Pérez-Perdomo, Rogelio (2012) *Gente Del Derecho Y Cultura Jurídica de América Latina*. Mexico City: IIJ-UNAM.

Pion-Berlin, David (1992) "Military Autonomy and Emerging Democracies in South America." *Journal of Comparative Politics* 25(1): 83–102.

Pou Giménez, Francisca (2010) "Género Y Protección de Derechos En México: Virtualidad Y Límites de La Jurisdicción Constitucional." In Juan Antonio Cruz Parcero and Rodolfo Vázquez (eds) *Debates Constitucionales Sobre Derechos Humanos de Las Mujeres*. Mexico City: Fontamara, pp. 45–101.

Pou Giménez, Francisca (2012) *Judicial Review and Rights Protection in Mexico: Assessing the Recent Amparo Constitutional Reforms*, http://papers.ssrn.com/sol3/papers.cfm?abstract_id=2210959 (accessed June 29, 2016).

Pozas-Loyo, Andrea (2012a) *Constitutional Efficacy*, PhD thesis, New York: New York University, Department of Politics.

Pozas-Loyo, Andrea (2012b) "Los Jueces Constitucionales Latinoamericanos Frente Al Espejo: Sobre La Procedencia de Juzgar La Constitucionalidad de Una Reforma Constituciona." In Adriana Luna, Pablo Mijangos, and Rafael Rojas (eds) *De Cádiz Al Siglo XX: Dos Siglos de Constitucionalismo En México E Hispanoamérica*. Mexico City: CIDE-Taurus.

Pozas-Loyo, Andrea and Julio Ríos-Figueroa (2011) "The Politics of Amendments Processes: Supreme Court Influence in the Design of Judicial Councils." *Texas Law Review* 89(7): 1807–1833.

Rath, Thomas (2013) *Myths of Demilitarization in Postrevolucionary Mexico, 1920–1960*. Chapel Hill, NC: University of North Carolina Press.

Ríos-Figueroa, Julio (2007) "Fragmentation of Power and the Emergence of an Effective Judiciary in Mexico, 1994–2002." *Latin American Politics Society* 49(1): 31–57.

Ríos-Figueroa, Julio (2012) "Sociolegal Studies on Mexico." *Annual Review of Law and Social Science* 8: 307–321.

Ríos-Figueroa, Julio (2016) *Constitutional Courts as Mediators: Armed Conflict, Civil-Military Relations, and the Rule of Law in Latin America*. New York: Cambridge University Press.

Ronfeldt, David (1985) *The Modern Mexican Military: Implications for Mexico's Stability and Security*. Santa Monica, CA: Rand.

Schedler, Andreas (2013) *The Politics of Uncertainty: Sustaining and Subverting Electoral Authoritarianism*. New York: Oxford University Press.

Searle, John R (2010) *Making the Social World*, New York: Oxford University Press.

Serra, Narcís (2010) *The Military Transition: Democratic Reform of the Armed Forces*. New York: Cambridge University Press.

Serrano, Mónica (1995) "The Armed Branch of the State: Civil-Military Relations in Mexico." *Journal of Latin American Studies* 27(2): 423–448.

Staton, Jeffrey K. (2004) "Judicial Policy Implementation in Mexico City and Mérida." *Comparative Politics* 37(1): 41–60.

Staton, Jeffrey K. (2010) *Judicial Power and Strategic Communication in Mexico*. New York: Cambridge University Press.

Tobler, Hans Werner (1971) "Las Paradojas Del Ejército Revolucionario: Su Papel Social En La Reforma Agraria Mexicana, 1920–1935." *Historia Mexicana* XXI(1): 38–79.

Weldon, Jeffrey (1997) "The Political Sources of Presidentialism in Mexico." In Scott Mainwaring and Matthew Soberg Shugart (eds) *Presidentialism and Democracy in Latin America*. Cambridge, MA: Cambridge University Press, pp. 225–258.

Zambonelli, F., N. R. Jennings, and M. Wooldridge (2003) "Developing Multiagent Systems: The Gaia Methodology." *ACM Transactions on Software Engineering and Methodology* 12(3): 317–370.

2

THE LAW AS POWER

Strategic litigation in Mexico

Pedro Salazar Ugarte

I

This chapter aims to identify the state of strategic litigation in Mexico at the beginning of the twenty-first century. It highlights the political and institutional conditions that make this kind of legal phenomenon possible and asks what role the Mexican Supreme Court of Justice should assume to support those conditions. Therefore, a series of definitions is given first, along with a characterization of this kind of advocacy. A theoretical reflection is then carried out about its potential importance in a constitutional democracy. The Mexican political and legal context in Mexico over recent years is reconstructed in Section III and finally, in Section IV, some cases of strategic litigation in Mexico are mentioned as examples. It is important to acknowledge that the selection of these cases was made with attention to their specific relevance to human rights' protection in Mexico. There was no statistical or exemplary selection of cases, nor do they pretend to be representative of other litigations. They are solely examples to illustrate the main ideas of this chapter.

II

Strategic litigation is located within the context of "public interest law." In other words, it falls under the category of actions dealing with the teaching and practice of law in a way that has impacted on the public sphere of a given society. Specifically, strategic litigation—as dealt with in this chapter—is placed within the sphere of the defense of human rights.[1] Some of the definitions proposed by scholars and activists on this matter are discussed below.

From a broad perspective, Luis Miguel Cano and Graciela Rodríguez (2007) hold that strategic litigation is:

> a subdivision of the group that makes up the paradigmatic defense of human rights. The scope of the latter is wider when it includes the protection of the fundamental rights that can be attained in ways other than through legal channels.[2]

In line with this definition, Diego R. Morales (2010) states that:

> strategic human rights litigation is a tool that has been used by victims, civil organizations and certain State agencies—like Public Prosecutor's Offices and Ombudsman's Offices—to protect human rights through the use of legal systems and international mechanisms in the (Latin American) region over the last 30 years.[3]

Meanwhile, in specific terms of protecting children's rights, Patrick Geary (2008) holds that strategic litigation:

> sometimes also called impact litigation, involves selecting and bringing a case to the courtroom with the goal of creating broader changes in society. [...] This means that strategic litigation cases are as much concerned with the effects that they will have on larger populations and governments as they are with the end result of the cases themselves.[4]

Finally, according to Juan Carlos Gutiérrez, Silvano Cantú, and Tatiana Rincón (2012), strategic human rights litigation "should be understood as the set of judicial activity actions aimed at guaranteeing the justiciability of human rights before national or international agencies, according to each case." For these authors:

> [T]he difference [between this and] classic legal activism lies in the development of new features for handling cases, as it seeks to incorporate international standards on human rights into court decisions, especially those found in treaties signed and ratified by the State.[5]

These definitions make it possible to identify the basic characteristic aspects of this issue. To begin with, we know that the defining trait of strategic litigation does not lie in the agency that promotes it. There can be diverse actors in this action: individual lawyers, civil society organizations, legal clinics, academic institutions, and even public or state agencies. Second, we know that the core issue of the type of litigation in question is human rights, which leads us to affirm that the ultimate and general aim of these actions is to protect these fundamental legal rights. However, there is another desired consequence that highlights an educational pursuit aimed at citizens in general: strategic litigation purports to tell citizens of the importance of rights and the potential value of the law as an instrument that offers them protection.[6]

Therefore, the search for an effect that transcends those actors involved in each specific case is another distinctive trait of this kind of litigation. It is thus inserted within the framework of actions directed at public interest. Some authors call this high impact litigation, and even assert that there are other modalities viewed as structural litigation.[7] Another characteristic component of this type of action is that judicial authorities carry it out. Therefore, it is possible to say that the instrument of action is the law, and the judicial branch is the ideal means for dealing with it. This implies recognizing human rights as justiciable rights (at least in the states that have adopted the model of a constitutional democracy). Finally, various authors concur in stressing that strategic human rights litigation has a national dimension, but is also carried out through international instruments and agencies.

In Latin America, there are various organizations specifically devoted to this kind of litigation. Such is the case of the Center for Justice and International Law (CEJIL) with central offices in four countries (the United States, Costa Rica, Argentina, and Brazil); the Centro de Estudios Legales y Sociales [Center for Legal and Social Studies] (CELS) in Argentina; the Comisión Colombiana de Juristas [Colombian Commission of Jurists] in Colombia; or the Myrna Mack Foundation in Guatemala.[8] There are also clinics at prestigious universities in the region (Diego Portales in Chile, Universidad de Palermo in Argentina, and Universidad de Quito in Ecuador, to name a few) that do this kind of litigation. Mexico also has this type of institution, as will be seen below: both non-governmental organizations (NGOs) such as the Asociación Nacional de Abogados Democráticos [National Association of Democratic Lawyers] (ANAD); the Centro de Derechos Humanos Miguel Agustín Pro Juárez [Miguel Agustín Pro Juárez Center for Human Rights] (ProDH); the Centro de Derechos Humanos de la Montaña "Tlachinollan" ["Tlachinollan" Mountain Center for Human Rights]; the Comisión Mexicana de Defensa y Promoción de los Derechos Humanos [Mexican Commission for the Defense and Advocacy of Human Rights] (CMDPDH); and FUNDAR Centro de Análisis e Investigación [FUNDAR Center for Research and Analysis].[9] There are also university clinics at institutions like the Centro de Investigación y Docencia Económicas [Center for Research and Teaching in Economics] (CIDE) and law firms like Litiga Olé devoted specifically to this field.[10]

III

Human or fundamental rights are the core element of what we call constitutional democracies. These systems adopt a model of political organization that aims toward two analytically different objectives: to *limit* political power, and to *distribute* it among citizens based on an effective guarantee of the fundamental rights of the people who form said community.

Individuals, as beneficiaries of these rights—especially those who have a citizen status—are the main actors of society and not only electors of their government. This demands people's participation in different venues (not only in government or representative bodies), as well as an attitude of constant vigilance and following up on the tasks of those managing life in society. To do this, there are mechanisms and institutions aimed at citizen participation and the accountability of the ruling class. Strategic litigation implies the use of citizen participation mechanisms that strive to exert influence on an especially sensitive and important issue like human or fundamental rights guarantees. It is a type of participation through law and differs, in this sense, from other forms of political participation while preserving a dimension that is unavoidably political. Legal cases are just one part of a broader action that involves a complex political strategy although the outcomes and effects of strategic litigation are inevitably uncertain for those who file said cases. The political aim of the action undertaken is upheld even though it is not possible to guarantee the success—or the specific significance—of the effects of the legal case. Political action frequently transcends and outlives legal disputes.

To understand the specific niche in which strategic litigation is incorporated as a form of citizen participation and its political–legal dimension, the basic structural design of constitutional democracies must be considered. These democracies are based on a complex design that basically includes—with the particularities and uniqueness of each country—the following institutions:[11]

a A—in most cases written—constitution is viewed as the supreme law of legal order and the contents of which is protected by a guarantee of constitutional rigidity. In theory, a constitution must be a clear, accessible document that brings together people's rights (substantive dimension) and also includes the blueprints of the state apparatus (organic/political dimensions). The constitutions of many Latin American countries have extended their substantive dimension to include international human rights treaties. The set of provisions set forth in the constitution and related treaties are known as a "constitutional block."[12]
b The core content of this type of constitution—in keeping with the classical definition set forth in the 1789 French Declaration, which states that "any society in which the guarantee of the rights is not secured, or the separation of powers not determined, has no constitution at all"—is, on one hand, the principle of the separation of state powers (in which the legislative branch plays a more important role than the executive branch in terms of creating collective laws and as the main holder of political representation while the judicial branch is the ultimate guarantor of the principle of impartiality and

the protector of the constitution) and, on the other, at its core, human or fundamental rights—to freedom, as well as social and political rights, both of which constitute the organic and substantive dimensions of a constitution.

c While the division of powers is an initial guarantee of rights, constitutional democracies have several institutions dedicated to this same purpose, ranging from institutes devoted to ensuring transparency in government administration to figures like ombudsmen with the specific task of providing non-jurisdictional protection of people's rights. These institutions are channels that enable people to protect their rights.

d As a guarantee of the content of the constitution as a whole (and of rights in particular), it makes provisions for judges to be in charge of the delicate task of performing the "constitutional review of the laws," in addition to the separation of powers and other legal and non-jurisdictional protection mechanisms. Known as constitutional justice, constitutional review is central to constitutional democracies and is usually performed by special tribunals or courts, but can also be the diffused responsibility of ordinary judges.

e The above implies that constitutional democracies have discarded the principle that characterized "legislative Rule of Law," which was based on the legislators' sovereignty. In a constitutional democracy, most policies (regardless of how far-reaching they may be) are placed under the constitution and decisions are subject to a review of constitutionality.[13] This is necessary so that fundamental rights can be genuine "trump cards"—to paraphrase Ronald Dworkin (1978)—opposite the political power of the majorities and of governments.[14]

f The democratic aspect of the model—the form of government—is manifest in "universal procedural values," which are the "minimum" institutions and procedures needed, according to Norberto Bobbio's theory (1999), that typify a democracy:

  i all adult citizens without distinction of any kind must be granted political rights;
  ii citizens' votes must carry the same weight;
  iii all holders of political rights must be free to vote according to their own views;
  iv citizens must also be free in the sense that there should be conditions to choose from among various solutions, that is, between parties with different and alternative programs;
  v in both elections and collective decisions, the majority rule must apply;
  vi no decision adopted by a majority should limit the rights of the minority, especially if the law in turn becomes a majority in terms of equal conditions.

The model works on the basis of balancing constitutionalism and democracy in a way that is fundamentally expressed in this series of institutions. The constitutional factor plays a very important role because it imposes limits on and connections between democratic government body decisions in order to position fundamental rights at the core of state actions. From this perspective, supporters of constitutional democracy declare that "democracy can only be justified if it is subjected to constitutional restrictions"[15] and human or fundamental rights are the guiding light of all public policies. In this aspect, citizen participation mechanisms like strategic litigation are incorporated and have significance. Enabling judges to expand human or fundamental rights guarantees contributes to the workings and consolidation of constitutional democracy. Making use of the law and having recourse to various institutions that guarantee these rights, litigants give life to constitutional democracy.

The specific topic of constitutional justice—which is one area of strategic litigation *par excellence*—deserves particular mention. Theoretical supporters of constitutional democracy, like Luigi Ferrajoli, Robert Alexy, or Ronald Dworkin, are resolute defenders of judges undertaking the constitutional review of laws. On the other hand, there are voices like those of Jeremy Waldron or Roberto Gargarella who warn that it is an elitist court institution that imposes unjustified restrictions on democratic participation and representation. Although this interesting discussion is not the object of this chapter,[16] it is true that—of interest to us now the primary role of constitutional review is to defend human or fundamental rights in the face of decisions made by the political majorities in office, or by public and private powers in general. To this extent, judges in a constitutional democracy play an important political role because they can impose their constitutional interpretation on the political majorities. Oftentimes, the purpose of strategic litigation is precisely to activate these counter-majority control mechanisms.

Most of the Latin American constitutions enacted in the 1990s and 2000s (and older ones like the 1917 Mexican Constitution) formally ascribe to democratic constitutionalism. The same applies to constitutions that were revived after military dictatorships (like the 1980 Chilean Constitution) and, despite their particular complexity, those based on the so-called "New Latin American Constitutionalism" (Venezuela, 1999; Ecuador, 2008; and Bolivia, 2009). In every case and despite certain key differences, each constitutional design contains human or fundamental rights and the corresponding institutions that guarantee these rights by including some kind of legal constitutionality review. Moreover, all the constitutional documents incorporate the rule of political democracy. Therefore, constitutional democracy is formally the model that prevails in most states of the region. However, looking at reality, authoritarian logic continues to prevail throughout the continent and human or fundamental rights are violated every day. In practice, the constitutional democratic model is still an unfulfilled promise. Latin America is a good reminder for two things: that institutional designs should not be confused with sociopolitical realities; and that the promulgation of laws is different from (and not always accompanied by) their enforcement. In *El perfil del hombre y la cultura en México* [Profile of Man and

Culture in Mexico],[17] Samuel Ramos (1934) gleans a phrase by André Siegfried that reminds us that this is an old problem in these lands:

> It is only in South American countries, where the Constitution is disregarded every day of the year, that one hears so much talk about it! Eminent jurists discuss with learning and knowledge the text of the law which politicians take so lightly. Apparently the majesty of the law is simply a matter of words.[18]

This applies to both the agenda of fundamental rights and the laws aimed at regulating access to and administration of power. Strategic litigation is presented as a tool for confronting and overcoming this gap between laws and facts. Under the implicit premise that law can be a powerful instrument to change reality, advocates of strategic litigation try to bring about decisions that have a structural impact on human rights protection. In other words, they try to make constitutional promises real for people's lives. This is an issue of justice because, as Amartya Sen (2012) said, "justice is ultimately connected with the way people's lives go, and not merely with the nature of the institutions surrounding them."[19] From this perspective, strategic litigation on human rights is a legal action with a political dimension and a vocation for social impact. Furthermore, it is an action aimed at consolidating constitutional democracies.

If we acknowledge that, as Norberto Bobbio would say, law and power are two sides of the same coin,[20] strategic human rights litigation emerges as proof of this in the field of citizen participation mechanisms. As Luis Miguel Cano and Graciela Rodríguez hold:

> [E]very time strategic litigation is initiated for the defense of human rights, an ordinary person can become a real factor of power just by using the power that the law and rights endowed to him or her to limit public and/or private powers that impinge upon those basic ones that any democratic regime should protect.[21]

The law, in effect, becomes an instrument of power to limit powers.

Experts in the field stress the need for legal actions—litigation, strictly speaking—with media actions and policies that enhance the impact of the legal action. This political dimension forms an essential part of the strategy characterizing this kind of action. As CELS (2008) points out:

> [A]central element in obtaining a positive result in legal motions—of strategic litigation—is the possibility of putting forward political issues along with judicial issues in such a way the solution of the legal case contributes to transforming the institutional deficiencies, State policies or social problems that gave rise to the claim.[22]

This gains significance if we underline that the institutional transformations sought are grounded because there are situations in which the law—and rights—are a dead letter; or legal uncertainty regarding human rights; or legal obstacles and/or policies for them to be effectively guaranteed; or a lack of knowledge or deliberate disregard of international standards on rights protection. It should be expressly noted that these transformations include situations in which the neglected rights are politically or economically charged, as in the case of social rights.[23]

In summary, strategic human rights litigation is a form of citizen participation—unlike other forms of civil political actions that can be aimed at influencing the design and practices of institutions that guarantee human rights—by using the law as an instrument to extend rights protection. By activating legal remedies or constitutional actions, those who set this kind of litigation in motion intend to push forward political action with high social impact that, due to the thematic nature of the action, can potentially contribute to the consolidation of constitutional democracy. Whether acting on a national level—before ordinary judges and/or national Supreme or Constitutional Courts or Tribunals—or on an international level—usually before the Inter-American Court of Human Rights in the case of Latin America, the litigants' objective goes beyond the case at hand and aims at influencing the creation of laws, interpretations, legal practices, and policies that enhance effective human rights protection. This often implies orchestrating a series of parallel actions—involving other social or political actors—that take place before, during, or after litigation. This is part of the strategy for bringing the case and its prosecution before the courts[24] and publicizing the outcome is a very important aspect of this.

IV

Institutional transformations in the political and judicial spheres have taken place in Mexico over the last four decades, making it possible to assert that—at least formally—the country adheres to democratic constitutionalism. In this context, strategic human rights litigation gains significance and can possibly exert influence. I believe it is a tool that is not aimed at democratizing a political system, but rather at consolidating a constitutional democracy. We will now look into some of the legal and material conditions that allow strategic litigation to play this role nowadays in Mexico.

IV.I

Mexico went from being a single-party system to a multi-party democracy owing to a set of electoral reforms that took place over the space of two decades (1977, 1986, 1990, 1994, and 1996), making it possible to have consolidated and competitive political parties, on one hand, and institutions and rules that process and allow competition, on the other.[25] While there have certainly been moments of intense tension and political crisis—simply recall, for instance, the 2006 post-election conflict—it is true that after a long period of hegemony of a single party, the fight for political power at all levels of government in Mexico in the twenty-first century takes place through citizen elections. Among other things, this has allowed for the alternation of power in executive positions—symbolically, the presidency of the Republic—and the presence of constant and growing plurality in legislative bodies. Hence, it can be said that Mexico has made the transition to democracy, which is the form of government currently in force in the country.

IV.II

Along with this political transformation, the country has also experienced in-depth legal transformation of its legal system.[26] Giving an account of this transformation helps to better understand the context that gives way to the emergence of strategic human rights litigation, as well as the obstacles and challenges it faces. To begin, we will focus on the dogmatic sections of the Mexican Constitution and their evolution. Ever since 1857, the constitution has included an extensive list of rights: the abolition of slavery (Art. 2), academic freedom (Art. 3), freedom of choice of profession (Art. 5), freedom of expression (Art. 6), the right of petition (Art. 8), the rights of assembly and association (Art. 9), freedom of transit (Art. 11), the abolition of hereditary titles (Art. 12), due process of law (Arts. 13 to 20 and 24), communications privacy (Art. 25), and right to private property (Art. 27). In fact, Article 1 sets forth the need to establish the "rights of man"—according to the terminology of said document—as the foundations for social institutions. This resolution would go on to be included in the text of the 1917 Constitution, which endorsed the obligation of "all the laws and all the country's authorities" to "respect and uphold the guarantees—which would be the term to be used in the human rights decades—granted by the constitution."

However, taking into account the organic dimension of the constitution—and rights guarantees in particular—we find that over a long period of time these were conditioned by other strategic needs of a state in its development stages. The prevailing political and legal culture in the country gave rights secondary status as "reflex actions" of the will of the state—following the public law tradition dominant in the German and Italian doctrine of the late nineteenth and early twentieth centuries. This tendency would have a highly significant negative impact on the 1917 Mexican Constitution's main contribution to modern constitutionalism: the inclusion of social rights (originally the right to land and the right to work) along with the rights of freedom, liberty, and political rights. This social element—most clearly set forth in Articles 27 and 123 of the 1917 Constitution—would become one of the most distinctive qualities that would make this constitutional document a global example. However in practice, these rights would be politically conditioned to the agenda of important actors and therefore considered "programmatic rights" or at least strategic principles of the ruling political project and not as binding legal laws. Basically, the justiciability of rights was ignored.

Accordingly, for a long period of time, the Mexican Constitution was a non-effective legal instrument: a set of laws inspired by a political movement and cloaked in emancipatory rhetoric that would be of no use in organizing a democratic, social, and liberal country, but to mask the authoritarian and unequal reality that characterized it. The national political culture would ripen the theory that social rights were not justiciable while the authoritarian attitude of the political system inhibited the enabling conditions of what we call strategic human rights. In practice, this went beyond the social agenda because liberal-tending rights were sequestered by the authoritarian political regime and political rights did not even have any formal remedy of protection.[27] In practice, the constitutionalized rights lacked effective observance and the possibility of going before the courts to demand that rights be guaranteed was not an option because there were no legal remedies to do so and because the judiciary itself operated under an authoritarian rule (due to both its dependency on the Executive Branch and the prevailing legal culture).

The same thing happened with other rights that, as time went by, would be incorporated into the constitutional text in the twentieth century. For instance, the right to information (1977), the right to work in a dignified and socially useful way (1978), the right to choose the number and spacing of children (1980), the children's right to physical and mental health (1980), the right of all people to health (1983), the right to family housing (1983), and the right to a healthy environment (1999). All of these rights entered the constitution under specific circumstances and served as a tool to overcome the political conflicts of the time, but were still without any effective guarantees. Especially since the possibility of demanding in court that rights be guaranteed was out of the question, during a long authoritarian period and the first years of democratization, law and justice were not tools that would make rights a reality. It is only necessary to observe that the rights protection mechanism *par excellence*—known as the *Amparo* Trial—had relative or exclusive effects for the person who filed it. Hence, the potential impact of this legal remedy was extremely limited, even in cases in which justice was sought and it was possible to obtain protection.

In the first decade of the twenty-first century, other rights were incorporated into the constitutional text, such as the right to non-discrimination (2001), the rights of indigenous peoples (2001), compulsory preschool and middle school education (2001), the prohibition of the death penalty (2005), the right of reply (2007), and the protection of right to personal data (2010). Some of these rights would be complemented by the creation of institutions that guarantee these rights, like the Consejo Nacional para Prevenir y Combatir la Discriminación [National Council to Prevent and End Discrimination] or the Instituto Federal de Acceso a la Información y Protección de Datos Personales [Federal Institution of

Access to Information and the Protection of Personal Data], but others would remain unregulated (like the right of reply)[28] or would simply be laws without any practical impact (like the two levels of compulsory schooling). However, over the years, the dogmatic section of the constitution certainly has been reinforced and, with it, the basic foundations have been set so that the Mexican people can make—politically and legally—claims regarding their rights.

This tendency was crowned with an important human rights reform in June 2011.[29] The potential scope of this constitutional process emerged in the shape of five strategic pillars: (a) extending the set of human rights; (b) broadening the concept of holding rights; (c) stipulating the obligations of the authorities; (d) strengthening (jurisdictional and non-jurisdictional) protection institutions; (e) accentuating the protection of rights in public policies.[30] The significance and potential scope of this constitutional process was embodied in Article 1 of the reformed constitution:

> In the United Mexican States, all individuals shall be entitled to the human rights granted by this Constitution and the international treaties signed by the Mexican State, as well as to the guarantees for the protections of these rights. Such human rights shall not be restricted or suspended, except for the cases and under the conditions established in this Constitution itself.
>
> The provisions relating to human rights shall be interpreted according to this Constitution and the international treaties on the subject, working in favor of the protection of people at all times.
>
> All authorities, in their areas of competence, are obliged to promote, respect, protect and guarantee human rights, in accordance with the principles of universality, interdependence, indivisibility and progressiveness. As a consequence, the State must prevent, investigate, penalize and redress violations of human rights, according to law.
>
> Slavery shall be prohibited in the United Mexican States. Any individual who is considered a slave in a foreign country shall be freed and protected by law by simply entering national territory.
>
> Any form of discrimination, based on ethnic or national origin, gender, age, disabilities, social status, medical conditions, religious beliefs, opinions, sexual orientation, marital status, or any other form, that violates human dignity or seeks to annul or diminish the rights and freedoms of the people is prohibited.

IV.III

I will discuss the significance and scope of this constitutional law below, but now to conclude the contextual panorama of the conditions that evolved to make strategic human rights litigation possible in Mexico, I will give a summary account of another series of reforms that are not centered on the dogmatic section, but on the organic dimension of the constitution. These reforms have made it possible to overcome—albeit gradually and still insufficiently—the ideological and legal obstacles that had led to rights having no legal recourse.

One turning point took place in the last decade of the twentieth century when the Supreme Court of Justice of the Nation (SCJN) acquired the powers of the Constitutional Court and attained an acceptable degree of autonomy from the other two government branches. In this way, constitutional review was perfected for laws that for a long time in Mexico had only come about through the *amparo* trial. But as mentioned above, it was a constitutional review without general effects or *erga omnes*. Hence, its scope was limited and its effectiveness weakened. Therefore, it was not wrong to say that constitutional justice, strictly speaking, was introduced into the Mexican constitutional system when the Supreme Court was granted the power to rule on unconstitutionality cases and constitutional disputes—with potentially *erga omnes* effects—through a legal reform implemented in 1987 and especially through the constitutional reforms that took place in 1994 and 1995.

At first, cases involving issues regarding constitutionality or requiring a direct interpretation of the constitution were placed in the hands of the Supreme Court. In 1994–1995, the court attained the power to handle both actions of unconstitutionality against "general laws" and constitutional controversies between different branches of the state. Thus, by being able to declare a law unconstitutional or rule on a controversy with general effects (with the vote of eight of the eleven justices), the SCJN was formally instituted as a Constitutional Tribunal. This established the regulatory bases that broadened the potential impact of constitutional controversies on human rights issues. Although its potential impact was closed off to litigants, since only institutional actors—legislators, general attorney's office, and political parties—could file actions of unconstitutionality, in 2006, it was opened to ombudsmen (known in Mexico as Comisiones de los Derechos Humanos [Human Rights Commissions]).

In terms of political rights, a specialized court with the constitutional powers to offer protection of these rights was created in 1996: the Tribunal Electoral del Poder Judicial de la Federación [Federal Electoral Court]. In this scope, the laws and interpretations of this judicial body began to make inroads for litigating cases that would expand the political rights of Mexican citizens. Furthermore, this process of institutional transformation to offer human rights guarantees was complemented in general by the creation of other institutions and the enactment of other procedural reforms, specifically the constitutional foundations for establishing a National Human Rights Commission in 1999 and similar bodies in the states that form part of Mexico. These non-jurisdictional institutions guaranteeing rights have become a channel for denouncing rights violations. As mentioned above, in 2006 these institutions attained the legal status to bring actions of unconstitutionality—against laws and international treaties that violate the rights recognized in the constitutional block—cases before the Supreme Court of Justice. Thus, they became institutions capable of initiating strategic litigation.

A few days before the 2011 human rights reform, an important constitutional reform was passed, changing the rules and scope of the *amparo* trial. This reform—along with secondary legislation passed in 2013—sets the basis for this rights instrument to truly become a legal tool with high impact,[31] something that until then had been structurally impossible. The new *amparo* that admits class action lawsuits and empowers any judge to carry out a constitutional review with potential effects *erga omnes*, in addition to its substantive basis on the human rights contained in the constitutional block, may become a powerful instrument to stimulate strategic litigation in Mexico.

Despite the existence of jurisdictional and non-jurisdictional institutions dedicated to guarantee rights and changes of the rules protecting these rights, it must be pointed out that there is some cultural resistance to change. Many Mexican judges at different levels of the judiciary—from state courts to the Supreme Court—still work under the old model in which state power has priority over people's rights. In this sense, these judges pose an obstacle to the legal feasibility and political impact of strategic litigation. In a way, as Ana Laura Magaloni (2007) observes, we have twenty-first-century institutions that are controlled by judges with a nineteenth-century mentality. A change in attitude is a necessary condition for human rights to begin to populate the national public sphere. The Supreme Court could play a vital role in this process, but it will only be possible if the composition of this collegiate body is changed. Judges with open minds toward the human rights agenda are needed and this type of judge cannot currently be found in the judiciary. Hence, renovation must come from without.[32]

IV.IV

Mexico's political transition and legal transition have come about together with other processes relevant to the topic at hand. One of them is fundamental and has also faced much resistance in the judiciary: the internationalization of the human rights agenda. Despite being a condition needed for advancing strategic litigation and despite the nationalism that prevails in the Mexican legal sphere, a gap has opened up regarding the possibility of taking Mexican rights violation cases to international levels—especially in the Inter-American Commission and Court. This was a process that led to the recognition of the contentious jurisdiction of the Inter-American Court of Human Rights in 1998 and the adherence to and ratification of various international human rights instruments. Natalia Saltalamacchia and Ana Covarrubias (2011) describe the evolution of this process as follows:

> Through the interaction of national and international factors over six decades (…), Mexico went from taking a defensive position to a proactive one before the international human rights system.
>
> (…)

> For human rights to become a priority in Mexico's foreign policy, a process must first be carried out for Mexicans to familiarize themselves with this model and adopt it as a lens to interpret their own political and social situation. This socialization of human rights in Mexico began in the 1980s, mainly led by civil society organizations, and spread to political parties and the ruling class.
>
> (...)
>
> [Moreover] the changes in Mexico's foreign policy coincided with transformations in the international order that boosted transnational human rights networks' capacity of influence.[33]

The background to this process partially explains the vein along which the human rights reform was approved in 2011. Even though it stems from a national political process driven by activists and academics, the reform clearly shows strong international guidance. It is quite fitting to maintain that the touchstones of all the modifications made to the Mexican Constitution are criteria, principles, and institutions which guarantee human rights that have evolved under the domain of international organizations; and this can only be explained by the process described by Saltalamacchia and Covarrubias (2011). It also involves important transformations in legal activities that in turn offer enormous potential for the issue at hand, but have run up against strong resistance from the judiciary and Mexican lawyers. Once again, because of its institutional standing and the public visibility of its decisions, the Supreme Court could be a determining factor in overcoming said opposition. If so, it will open doors for the successful implementation of strategic human rights litigation.

The constitutional foundations for this transformation already exist. On examining Article 1 of today's constitution, we see that not only does the so-called "constitutional block" apply, but constitutional interpretation in Mexico should also take place in accordance with international human rights instruments and always conforming to the "*pro persona*" principle (that obligates all state authorities to offer the highest possible level of protection). This opens up scores of substantive and procedural possibilities for strategic litigation in Mexico, including the paths that some litigants had already attempted and exercised before this reform—as seen in the cases included in the following section—but that now have much better prospects. But again, this can only occur if the culture and the essence of jurisdictional activities change.

IV.V

One last basic condition for strategic human rights litigation is—unfortunately—a reality that has kept 52 million people in Mexico living in poverty (46 percent of the population) and that admits the structural inequality that lets the poor live alongside the richest man in the world. These figures point at the violation of the most elementary principle of justice and herald the massive violation of social human rights in the country. Under this perspective, there are many reasons to launch strategic litigation suits in order to meet and extend the guarantees of these violated rights. In this sense and for the wrong reasons, strategic litigation has a wide margin of possibilities.

At the same time, Mexican society on entering the second decade of the twenty-first century has been marred by growing violence and rampant impunity. The statistics are horrifying: 70,000 homicides during the administration of Felipe Calderón Hinojosa, thousands of people missing or displaced. Some of these people were the victims of crime (which implies a state that has neglected its generic obligation to offer security) while many others have been victims of state violence directly (making the state a criminal or negligent entity that fails in fulfilling its obligation to respect human rights). This regrettable reality, which implies that torture, disappearances, and executions at the hands of public authorities will once again be on Mexico's agenda, sets the basis—yet again for the wrong reasons—for the design and implementation of strategic human rights litigation. It is hard to know how this difficult stage in Mexican history will be dealt with in the future; but it is foreseeable that both national and international human rights law instruments will often be resorted to.[34]

V

There is a degree of unpredictability with any choice, especially when there are no indisputable criteria to aid in the decision. This is the main problem I have faced in selecting for this chapter a few cases—as well as dismissing others—that allow a better comprehension on how strategic human rights litigation works in Mexico. I present the following examples of successful strategic litigations without intending them to be a representative sample or a ranking of this type of legal actions. I am well aware that there are other examples, and that the selection could have been different and responded to stricter and less subjective methodological criteria, but the aim I set for this chapter was to evince the conditions that make this type of litigation possible, as discussed below.

In choosing these cases, I did not consider litigants' intent or the strategy used, but rather focused on their impact. I have made emphases on the fact that they are "successful" cases. This success does not depend on the will of the actors nor does it necessarily respond to their original intentions. I believe litigation is successful when it has institutional (political and/or legal) effects aimed at extending rights or their guarantees even though said effects may not be the ones sought, expected, or desired by their litigants.[35] Likewise, I have taken the use of international laws or proceedings into account as part of the grounds, argument, or litigation channel. Some cases reveal Mexican judges' resistance against using this type of instrument while other cases show signs of these officials' potential empowerment of international instruments (for example, to offer social rights protection).

It should be noted that I have disregarded cases filed by public institutions—Comisiones de los Derechos Humanos [Human Rights Commissions] or the Procuraduría General de la República [General Attorney's Office]—and focused on lawsuits initiated by civil organizations or lawyers. Except for one case of an electoral nature, these cases have been processed through *amparo* lawsuits. Nor have I considered cases with high media impact and a potential legal impact, but those with the primary (and probably exclusive) aim of defending the specific cause of the person involved, like the case of the release of French national Florence Cassez.[36] The four cases selected simply reflect my intention of showing the phenomenon as it exists in Mexico and its potential in the process of consolidating constitutional democracy.

Finally, I thought it would be interesting to offer an array in terms of the issues dealt with on those cases. Therefore, I chose cases dealing with a variety of issues: due process, political rights, social rights, and enforced disappearance of persons: the Acteal, Castañeda, Mininuma and Rosendo Radilla cases.

Case 1: Acteal and due process

On December 22, 1997, forty-five indigenous persons were brutally murdered in Acteal, Chiapas, and seventy-five people were accused and imprisoned for these deeds. Ten years later, a lawyer, Javier Cruz Angulo, backed by the Centro de Investigación y Docencia Económicas Clínica de Interés Jurídico [Legal Interest Clinic], went before the judiciary to denounce serious violations in the legal proceedings that supported these accusations. This lawsuit was presented before the Consejo de la Judicatura [Council of the Federal Judiciary] on the grounds of the corresponding judges' negligence in not rendering a judgment against the accused for nine years. On August 2, 2009, the Supreme Court decided to become involved in the case because it dealt with an issue "of paramount interest, reflected in the possible effects or disruption of social or political values, as well as those of general coexistence or welfare." Ruling on the Direct *Amparo* 9/2008 on August 12, 2009, the First Chamber of the Supreme Court of Justice decided to protect the detained by ordering their release.

Public opinion was surrounded by a great deal of controversy over this case. In a press release addressed to the public, CIDE itself explained the reasons why its public interest clinic had accepted the case (the right to a speedy trial, the right to be assisted by an interpreter, the principle of the presumption of innocence, and the rules of due legal process in general had been violated). Above all, CIDE declared the object of the lawsuit: "to establish precedents that will improve the quality of criminal proceedings in Mexico." The goal was achieved in the end, a fact worth celebrating because, as Ana Laura Magaloni (2007) declared at the time:

> As long as the guilt or innocence of the prisoners accused as the perpetrators of the Acteal massacre is being debated in the political and ideological arena

> and not based on the evidence and the legal process, the Mexican criminal system might continue to be what it is: a relentless and systematic mill of injustices that almost unfailingly guarantees impunity.[37]

With this lawsuit, CIDE and Angulo contributed to take the discussion to the realm of law and rights. Thus, they furthered the consolidation of Mexican constitutionalism. Although the case did not acquire international renown, it can be considered a successful strategic litigation in view of its significance and impact.

It is important to note that the case of the Acteal community established an important judicial precedent that allowed due process in the country to be strengthened. In fact, the jurisprudential theses that were emitted have served as grounds for the liberation of many other people—whether indigenous or not—who were detained without adequate observance of the due process standards.

Case 2: The Castañeda case and political rights

This case is interesting because it touches upon political rights issues. Moreover, it gained international attention and was the first case in which the Inter-American Court of Human Rights issued an indictment against the Mexican State. The motives for the lawsuit arose when Mr. Jorge Castañeda Gutman went in March 2004 before the Mexican authority in charge of election administration to register as an independent presidential candidate. This authority refused his registry since Mexican legislation only grants national political parties the right to register candidates for federal office; so Castañeda and his attorney, Santiago Corcuera, filed for an *amparo* with the federal judiciary. As previously explained in this chapter, this remedy was rejected because it was not the ideal channel for protecting political rights. As part of his litigation strategy, Castañeda contested the judge's refusal before the Supreme Court. In August 2005, after the court declared that his request for an *amparo* did not proceed, Castañeda went before the Inter-American Human Rights Commission.

In the complaint filed with international agencies, he argued the violation of two rights contained in the Inter-American Declaration of Human Rights (political rights and access to justice). On December 12, 2006, after the presidential elections in Mexico had concluded, the commission admitted the case and on March 21, 2007, presented it before the Inter-American Court. This information is important because it substantiates the nature of the case in question because even though it was evident that the client's principal objective could not be met, Corcuera continued to fight the case. Finally, on August 6, 2008, the court issued its judgment. Although the court did not rule in the claimant's favor in terms of the main case itself—the right to register as an independent presidential candidate—it did concede the claimant was right to protest against the denial of justice that led to his not being able to obtain an *amparo* from the electoral authority's decision.

This case is another example of strategic litigation considering that in addition to its international nature and the strategic purpose implicitly declared by the actors, it brought about a change in the Mexican constitution to establish the Juicio de Protección de los Derechos Político Electorales del Ciudadano [Citizens' Claim for the Protection of Political Rights] as a constitutional protection remedy aside from the *amparo* (which would be managed by the Electoral Court) and significantly had a bearing on the debate that led to the approval of the 2012 electoral reform that finally included the figures of independent—or citizen—candidates for federal offices in Mexico. The Castañeda case and the Inter-American Court's legal argument prompted a debate that led to the enactment of new laws for registering candidates to elected office. To this extent and regardless of the claimant's original intent, it gradually acquired the status of being a successful strategic litigation.[38]

Case 3: Mininuma and social rights

This case is a judicial and historical exception to Mexican courts' tendency to view social rights as non-justiciable. To a certain extent, it is also a precedent to the 2011 *amparo* reform because the case's judge—against legal tradition and precedents—decided to grant collective—and not individual—legal protection. It all began when a social organization called Centro de Derechos Humanos de la Montaña Tlachinollan [Tlachinollan Mountain Human Rights Center] went to ask the Seventh District judge in the State of Guerrero on behalf of the Na Savi (Mixtec) indigenous community, Mininuma, in the Metlatónoc municipality, to help put an end to the continued violation of community members' right to health. The basis of their petition was simple and uncompromising: the lack of a health clinic in the community and in the surrounding areas.

This is a typical case of strategic litigation in which an *amparo* lawsuit was coupled with other political, social, and media actions. There had been an arrangement approved in 2003 for the community to get a healthcare center although the *amparo* was not filed until four years later, in 2007. To do this, they first persuaded state health to provide them with a written refusal, denying them a clinic of their own. Once this was obtained, they could then proceed to request a legal *amparo* against said refusal. Furthermore, the contents of the lawsuit made tactical use of international human rights law, especially in presenting arguments that would most likely establish the justiciable nature of economic, social, and cultural rights (ESCR).

On July 11, 2008, against all odds, the judge granted them an *amparo*. The violated rights the judge took into account were: the right to health and the right to non-discrimination (as interdependent rights). The case was based on various international treaties and instruments. As Rodrigo Gutiérrez and Aline Rivera (2009) stated:

> [T]he importance of the Mininuma lawsuit lies in that with it, the old paradigm—that denies social rights justiciability—was challenged and, by making use of the new theoretical ESCR constructions, it was possible to make progress in court regarding the possible justiciability of ESCR and thus, reconsider them genuine fundamental rights.[39]

From this perspective and beyond the particularities of the case, Mininuma is another example of successful strategic human rights litigation that was particularly fruitful in the context of Mexico.

Furthermore, given that this case is about economic, social, and cultural rights, and that for decades Mexican judges had decided in the sense that these rights were only programmatic, and thus non-justiciable, this decision sets an important precedent for developing a new perspective on the effective guarantees for these rights. With the decision of Mininuma, a court's decision allowed other cases containing violations of the right to education, health, access to water, etc.

Case 4: Rosendo Radilla and forced disappearance

Prosecuted by the Comisión Mexicana de Defensa y Promoción de los Derechos Humanos A.C. [Mexican Commission for the Defense and Advocacy of Human Rights], this case has been the one with the most impact on the Mexican legal system. This is basically for two reasons: (a) because it served as a starting point for the Inter-American Court of Human Rights to remind Mexican judicial authorities of their obligation to observe and carry out the so-called "review for compliance"; and (b) its effects were heightened with the approval of the 2011 constitutional reform on human rights.[40]

The case reached the Inter-American Commission in November 2001 and was presented before the Inter-American Court in March 2008. A judgment was pronounced in November 2009 and published on December 15, 2009. Mexico already had knowledge of this judgment before the 2011 reform was passed, but there was still a great deal of resistance to it. With the enactment of said reform, the branches of government that showed resistance of any kind would be forced to relent. This was best seen in the Supreme Court debate on the scope of the Inter-American Court's judgment in August 2010, which determined that said ruling imposed an obligation to carry out a review of compliance that would be in the hands of all the judges of the nation, regardless of the fact that a few months before the 2011 constitutional reform, the Supreme Court itself had ruled the opposite, with a vote of six to five. The reform undoubtedly was a factor that set off the effects of the Rosendo Radilla case.

This is a case of forced disappearance of people during Mexico's so-called "dirty war" in the 1960s. Mr. Radilla, a musician and left-wing political activist, disappeared at the hands of the Mexican army. His relatives embarked on a long legal battle that included complaints filed before administrative authorities and the

Comisión Nacional de los Derechos Humanos [National Human Rights Commission], as well as criminal lawsuits. This process ended with an Inter-American Court of Human Rights ruling that found the Mexican State guilty. This sentence included the imposition of carrying out legal reforms (to restrict military jurisdiction) and several administrative actions (of which we can highlight the search for the missing person and those responsible for his disappearance, as well as paying compensation to his relatives). According to the court, Mexico violated Radilla's rights to personal liberty, physical integrity, life, and juridical personality.

The legal and political effects of this ruling are still in the process of taking shape. This case was destined to transform the way Mexican judges think and argue when human rights are involved. As Gutiérrez, Cantú, and Rincón (2012) claim:

> the precedents set by Radilla's case will undoubtedly be seen in the demands of the movement of victims of crimes committed during the "dirty war", as well as in the defense of cases of human rights violations inflicted on civilians by the military who have extended military jurisdiction.[41]

Unfortunately, by 2013, cases like these were continuing to occur in the context of the wrongly named "war against organized crime."

VI

Even though such cases exist, the truth is that, as Miguel Pulido pointed out:

> experiences of strategic litigation are actually scarce in our country. The number of documented precedents do not coincide with the fashionableness of the term or, at least, there is a category used to define practices from a legal perspective that are not necessarily strategic litigation or that could be variables with very specific particularities.[42]

One explanation of this is that, unlike what happened in countries like Argentina or Colombia—where the phenomenon is widespread—in Mexico, there are strong procedural and substantive limitations to introducing this type of legal remedy. As mentioned above, constitutional actions can only be instigated by certain institutional actors; and the *amparo*, the lawsuit to protect rights *par excellence*, had relative effects (only valid for the litigant), among other restrictions. However, this is also due to the fact that there is a strong cultural resistance to it, especially in the judicial sector. In this particular aspect, the Supreme Court of Justice bears primary responsibility.

Now after some landmark changes since 2011, things might improve constructively. On one hand, there are new constitutional laws regarding human rights resulting from the reforms mentioned and which led to the new text of Article 1 as cited in this chapter. The elements and principles contained in this law—constitutional block, treaty-compliant interpretation, the pro persona principle, state obligations, etc.—have implanted bases in Mexican law, which are similar to those in the 1991 Colombian Constitution and the 1994 Argentine Constitution. It can be supposed that each of these served as a basis for strategic litigation in said countries. Now there are better regulatory elements for adopting this kind of legal action in Mexico. This is even more evident if we consider that the constitutional and legal bases of the *amparo* have changed. Specially by broadening the scope of this legal remedy—both in terms of what is its scope and effects and what it changes in regard to legal personality—there are now bases to make the *amparo* the ideal instrument to initiate new strategic litigations. Now what is needed is to encourage a cultural change in Mexican jurists, lawyers, and judges in particular.

Another consideration—which deserves an essay of its own—relates to the fleeting desirability of strategic litigation. The contradiction is that even though it is good that conditions for making this kind of litigation possible are emerging, the best thing that could happen is for it to be a short-lived phenomenon. The ideal situation would be to live in a society in which there were few injustices needing to be addressed by law. This would entail decent living conditions for people and the effective guarantee of their fundamental rights. Such a situation is—ideally—achieved through policies, as well as by law. If effectively carried out, strategic litigation can be a contributing factor. But, in order for this to happen, strategic litigation should be a singular and extraordinary remedy. Otherwise, it would become meaningless and lose its potential impact. Successful strategic litigation should bring about changes in laws, in institutions, and in the culture that gave rise to the unfair situation and in this way contribute to overcoming these problems. To this extent, strategic litigation should be a remedy that is well thought out, well planned, and well executed—something like sharpshooting.

The necessary exceptionality of strategic litigation is different if we think about the Inter-American system for the protection of human rights. To date, the Inter-American Commission and Court have, in general, been an ideal space in which to channel successful strategic litigations. But they have been successful precisely because only extraordinary and singular cases reach these bodies. Otherwise if, given the failure of the legal systems of the different countries that form part of the system, the court became a type of "last resort" for unresolved disputes, the system would most probably collapse. The sad irony is that it would be a collapse instigated and sponsored by the autocrats of the region and that could be reinforced by excessive litigation by people who suffer from this same ruling class.

Notes

1 It is quite possible to imagine strategic litigation aimed at promoting various types of goods or interests. However, in this paper, I will focus on the form of litigation that strives to protect human rights and advance their agenda.

2 L. M. Cano and G. Rodríguez, "Del litigio estratégico como estrategia democrática" [On Strategic Litigation as a Democratic Strategy]. In OACNUDH, *El litigio estratégico en México: la aplicación de los derechos humanos a nivel práctico. Experiencias de la sociedad civil* [Strategic Litigation in Mexico: The Application of Human Rights in Practice. Experiences in Civil Society] (2007), 139.

3 D. Morales, "¿Qué es el litigio estratégico en derechos humanos?" [What is Strategic Human Rights Litigation?]. (Nexus, El Juego de la Corte, 2010), available at http://eljuegodelacorte.nexos.com.mx/?p=467 <website> (accessed July 13, 2016). Morales headed the Centro de Estudios Legales y Sociales de Argentina (CELS). Dedicated to strategic litigation and widely recognized in Latin America, this organization published *Litigio estratégico y derechos humanos. La lucha por el derecho* [Strategic Litigation and Human Rights] (Buenos Aires: Siglo XXI editores, 2008).

4 P. Geary, *Children's Rights: A Guide to Strategic Litigation* (Child Rights Information Network (CRIN), 2008), 6.

5 Juan Carlos Gutiérrez et al., *Litigio estratégico en Derechos Humanos. Modelo para armar* [Strategic Human Rights Litigation: A Model to Create] (Mexico City: Comisión Mexicana de Defensa y Promoción de los Derechos Humanos A.C., 2012) 15. For these authors, this kind of litigation was generated by the publication of Jerome Frank's (1931) article entitled "Why Not a Clinical Lawyer-School?" (*University of Pennsylvania Law Review 81*: 907–923). In the United States, litigation clinics are well-established institutions and, as the authors themselves point out, were significantly transformed with the publication of Gary Bellow and Bea Moulton's (1978) text entitled *The Lawyering Process: Materials for Clinical Instruction in Advocacy*. (Mineola, NY: Foundation Press, 1978).

6 I would like to thank Ana Laura Magaloni for this important observation.

7 This latter type consists of strategic litigation aimed at changing public policy or influencing the implementation of governmental action in strategic areas, such as in the sphere of healthcare or public works (whether to promote or deter them). I would like to thank Francisca Pou for this observation.

8 Cf. V. Abramovich and P. Rodríguez, *Experiencias de Activismo de Derechos Humanos. Hecho en América Latina* [Experiences in Human Rights Activism: Made in Latin America] (Buenos Aires: Universidad de San Andrés, 2011).

9 I base my theory on references provided by J. C. Gutiérrez et al., op. cit., 21–22.

10 For more on this topic, cf. Suprema Corte de Justicia de la Nación, Escuela Libre de Derecho, *Clínicas de Derechos Humanos. Una alternativa para la educación jurídica y la sociedad* [Human Rights Clinics: An Alternative for Legal Education and Society] (Mexico City: ELD, SCJN, 2011).

11 I have elaborated on these theories in other works. Cf. among others, P. Salazar P., *La democracia constitucional. Una radiografía teórica* [Constitutional Democracy: A Theoretical Snapshot] (3rd ed.) (Mexico City: FCE, 2011) and P. Salazar, "El rompecabezas y el modelo. Claves para una segunda transición mexicana [The puzzle and the model. Keys for a second mexican transition]." in Sandoval E. Ruiz (ed.), *México 2010. Hipotecando el Futuro* [Mexico 2010: Mortgaging the Future] (New York and London: Taurus, 2010), 115–146.

12 This term originated in French. In the 1970s, the French Constitution ruled that the supreme law of the country would include the following: the Constitution of 1958, its preamble, and the 1789 Declaration of the Rights of Man and the Citizen, thus extending the set of provisions that recognize people's rights. Legal scholar Louis Favoreu christened the result "constitutional block."

13 In fact, the relationship between fundamental rights (protected and guaranteed by the constitution) and democracy is not exempt from tensions: rights are preconditions and conditions for democracy and, at the same time, limit democratic power. There is no absolute power in a constitutional democracy. The author who has best elaborated on

these theories the most in recent years is Luigi Ferrajoli. His complete theories can be found in his most recent publication: L. Ferrajoli, *Principia Iuris. Teoria del Diritto e della Democrazia* (Rome: Laterza, 2007). For Ferrajoli, rights are the substantial dimension of democracy. For other authors like Garzón Valdés, rights are a "*coto vedado*" [preserve] for democratic decisions. For Bovero, rights limit democratic power but do not form part of the democratic system except as preconditions (social rights) and conditions (the right to freedom and political rights) of said system (Cf. M. Bovero, *Una gramática de la democracia. Contra el gobierno de los peores* [Grammar of Democracy: Against one of the Worst Governments] (Madrid: Trotta, 2002); M. Bovero and L. Ferrajoli, *Teoria de la democrazia. Dos perspectivas comparadas* [The Theory of Democracy: Two Perspectives Compared], in Colección "Temas para la democracia" ["Topics on Democracy" Series], Conferencias Magistrales, 13 (Mexico City: Instituto Federal Electoral, 2001).

14 Cf. R. Dworkin, *Taking Rights Seriously* (Cambridge, MA: Harvard University Press, 1978).

15 E. Garzón Valdés, "El futuro de la democracia" [The Future of Democracy], Colección "Temas de la democracia", Conferencias magistrales 15 (Mexico City: Instituto Federal Electoral, 2007), 46.

16 There is a well-known academic discussion on this "counter-majoritarian" and elitist power of constitutional justice, which will not be rewritten here. However, it is worth noting that this controversy is an expression of the tension between democracy and constitutionalism. Cf. among others, the compendium edited by Jon Elster and Rune Slagstad, *Constitucionalismo y Democracia* [Constitutionalism and Democracy] (Mexico City: FCE, 1999) (original edition in English, Cambridge University Press, 1988). See also the work of Luigi Ferrajoli (in particular: L. Ferrajoli, op. cit.) For more reference, see R. Gargarella, "Pensando sobre la reforma constitucional en América Latina" [Thoughts on Constitutional Reform in Latin America]. In C. Rodríguez Garavito, *El derecho en América Latina. Un Mapa para el pensamiento jurídico del Siglo XXI* [Law in Latin America: A Map for Legal Thought in the Twenty-first Century] (Buenos Aires: Siglo XXI editores, 2011), pp. 87–108.

17 Samual Ramos, *El perfil del hombre y la cultura en México* [Profile of Man and Culture in Mexico] (Mexico City: UNAM, 1934).

18 A. Siegfried, *Amerique Latine*, cited in Samuel Ramos, *El perfil del hombre y la cultura en México* [Profile of Man and Culture in Mexico] (Mexico City: UNAM, 1934), p. 61.

19 A. Sen, *La idea de justicia* [The Idea of Justice] (Madrid: Taurus, 2010), p. 15.

20 Cf. N. Bobbio, *Teoria generale della politica* (Turin: Einaudi, 1999).

21 Cano and Rodríguez, op. cit., 141.

22 CELS, op. cit., 26.

23 Cf., among others, M. Villareal, "El litigio estratégico como herramienta del derecho de interés público" [Strategic Litigation as a Tool of Public Interest Law]. In OACNUDH, op. cit., 22–27.

24 It should be noted that not all cases should necessarily (or solely) be brought before the judiciary. In analyzing the possibility of setting strategic litigation in motion, the FUNDAR organization, for instance, take into account matters like "the choice of mechanism for the defense (judicial, quasi-judicial, jurisdictional, administrative, etc.) and others like the type of venue, issues, an appeal, etc." They believe that this "is extremely important since the potential for reaching success is also filtered, even by procedural aspects like the formal admission of evidence, (dispute) structure, technicalities." I would like to thank Miguel Pulido for this information.

25 R. Becerra, P. Salazar, and J. Woldenberg, *La mecánica del cambio político en México. Elecciones, Partidos y Reformas* [The Mechanics of Political Change in Mexico: Elections, Parties and Reforms] (3rd edn) (Mexico City: Cal y Arena, 2005).

26 Cf. Mari del Refugio González and S. López Ayllón, *Transiciones y diseños institucionales* [Institutional Transitions and Designs] (Mexico City: UNAM, 1999).

27 The *amparo* trial does not apply to protecting these rights. It was not until 1996 that a special trial was established for this matter (the Trial for the Protection of Electoral Political Rights under the auspices of the Electoral Court).

28 At least at the time of writing this text, this right has yet to be regulated (February 2013).

29 Cf. M. Carbonell and P. Salazar (eds), *La Reforma de Derechos Humanos de 2011. Un nuevo paradigm* [The 2011 Reform of Human Rights: A New Paradigm] (Mexico City: UNAM-Porrúa, 2012).

30 This idea is taken from the comments presented by Alan García at the Seminar on the Reform of Human Rights organized by the Supreme Court of Justice of the Nation (SCJN) at several venues nationwide on September 23, 2011. Professor García participated with the author of this chapter at the Casa de la Cultura Jurídica in León, Guanajuato.

31 A reform to secondary legislation was passed in 2013. This reform will have the following effects: (a) the *amparo* will be a remedy used to protect the human rights recognized by the constitution and international treaties; (b) the scope of *amparo* trial protection was extended (now it can be initiated by whoever can demonstrate having a legal interest or a legitimate interest in a specific case; that is, whoever argues he/she is the holder of an individual or collective right); (c) the *amparo* against laws extends the effects of sentences, which will now have general effects when jurisprudence establishes the unconstitutionality of a law (except in matters of taxes); and (d) it will now be possible to process an *amparo* trial electronically.

32 In Mexico, the SCJN is made up of eleven justices. To fill a vacancy—whether a justice is absent due to natural causes or his or her fifteen-year term in office has ended—the president presents the Senate with a shortlist of possible candidates. The Senate then votes on the new appointee. If a legislative majority is not attained for a candidate after two presidential shortlisted have been presented, the president selects and appoints one of his/her candidates (Articles 86 and 96 of the Constitution).

33 N. Saltalamacchia and A. Covarrubias (eds), *Derechos Humanos en Política Exterior. Seis casos latinoamericanos* [Human Rights in Foreign Policy: Six Cases from Latin America] (Mexico City: ITAM-Miguel Ángel Porrúa, 2011), pp. 199, 201, 203.

34 Cf. http://www.nexos.com.mx/?P=leerarticulo&Article=2102734. For information on the use of strategic litigation in Argentina during the country's transition to democracy after a period of military dictatorship, see C. Courtis, "El desarrollo del derecho de interés público en la Argentina: avances, obstáculos, desafíos" [The Evolution of Public Interest Law in Argentina: Progress, Obstacles, Challenges]. Iin F. González, *Clínicas de Interés Público y Enseñanza del Derecho. Argentina, Chile, Colombia, México y Perú* [Public Interest Clinics and the Teaching of Law: Argentina, Chile, Colombia, Mexico and Peru] (Diego: Facultad de Derecho. Universidad Diego Portales, 1985), pp. 69–93.

35 There are interesting cases like the so-called "*amparo* for intellectuals" against the 2007 electoral reform that, from the perspective proposed here, did not meet the criteria and will therefore not be included.

36 Ms. Cassez was accused of kidnapping, and convicted by Mexican judges and courts to serve a sixty-year prison sentence. However, her case reached the Supreme Court of Justice and she was released because her rights to due process had been seriously violated during her detention.

37 A, Magaloni, "A 10 años de Acteal" [10 Years after Acteal] (*Reforma*, Dec. 22, 2007).

38 From a certain perspective, this case can be classified as what Miguel Pulido calls "*Litigio Protagónico*" [Protagonic Litigation], which encompasses lawsuits filed by personalities or organizations that in addition to seeking a desired result, use the case as a way to promote their own personal or program agenda. The examples Pulido offers include: an *amparo* filed by Ignacio Burgoa requesting to know the amount of the

external debt run up during President López Portillo's administration (arguing his right to exercise the constitutional rights contained in Articles 6 and 8); the so-called "*amparo* for intellectuals" against the 2007 electoral reform or the *amparo* presented by the Mexicanos Primero organization to know the salaries of teachers affiliated to the SNTE (National Teacher's Union).

39 R. Gutiérrez and A. Rivera, "El caso 'Mininuma': un litigio estratégico para la justiciabilidad de los derechos sociales y la no discriminación en México" [The "Mininuma" Case: Strategic Litigation for the Justicability of Social Rights and Non-Discrimination in Mexico], *Revista de la Facultad de Derecho* (Mexico City: UNAM, 2009), available at www.juridicas.unam.mx/publica/librev/rev/facdermx/cont/251/pr/pr5.pdf (accessed July 13, 2016). This text gives an excellent reconstruction of the case and its legal and political effects.

40 For more information on the case, cf. Gutiérrez, op. cit.;*La sentencia de la Corte IDH caso Radilla Pacheco vs Estados Unidos Mexicanos* [The IAHR Court Judgment: Radilla Pacheco vs United Mexican States Case] Comisión Mexicana de Defensa y Promoción de los Derechos Humanos A.C., AFADEM, 2010. It should be noted that similar cases appeared after this case (the Fernández Ortega et al. case; the Rosendo Cantú case, both in 2010).

41 Gutiérrez, op. cit., p. 133.

42 M. Pulido, "Revisión de casos de litigio estratégico. Delimitación de la muestra. Autoidentificación o heteroidentificación" [A Review of Strategic Litigation Cases: A Delimitation of the Sample – Self-Identification or Hetero-Identification], mimio.

References

Abramovich, V. and P. Rodríguez (2011) *Experiencias de Activismo de Derechos Humanos. Hecho en América Latina* [Experiences in Human Rights Activism: Made in Latin America]. Buenos Aires: Universidad de San Andrés.

Becerra, R., P. Salazar, and J. Woldenberg (2005) *La mecánica del cambio político en México. Elecciones, Partidos y Reformas* [The Mechanics of Political Change in Mexico: Elections, Parties and Reforms] (3rd edn). Mexico City: Cal y Arena.

Bobbio, N. (1999) *Teoria generale della politica.* Turin: Einaudi.

Bovero, M. (2002) *Una gramática de la democracia. Contra el gobierno de los peores* [Grammar of Democracy: Against one of the Worst Governments]. Madrid: Trotta.

Bovero, M. and L. Ferrajoli (2001) *Teoria de la democrazia. Dos perspectivas comparadas* [The Theory of Democracy: Two Perspectives Compared], Colección "Temas para la democracia" ["Topics on Democracy" Series], Conferencias Magistrales. Mexico City: Instituto Federal Electoral, p. 13.

Cano, L. M. and G. Rodríguez (2007) "Del litigio estratégico como estrategia democrática" [On Strategic Litigation as a Democratic Strategy]. In Oficina De Alto Comisionado De Las Naciones Unidas (OACNUDH) (eds), *El litigio estratégico en México: la aplicación de los derechos humanos a nivel práctico. Experiencias de la sociedad civil* [Strategic Litigation in Mexico: The Application of Human Rights in Practice. Experiences in Civil Society] Mexico City: UN-OHCHR, p. 139.

Carbonell, M. and P. Salazar (eds) (2012) *La Reforma de Derechos Humanos de 2011. Un nuevo paradigm* [The 2011 Reform of Human Rights: A New Paradigm]. Mexico City: Universidad Nacional Autónoma de México (UNAM)-Porrúa.

Centro de Estudios Legales y Sociales de Argentina (CELS) (2008) *Litigio estratégico y derechos humanos. La lucha por el derecho* [Strategic Litigation and Human Rights]. Buenos Aires: Siglo XXI editores.

Courtis, C. (1985) "El desarrollo del derecho de interés público en la Argentina: avances, obstáculos, desafíos" [The *Evolution* of Public Interest Law in Argentina: Progress, Obstacles, Challenges]. In F. González (ed.) *Clínicas de Interés Público y Enseñanza del Derecho. Argentina, Chile, Colombia, México y Perú* [Public Interest Clinics and the Teaching of Law: Argentina, Chile, Colombia, Mexico and Peru]. Diego: Facultad de Derecho, Universidad Diego Portales, pp. 69–93.

Dworkin, R. (1978) *Taking Rights Seriously*. Cambridge, MA: Harvard University Press.

Elster, Jon and Rune Slagstad (1999) *Constitucionalismo y Democracia* [Constitutionalism and Democracy]. Mexico City: FCE.

Ferrajoli, L. (2007) *Principia Iuris. Teoria del Diritto e della Democrazia*. Rome: Laterza.

Garzón Valdés, E. (2007) "El futuro de la democracia" [The Future of Democracy], Colección "Temas de la democracia", Conferencias magistrales 15. Mexico City: Instituto Federal Electoral.

Geary, P. (2008) *Children's Rights: A Guide to Strategic Litigation*. London: Child Rights Information Network (CRIN).

González, Maria del Refugio and S. López Ayllón (1999) *Transiciones y diseños institucionales* [Institutional Transitions and Designs] (3rd edn). Mexico City: UNAM.

Gutiérrez, Juan Carlos et al. (2012) *Litigio estratégico en Derechos Humanos. Modelo para armar* [Strategic Human Rights Litigation: A Model to Create]. Mexico City: Comisión Mexicana de Defensa y Promoción de los Derechos Humanos A.C.

Gutiérrez, R. and A. Rivera (2009) "El caso 'Mininuma': un litigio estratégico para la justiciabilidad de los derechos sociales y la no discriminación en México" [The "Mininuma" Case: Strategic Litigation for the Justiciability of Social Rights and Non-Discrimination in Mexico] In *Revista de la Facultad de Derecho*. Mexico City: UNAM, available at www.juridicas.unam.mx/publica/librev/rev/facdermx/cont/251/pr/pr5.pdf (accessed July 13, 2016).

Magaloni, A. (2007) "A 10 años de Acteal" [10 Years after Acteal]. *Reforma*Dec. 22, available at http://fredalvarez.blogspot.mx/2007/12/acteal_23.html (accessed June 27, 2016).

Morales, D. (2010) "¿Qué es el litigio estratégico en derechos humanos?" [What is Strategic Human Rights Litigation?]. *Nexos, El Juego de la Corte*, available at http://eljuegodelacorte.nexos.com.mx/?p=467 (accessed June 27, 2016)

Pulido, M., "Revisión de casos de litigio estratégico. Delimitación de la muestra. Autoidentificación o heteroidentificación" [A Review of Strategic Litigation Cases: A Delimitation of the Sample – Self-Identification or Hetero-Identification], mimio.

Ramos, Samuel (1934) *El perfil del hombre y la cultura en México* [Profile of Man and Culture in Mexico]. Mexico City: UNAM.

Rodríguez Garavito, C. (2011) *El derecho en América Latina. Un Mapa para el pensamiento jurídico del Siglo XXI* [Law in Latin America: A Map for Legal Thought in the 21st Century]. Buenos Aires: Siglo XXI editores.

Salazar, P. (2011) *La democracia constitucional. Una radiografía teórica* [Constitutional Democracy: A Theoretical Snapshot] (3rd edn). Mexico City: FCE.

Salazar, P. (2010) "El rompecabezas y el modelo. Claves para una segunda transición mexicana [The Puzzle and the Model. Keys for a Second Mexican Transition]." In Sandoval E. Ruiz (ed.) *México 2010. Hipotecando el Futuro* [Mexico 2010: Mortgaging the Future]. Madrid: Taurus, pp. 115–146.

Saltalamacchia, N. and A. Covarrubias (2011) *Derechos Humanos en Política Exterior. Seis casos latinoamericanos* [Human Rights in Foreign Policy: Six Cases from Latin America]. Mexico City: ITAM-Miguel Ángel Porrúa.

Sen, A. (2010) *La idea de Justicia* [The Idea of Justice]. Madrid: Taurus.

Suprema Corte de Justicia de la Nación, EscuelaLibre de Derecho (2011) *Clínicas de Derechos Humanos. Una alternativa para la educación jurídica y la sociedad* [Human Rights Clinics: An Alternative for Legal Education and Society]. Mexico City: Escuela Libre de Derecho (ELD) and Supreme Court of Justice of the Nation (SCJN).

Villareal, M. (2007) "El litigio estratégico como herramienta del derecho de interés público" [Strategic Litigation as a Tool of Public Interest Law]. In Oficina De Alto Comisionado De Las Naciones Unidas (OACNUDH) (eds) *El litigio estratégico en México: la aplicación de los derechos humanos a nivel práctico. Experiencias de la sociedad civil* [Strategic Litigation in Mexico: The Application of Human Rights in Practice. Experiences in Civil Society]. Mexico City: UN-OHCRC, pp. 22–27.

3

ARE MEXICAN JUSTICES TRUE ARBITERS AMONG THE POLITICAL ELITES?

An empirical analysis of the court's rulings from 2000–2011

Andrea Castagnola and Saúl López Noriega

There is general consensus that the 2000 presidential election represented the concrete embodiment of the birth of Mexican democracy after the Institutional Revolutionary Party (PRI) lost the presidency after being more than seventy years in office. The change of ruling party in governance had a significant impact on all the country's political institutions and the Supreme Court was no exception. But to what extent did the emergence of democracy in the country allow Mexican justices to be a true arbiter in mediating intra-elite conflicts? Do justices' party loyalties still affect the way a justice votes? The objective of this chapter is to examine the voting behavior of the justices on politically sensitive cases, those that arise from conflicts among the different levels and branches of government, and between different political parties. We argue that the political context and ideology of justices can affect the way a justice votes as well as the particularities of the constitutional design of each means of constitutional control. We answer these questions by analyzing Supreme Court rulings from 2000 to 2011 on constitutional controversies and constitutional actions on organic issues. The literature has traditionally considered that, overall, unconstitutional rulings are a sign of judicial independence and in this case, due to the particularities of the Mexican political context of divided government and high institutional stability, we would follow that idea.

Since 1929 the Revolutionary National Party, the predecessor of the PRI, has been appointing all the justices to the court without any institutional or political constraint, except from those that guaranteed political equilibrium inside the party. In fact, by 1933 the unwritten prerequisite to remain on the bench was to be affiliated to the PRI (Cabrera Acevedo 1998). During PRI supremacy, the court, as well as the Congress (Casar 1999), was merely a rubber stamp since it became more like an institutional office extension of the party rather than an independent body (Magaloni 2003; Magaloni 1997), or as what Beatriz Magaloni (2003) refers to as a partisan system of elite circulation.[1] Intra-elite conflicts, both horizontal and vertical, were often resolved by the president's office rather than in the Supreme Court; therefore it is no surprise that only fifty-five constitutional controversies reached court between 1917 and 1994. This represents fewer than one controversy per year (Cossío 1998).

Society strongly acclaimed the end of PRI hegemony on the court because changes in court membership could bring changes in the policy outcomes of its rulings as well as in the judicial behavior of the justices. However, existing research presents inconclusive evidence about that assumption. Even though Julio Ríos-Figueroa (2007) finds that unconstitutional rulings against the PRI increase when there is more fragmented power, Arianna Sánchez et al. (2011) find that on controversies justices have favored PRI even after the electoral defeat of 2000. In this paper we analyze the controversies and constitutional actions of the justices' vote on particular decisions so as to make predictions about the justices rather than the court as a collegiate body.

The paper proceeds as follows. Section I briefly discusses the literature on judicial behavior, paying special attention to the studies carried out in Latin America. Section II presents the model of judicial behavior that can be applied to the Mexican case, taking into account the particularities of the political and institutional context. The literature would predict that in a stable politically institutional context with a fragmentation of political power it is expected that justices would not be constrained in their decisions by external actors and thus not fear to argue against the ruling party. Section III presents descriptive evidence about Supreme Court rulings on controversies and actions. We have created an original data set of more than 1,000 cases from 2000 to 2011. Overall, justices have been deferential to the ruling party and justices appointed during the National Action Party (PAN) administration have been the most aggressive in their decisions, contrary to justices appointed during the PRI administrations. Section IV presents the results of a random intercept logistic model that predicts the probability of a justice to rule unconstitutionally under different scenarios. During the twelve years analyzed we found that, even under divided government, justices favored the ruling party in detriment to the former hegemonic PRI. Section V discusses the main contributions of our findings to the existing literature.

I Explaining judicial behavior in consolidating democracies

American scholars have long been studying the voting behavior of their justices by examining whether legal doctrines, attitudinal preferences, or external factors guide the decisions they make.[2] Legal scholars have traditionally studied how legal doctrines influence the decisions justices make and conclude that they vote in accordance with legal principles (Gibson 1978; Posner 2008; Ulmer 1973).

Under this model, *stare decisis* or precedent becomes central to this approach since justices' decisions should be consistent with past decisions (Dworkin 1978; Gillman and Clayton 1999; Kahn 1999). But because precedents can often be found on both sides of a case, scholars started to argue that justices use precedent to indirectly achieve their policy preferences.

The attitudinal model, clearly exposed in Jeffrey Segal and Harold Spaeth's (2002) influential book, was a very powerful attack on the legal model since they showed that legal doctrine does not represent a constraint when deciding on a case; but rather it is the justices' own beliefs and values that affect the decision; what they call "sincere voting". The general idea is that because the law is ambiguous and there is often no clear precedent, justices can incorporate their personal views in the development of a law or the decision of a case, thus using legal views as smoke screens to cover their personal preferences. Numerous scholars from within and outside the US have tested these assumptions bringing interesting results to the debate about whether or not the justices own preferences matter when deciding on a case (Rohde and Spaeth 1976; Segal and Spaeth 2002; Segal et al. 1995; Spaeth 1961, 1964 for example; Ostberg and Wetstein 2007).

But the attitudinal model supremacy was soon challenged when the strategic voting model introduced a more complex scenario into the decision-making process: external constraints (Epstein and Knight 1998). The main underlying assumption in the strategic model is that justices are political actors and therefore subject to influence from external actors. Even though most of the literature focuses on the influence of other branches of government (known as the separation-of-power model), there are other research studies that identified other possible external influences on justices' decisions, such as the majority coalition in the court (see for example, Maltzman et al. 2000) or public opinion (see for example, Clark 2009; Staton 2010; 2005). In the separation-of-power model, scholars evaluate how constraining the interests and preferences of the president and Congress can be when achieving their policy preferences on the decision. Most of the empirical research combines both the attitudinal and the strategic model. However, a recent study tests the three approaches simultaneously so as to provide a more comprehensive approach (Bailey and Maltzman 2011).

II Approaches for developing democracies

Even though in the American literature there is general consensus that justices are political actors that pursue policy goals (Baum 1997; 1957; Epstein and Knight 1998; 2002; and Weingast 1992; Maltzman II et al. 2000; Spiller and Gely 1990; Wahlbeck et al. 1998), it is not clear whether that assumption still holds in new democracies in which justices do not necessarily have the institutional protections to secure the independence of their decisions. In fact, most of the existing research on judicial politics in new democracies reveals that executives have proven to be relevant actors in explaining judicial independence due to their constraining role in justices' decision-making process (Chávez 2004b; Ginsburg 2003; 2005; Helmke and Ríos-Figueroa 2011; Iaryczower et al. 2002; Magaloni and Sánchez 2006; Pérez Liñán and Castagnola 2009; Ramseyer and Rasmusen 2003; Figueroa 2007; Rodríguez-Raga 2011; 2008; Verner 1984; and Scher 2008). So basically, most of the theory of judicial intra-branch relations in developing countries focuses on the executive–court relation.[3]

The starting point of the separation-of-power model is that in new democracies with unsecure institutional contexts, justices would vote strategically by ruling in favor of the government as a way of circumventing reprisals (Chávez 2004b; Helmke 2005; Iaryczower et al. 2002; Larkins 1996; and Sánchez 2006; Ríos-Figueroa 2007; Sánchez et al. 2011). Therefore, justices are significantly constrained by the preferences of other branches of government, especially the executive example in those countries with strong *presidentialism.* [4]

The underlying assumption is that the independence of the judiciary (measured as rulings against the government) is strongly related to whether or not there is political fragmentation within other branches of government; what political scientists refer to as divided government. The idea is that, under divided governments, justices are less likely to be punished for their rulings against the government, either because it becomes difficult for the government to overrule those unfavorable decisions or because the ruling party does not have the majority in Congress for impeaching a justice (Chávez 2004b; Iaryczower et al. 2002; Ríos-Figueroa 2007).[5] So basically, justices who lack independence in strong administrations would rule in favor of the government as a way to circumvent reprisals. Gretchen Helmke (2005) finds that in Argentina it is precisely the justices who lack independence in weak administrations who are the ones that rule against the government during the final months. The author solves this puzzle by arguing that when a weak government approaches the end of the term justices are politically motivated to vote against the current government and in favor of the incoming one, what she calls *strategic defection*. In the case of Mexico, Julio Ríos-Figueroa (2006) finds consistent support for the fragmentation hypothesis since, between 1994 and 2002, the probability that the court rules against the ruling party increases as the degree of political fragmentation increases as well.[6] Sánchez et al. (2011) extend their sample of constitutional rulings up to 2007 and find that the fragmentation hypothesis does not apply to constitutional controversies but only to constitutional actions.

Even though the existing research on new democracies has consistently shown that justices would behave strategically under unsecure institutional contexts, Santiago Basabe-Serrano's (2012) original research on the Ecuadorian Constitutional Court presents a different story of voting patterns. He argues that in the context of extreme institutional instability, like Ecuador between 1999 and 2007, justices do not have any incentive to behave strategically since they know that a change in the ruling administration would inevitability produce a reshuffle in the court, regardless of the way justices vote. Under this scenario, the most rational behavior for the justices is to vote sincerely since it would allow them to maintain a reputation among the legal community to which they belong (Basabe-Serrano 2012).

Based on the mixed evidence of existing research, scholars in Latin America would conclude that the following three factors can contribute to predicting when justices would behave strategically: (1) whether or not the ruling party has a majority of seats in Congress (i.e. this refers to the fragmentation hypothesis); (2) whether or not the ruling government is approaching the end of the term (i.e. this refers to the timing hypothesis whether it is a "traditional" or strategic defection); and (3) the degree of institutional instability (i.e. this refers to the hypothesis of extreme institutional instability vs. medium or low instability).

II A model of judicial behavior for the Mexican Supreme Court: Effects of political context and constitutional design

Analysis of the Mexican Supreme Court rulings takes place under a context of political fragmentation and of low institutional instability. Regarding the first feature, many authors claim that the turning point in the long history of a subservient court was the decay of the hegemony of the PRI in the political arena, and the subsequent fragmentation of political power (Magaloni 2008; Figueroa 2007). At the national level, decay of the PRI started in 1988 when the party lost for the first time its two-thirds majority in the lower house (it continued in 1997 when they lost the single majority) and ended in 2000 when the PRI lost the presidency (Ríos-Figueroa 2007). At the state level, the end of supremacy of the PRI materialized by 1994 when the party had already lost three of the thirty-one gubernatorial elections and 20 percent of the municipalities of the country (Magaloni 2003). This new scenario of electoral pluralism brought new challenges to the old centralized system of dispute resolution in which neither the opposition parties (PAN and the Party of the Democratic Revolution (PRD) nor the different factions of the PRI[7] were willing to accept the old rules of the game for solving problems between the federal and state administrations or between the executive and the legislative branches.

Regarding the second feature of the Mexican political context, the institutional stability of the court, there is general consensus that the 1995 judicial reform placed the Supreme Court at the center of the checks-and-balances system (Cossío 2001; Cossío 2000; Magaloni 2003, 2008). Before 1995, the court had virtually no power to review cases with high political content like electoral law and conflicts among different branches or levels of government. But that situation changed with the creation of the constitutional actions along with the expansion of power of the constitutional controversies. Constitutional reform attacked not only the deficit in the judicial review but also other very relevant aspects of the Supreme Court like the tenure system, the total number of sitting justices, and the creation of the Council of the Federal Judicature. All these changes in the institutional design ended up producing a more stable and independent court, what scholars would classify as low institutional instability. Even though there is not general consensus of whether the reform responded to the long-term incentives of the ruling PRI (i.e. to ensure that those who may come into power would not rule arbitrarily (Finkel 2008),[8] or use short-term incentives), it represented a turning point in the history of executive–court relations since the new institutional design allowed the emergence of a court independent of political power.

Under this new scenario, the literature, mainly the separation-of-power approach, would claim that the divided government and the low institutional instability would represent a very favorable setting for justices, and the default hypothesis to test would predict that the probability of a justice ruling against the ruler increases because justices cannot be punished for their decisions. If this is the case, then it is expected that the differences between the way each justice votes would not necessarily be associated with the appointing political parties but rather with the personal characteristics of justices such as their age or career background.

Along with the previous scenario, it is also necessary to consider whether or not the particularities of the constitutional design of constitutional controversies and constitutional actions can affect the way a justice votes. Scholars like Robert Dahl (1957) and Martin Shapiro (1964), for example, have stressed the institutional perspective of the analysis of judicial behavior by showing how institutions and rules can affect their behavior. In this case, it is important to take that perspective into account since the particularities of each means of constitutional control can explain the changes by the way justices vote on them.

On the one hand, constitutional controversies deal with problems between different levels of government, both horizontal (between, for example, the executive and the legislative) and vertical (between, for example, the state entity and the federal government) (Article 105, Section I). Controversies over specific actions or general norms are alleged to make a concrete constitutional violation and can be presented by federal, state, and municipal executives, or federal and state legislative branches, or the state judicial branch. The effect of the decision remains only between the parties (*inter partes* effect) involved, with a simple majority (six or seven votes), unless eight or more justices agree on the unconstitutionality of the norm, in which case that decision will have *erga omnes* effect.[9] On the other hand, constitutional actions deal with contradictions between a state or federal law, international treaty, and the constitution. In this case, actions should be presented within the first thirty days after the enactment of the law (*a posteriori*) and it is not necessary to have a concrete case since the court has abstract review. Actions can be presented by one-third of either chamber of Congress or local legislatures, political parties, the Attorney General, and the National Human Rights Commission (CNDH). As in the case of constitutional controversies, actions would only have *erga omnes* effect when eight or more justices vote against the constitutionality of the law; however, if that super majority is not reached the case is dismissed, meaning that the plaintiff would only have a favorable result with a super majority of votes since there is no *inter partes* effect with a simple majority.

In this sense, and in order to have a clearer description of these means of constitutional control, we can identify unconstitutionality claims as part of the Austrian–Kelsen model of constitutional justice; although this has evolved during the second half of the twentieth century, its root is present in several of the constitutional courts of Europe. So that unconstitutionality claims resemble Hans Kelsen's conception of the negative legislator, since it is an abstract, specialized, and objective control between two general laws—the constitution and a law—where it is not necessary to claim injury to a right or power, with the prospective outcome of expelling from the system the law that contradicts the constitution. Hence, unconstitutionality claims are very similar to the abstract judicial review of Germany, which in Article 93, Section 2 of the Constitution states:

> The Federal Constitutional Court decides: (…) 2. in case of differences of opinion or doubts on the formal and material compatibility of Federal law or Land law with this Basic law, or on the compatibility of Land law with other Federal law, at the request of the Federal Government, of a Land government or of one-third of the Bundestag members.
>
> *(Kommers 1997; Jackson and Tushnet 2006)*

Meanwhile, constitutional controversies have traits similar to judicial review, in the sense that they are a form of constitutional control that requires an injury claim or actual controversy and confrontation between two antagonistic parties. This means that it is a form of concrete and subjective control, since the legal power of a governing body or government branch is at stake. But unlike judicial review, constitutional controversies are not part of a system of diffuse constitutional justice. On the contrary, like unconstitutionality claims, it is a concentrated constitutional control. This means that only the Supreme Court can hear and rule on constitutional controversies. In addition, it should be noted that judgments on unconstitutionality claims disputes may have general effects by invalidating all or parts of the law, unlike the judicial review rule whose effect is *inter partes* and involves the non-application of the rule in question (Jackson and Tushnet 2006).

These differences in institutional design can condition the justices' vote since the particularities of controversies vis-à-vis actions can create a more unfavorable scenario for unconstitutional rulings. Specifically, we argue that it is more likely that justices would rule unconstitutional on an action than on a controversy. The reasons are threefold. First, the abstract review on actions can be less politically sensitive to conflicts since justices are solving constitutional contradictions between a law and the constitution; while on controversies they are solving specific political conflicts. In this second case, political conflicts are more evident than actions and thus justices may be deferential to the powers in conflict. So, if a justice rules unconstitutional on actions, it can always be argued that the decision was the result of a clear contradiction between the law and the constitution; but in the case of the controversies it is more difficult to argue that the unconstitutional vote depended only on an assessment of the skills and powers under scrutiny without a political purpose.

Second, even though on both actions and controversies there is an *erga omnes* effect when eight or more justices vote against the constitutionality of the norm, in the case of controversies there is still an *inter partes* effect when six or seven justices vote in that direction, while on actions this is not possible. This difference in the effect of the judgment can affect the strategy of both plaintiffs and justices since on controversies the players can seek to unlock the political conflict without trying to achieve general effects, while on actions there is a necessary search for an *erga omnes* effect; otherwise the case would be meaningless.

Third, there are a limited number of actors that can entitle an action rather than a controversy as well as on the topics that each actor can challenge. For example, in the case of actions, political parties can only contest electoral laws because they do not have any other legal means to attack them. In controversies, first the Supreme Court and then the constitution have included municipalities in the catalogue of actors entitled, which increases potential users to more than 4,000. This important difference can also affect the way justices vote because in the case of actions they can be sensitive to the fact that some of the plaintiffs do not have any other legal means of challenging the law and thus tend to vote against the constitutionality, especially when legislative minorities are promoting those cases; while in the case of controversies, it is not unreasonable to consider that justices would think more carefully when declaring as unconstitutional a norm because it can open too many gaps in the legal system.

III A description of unconstitutional rulings during the PAN administration

We created an original data set with all the Supreme Court rulings on constitutional controversies and constitutional actions on violations to the organic part of the constitution from 2000 to 2011.[10] During those twelve years there were over 1,000 cases: 65 percent controversies and 35 percent actions. From those cases justices voted more than 1,000 times (a total of 12,777 votes on controversies and 7,554 on actions) because in many cases there was more than one topic on which justices had to vote. For example, the constitutional controversy No. 109/2004 from May 2005 raised the question about whether or not President Vicente Fox could veto the budget approved by the lower house in which deputies discharged the observations raised by the president. That controversy involved five rounds of voting on different topics, and thus we coded each of those votes separately.[11] Our dependent variable is coded 1 for those decisions in which the justice declared a norm unconstitutional and 0 otherwise (dismissals due to technical deficits in the presentations were not included in the sample).

III.I Voting behavior by political actors and topic

Figure 3.1 reveals that Mexican justices have been, on average, more aggressive in their rulings against the PRI than the PAN.[12] Figure 3.1a shows that 2001 and 2006 were the two years that presented the highest confrontation rates between justices and the ruling party, as in those two years justices ruled against the PAN more than 50 percent of the time. In 2006 the presidential election was held in which the PAN, the incumbent party, was re-elected. Even though it might initially have looked as though the justices indicated that the court was disloyal to the incoming president, behavior in the following years shows a court that was deferential to the incumbent party, even in 2012 when the PAN lost the presidential elections. Regarding the behavior of the justices against the PRI, Figure 3.1b clearly shows that since the party left government in 2000 there has been a steadily increasing rate in the votes against the PRI, even in 2012 when the party won the presidential elections. Overall, there were more unconstitutional rulings on actions (33 percent) than on controversies (14 percent), which corroborates previous findings (Sánchez et al. 2011).

Regardless of the political parties involved in the docket, overall unconstitutional rulings on actions have been very stable during the whole period except in 2006 and 2007 in which justices increased the average of unfavorable rulings by 54 percent and 66 percent respectively (see Figure 3.2). A closer look at those years reveals that 85 percent of the unfavorable rulings on each of those two years were on tax issues presented by the Attorney General against state entities.[13] Even though between 2008 and 2011 the average of unconstitutional rulings reduced by half, a careful look discloses that between 75 percent and 90 percent of those decisions were on electoral laws, a highly sensitive topic for political elites.

Actions were presented on a wide range of issues[14] but the majority of unconstitutional decisions were on tax (51 percent) and electoral (39 percent) issues. Even though justices had an active role on electoral laws, that perception changes if we take into account the total number of votes on that topic. From the total number of decisions on electoral laws, justices ruled as unconstitutional only one out of five times. The most actively engaged actors were the political parties, the General Attorney, and local legislatures (see Table 3.1). The issues on which each of these actors focused their claims were clearly specified: political parties on electoral laws (99 percent), Attorney General on tax issues (74 percent), and local legislatures on three other main issues—administrative (38 percent), tax (38 percent), and electoral (21 percent). Interestingly, as Table 3.1 shows, more than half of all unconstitutional rulings favored the Attorney General, however that privileged position improves even more if we analyze the favorable ruling over the docket presented by that particular political actor rather than over the total

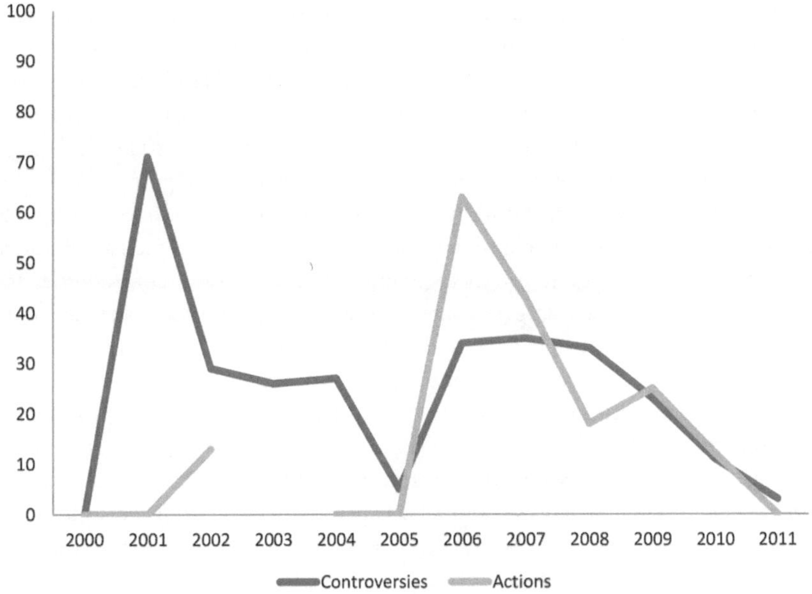

FIGURE 3.1A Unconstitutional rulings against the PAN (%)
Source: authors' own data.

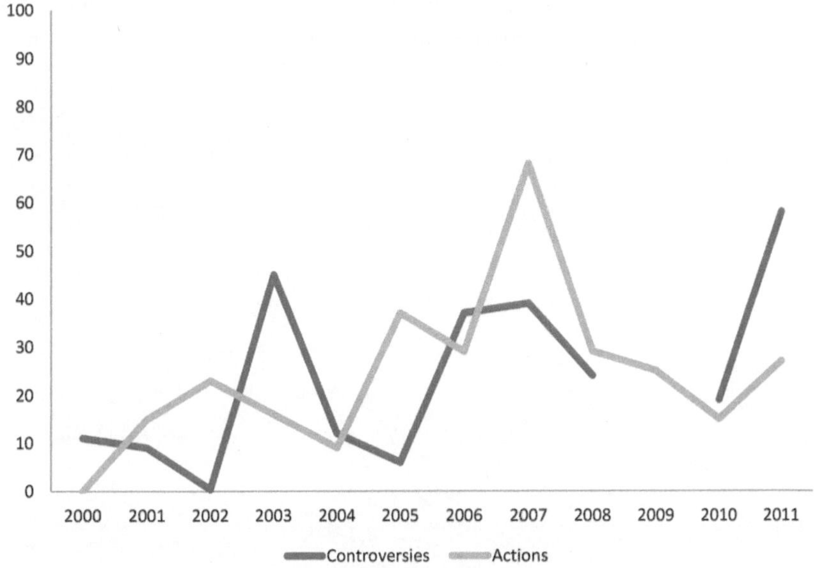

FIGURE 3.1B Unconstitutional rulings against the PRI (%)
Source: authors' own data.

docket. From the total of cases/decisions presented by the Attorney General, justices ruled favorably on 76 percent of those cases, a very successful rate.

Concerning constitutional controversies, the two most active years have been 2003 and 2006 in which justices declared 38 percent and 33 percent of the norm as unconstitutional, while the less active years were 2002 and 2005, declaring 1 percent and 5 percent of the norm unconstitutional (see Figure 3.2). Unlike actions, most of the unconstitutional rulings were on administrative issues (85 percent) and a small percentage on tax issues (14 percent).[15] Municipal executives have been by far the most proactive political actors in using controversies (see Table 3.1) and they have targeted their claims mainly against the state authority (56 percent) and against both state and federal authorities (39 percent). Likewise, municipal executives have had the most successful rate of favorable decisions: six out of ten unconstitutional rulings favored them (see Table 3.1). From all the controversies presented by municipal executives, the greatest number of favorable decisions was against the state (21 percent), since justices hardly ever ruled against both the state and federal authorities (0.4 percent). Most of those unfavorable decisions for local executives were taken in 2002, which explains why the court decreased their average of unconstitutional rulings to 1 percent.

The proactive role of municipalities in the use of controversies supports those studies that highlight their increasing role in the political arena (Selee 2012). The constitutional reform in 1999 elevated the status of municipalities to political entities, which placed them in a better position to intervene in the policy-making process within their jurisdiction. This institutional change, along with their increasing role in the democratization process, made them important actors in the

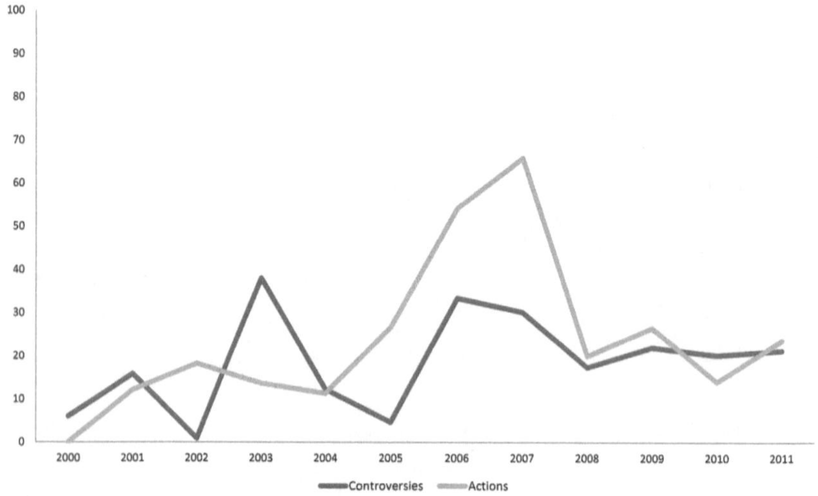

FIGURE 3.2 Unconstitutional rulings (%)
Source: Authors' own data

TABLE 3.1 Supreme Court docket according to the political actors involved as plaintiff in constitutional actions and controversies from 2000 to 2011

	Political Actors	*Docket*	*Favorable Rulings*
Actions	Political Parties	46%	27%
	Attorney General	24%	55%
	Local Legislatures	12%	4%
	Others	18%	14%
Controversies	Municipal Executives	69%	58%
	State Judiciaries	11%	18%
	State Executive	7%	6%
	National Executive	4%	7%
	Others	9%	11%

Source: Authors' own data.

political arena at state and federal levels. The Supreme Court supported the institutional strength by resolving certain constitutional disputes. The court confirmed that municipalities are an order of government created by the constitution as well as the federation and the states and accordingly have a range of powers that are outlined in the same constitution, the exercise of which is not conditioned by any institution of the federation or its respective federal entity.

III.II Voting behavior by justices' political proximity

Figures 3.3a and 3.3b capture the percentage of unconstitutional rulings by justices, regardless of the political parties involved, so as to explore which justices have been more aggressive in their rulings. Because of difficulties in measuring the political proximity of justices, we followed the American literature in the coding of their political affiliation: justices reflect the political preferences of the appointing executive (Hagle 1993; Spriggs and Wahlbeck 1995; Zorn and Van Winkle 2000).[16] Quite surprisingly, all the justices appointed during the PAN administrations have been those most aggressive on controversies while the justices appointed during the PRI administrations have been the friendliest (see Figure 3.3.a). Out of all unconstitutional rulings on constitutional controversies, 50 percent were against the PRI and 29 percent against the PAN. On the unconstitutional rulings against the PRI, 43 percent were from justices appointed by the PAN and 57 percent from the PRI, while from all unconstitutional rulings against the PAN, 33 percent were from justices appointed by the PAN and 67 percent from the PRI. This reveals that party identity matters to accounting for judicial behavior, since justices have been less aggressive in their rulings when their appointing political party was attacked. This behavior can explain why justices appointed during the PAN administration have a higher number of

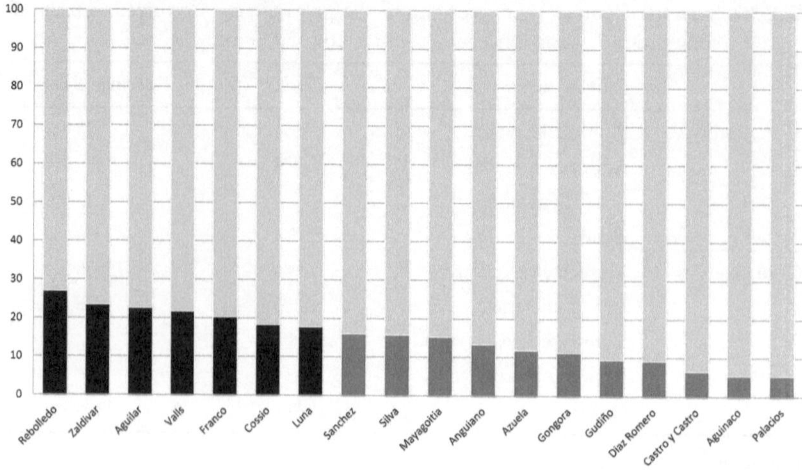

FIGURE 3.3A Unconstitutional rulings per justice on controversies (%)
Note: Grey bars correspond to justices appointed during the PRI administration and black bars to justices appointed during the PAN administration.
Source: Authors' own data.

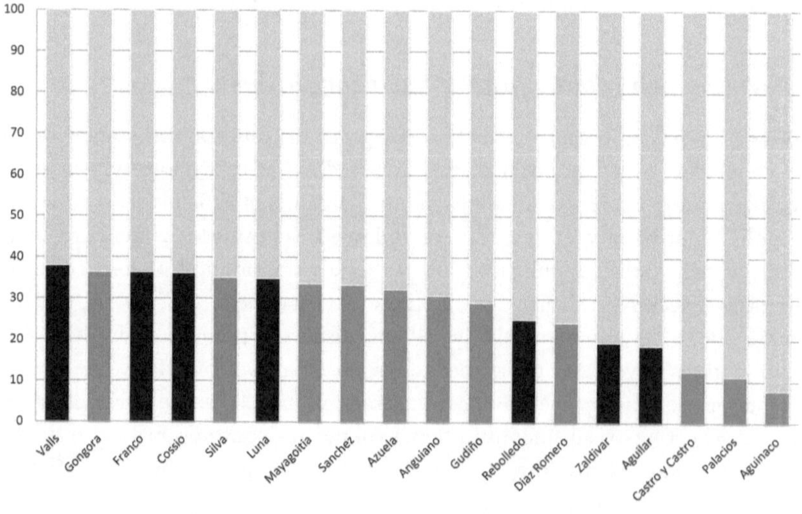

FIGURE 3.3B Unconstitutional rulings on constitutional actions
Note: Grey bars correspond to justices appointed during the PRI administration and black bars to justices appointed during the PAN administration.
Source: Authors' own data.

unconstitutional votes than those appointed by the PRI, since there were more rounds of votes on cases attacking the PRI than the PAN.

Regarding the unconstitutional rulings on actions, there is a more mixed pattern of voting behavior among the justices (see Figure 3.3.b). PAN-ist justices are still more aggressive on their rulings vis-à-vis the justices appointed by the PRI, however in this case Justices Góngora and Silva appointed by the PRI are among the first group, while Justices Pardo, Zaldívar, and Aguilar[17] are among the second group. The situation for these latter justices can be explained from the date on which they became Justices of the Supreme Court: Aguilar and Zaldívar began in late 2009 and Pardo in the first months of 2011. This means that their votes are not representative in consolidating a judicial proceeding, because the period of analysis concludes in December 2011. In this respect, the behaviors of Justices Góngora and Silva are more interesting. Even though both were appointed by the PRI, over the years they have shown a rather critical attitude to anachronistic interpretation models, conservative inertia, and authoritarian remnants in the administration of justice. It is important to recall that during their fifteen-year tenure, justices may significantly modify the way they understand and operate the constitution.

From all unconstitutional rulings, 52 percent were against the PRI while 12 percent were against the PAN. Contrary to controversies, there is no variation in the unfavorable rulings dependent on party identity of the justices since regardless of whether the PRI or the PAN were attacked, justices appointed by the PAN ruled against the political elites between 38 percent and 32 percent of the time, while justices appointed during the PRI were between 32 percent and 37 percent of the time. Once again, the PRI received the highest number of attacks.

IV An empirical account of Mexican justices mediating intra-elite conflicts

To what extent have Mexican Supreme Court Justices been a true arbiter in mediating intra-elite conflicts? To answer this question we model the voting behavior of the justices using two random intercept logistic regressions: one for constitutional controversies and the other for constitutional actions. This model, also known as a level-1 sampling model, allows us to account for the conditional dependence among the votes for the same justices by capturing the effect of omitted justice-specific factors (such as religious bias or social background—time-constant factors) that cause some justices to be more favorable to unconstitutional rulings than others (Raudenbush and Bryk 1992). Our dependent variable is coded 1 for those decisions in which the justice declared a norm unconstitutional and 0 otherwise (dismissals were not included in the sample). So the unit of analysis is a justice-decision—not a court-decision, as was carried out in previous studies (Ríos-Figueroa 2007; Sánchez et al. 2011). Therefore, one important contribution from this study is that we would present precise predictions about the behavior of the justices and not about the court as a whole.

Table 3.2 presents the list of independent variables that were included in both models. These variables can be sorted in four groups: (1) characteristics of the cases; (2) attributes of the plaintiff side; (3) attributes of the defendant side; and (4) attributes of the justices. Regarding the first group of variables we include in the two models a dummy variable—salience—that captures whether the decision of the justices is about a relevant case. Decisions were coded as salient when they: (a) focused on an issue that strongly polarized elites (for example, the "Televisa" law about the authority in charge of controlling the media market); (b) represent strong conflict between the political powers (for example, presidential veto on the budget); and (c) receive forceful attention from public opinion and the media (for example, the presidential decree closing the electric company "Luz y Fuerza del Centro"). For the constitutional actions model we included two additional dummy variables. The first variable identifies those cases that challenge an electoral law, while the second explores whether the action was against a law enacted by the current administration or the previous one. Traditionally, it is conceived that justices would more easily declare a norm unconstitutional if that norm was enacted by the previous administration rather than by the current one because the current government can impose threats on those justices who are hostile.[18]

TABLE 3.2 List of independent variables included in the regression models

Independent variables	*Model*	*Coding scheme*
Characteristics of the case		
Salience cases	C, A	1=Salience, 0=otherwise
Electoral laws	A	1=Electoral, 0=otherwise
Unconstitutional ruling on current norm	A	1=Current norm, 0=previous norm
Characteristics of the plaintiff side		
PRI claiming	C, A	1=PRI, 0=PAN
Other parties claiming	C, A	1=Other parties, 0=PAN
Municipalities claiming	C	1=Municipalities, 0=State and Federal
Characteristics of the defendant side		
Cases against PRI	C, A	1=PRI, 0=PAN
Cases against other parties	C, A	1=Other parties, 0=PAN
Cases against federal government	A	1=Federal, 0=State and Municipality
Characteristics of the justices		
PAN justices	C, A	1=PAN, 0=PRI
Judicial background	C, A	1=Judicial, 0=Political
Age	C, A	Number

Source: Authors' own data.

Note: C= Constitutional Controversies; A= Constitutional Actions.

Regarding the second group of variables, two dummy variables were included in both models to capture whether or not justices behaved differently according to the plaitiff's party identity. The dummy variable "PRI claiming" codes 1 for those decisions in which the PRI initiated the demand either by themselves or in a coalition with other parties excluding the PAN, while the "PAN claiming" variable captures 1 when the PAN initiated the demand either by themselves or in a coalition with other parties. The reference category is when other parties such as PRD or PT (Partido del Trabajo) initiated the demand.[19] An additional variable was included in the controversies model to explore whether justices behaved differently when a municipality presented a controversy. It is important to recall that during the time period of the analysis municipalities presented 69 percent of the controversies (see Table 3.1) while the federal government presented only 10 percent.

To capture the party identity of the defendant we follow a similar coding strategy as that employed for the party identity of the plaintiff side. We included in both models two dummy variables to capture those decisions against the PRI and the PAN (either alone or in a coalition with other parties) having as a baseline category those decisions against other parties. Two interaction variables were included in both models to predict the voting behavior of the justices in cases where the PAN tries to invalidate a norm enacted by the PRI and vice versa. For the constitutional actions model we included a special variable to capture whether the plaintiff is challenging a federal law.[20]

Finally we included three variables in both models to capture the effect of justices' special attributes: political proximity, background, and age. The proximity of the justice to the political parties can be determined by the political party of the appointing executive, since the idea is that the justice reflects the political preferences of the party of that executive (Hagle 1993; Spriggs and Wahlbeck 1995; Zorn and Van Winkle 2000). Therefore, PAN justices are those appointed during both Fox and Calderon administrations while the others are PRI justices. The judicial background variable identifies whether that justice comes from the judicial family, while the age variable captures the current age.

IV.I Judicial behavior on constitutional controversies

Table 3.3 presents the results of a random intercept logistic regression for the Supreme Court Justices rulings between 2000 and 2011 on constitutional controversies (Column 3.1) and constitutional actions (Column 3.2). The judicial behavior of justices on constitutional controversies reveals an interesting logic of power redistribution: the PRI will have a greater probability of obtaining a favorable outcome (either as plaintiff or defendant) when confronting minority parties, while the PAN will have a greater probability of obtaining a favorable ruling when attacking a norm passed by the PRI, but the opposite when that norm was passed by minority parties. So, basically there is no winner-takes-all, but rather partial winners: PAN over PRI when PAN is the plaintiff, PRI over minority parties on both

TABLE 3.3 Random intercept logistic regression for judicial behavior of Mexican Supreme Court Justices from 2000 to 2011

	3.1 Controversies	*3.2 Actions*
Characteristics of the cases		
Salience cases	−0.605***	0.205***
	(0.705)	(0.074)
Electoral laws	–	−1.389***
		(0.074)
Unconstitutional ruling on current norm	–	0.508***
		(0.119)
Attributes of the plaintiff and defendant sides		
PRI claiming	0.704***	−0.183
	(0.103)	(0.153)
PAN claiming	−0.218**	1.802***
	(0.093)	(0.108)
Cases against PRI	−0.297***	0.467***
	(0.114)	(0.120)
Cases against PAN	−0.002	−0.203*
	(0.090)	(0.108)
PAN vs. PRI	1.933***	−1.588***
	(0.132)	(0.128)
PRI vs. PAN	−0.217	−1.964***
	(0.150)	(0.372)
Municipalities claiming	−0.569***	–
	(0.064)	
Cases against federal government	–	−0.988***
		(0.127)
Attributes of the justices		
PAN justices	1.497***	0.457
	(0.417)	(0.326)
Judicial background	−0.421	−0.367
	(0.400)	(0.276)
Age	0.089***	0.010
	(0.012)	(0.014)
Constant	−7.650***	−1.862*
	(0.903)	(0.968)
/lnsig2u	−0.662	−1.547***
	(0.425)	(0.593)
Number of observations	12777	7554

Source: Authors' own data.

Note: *** $p<0.01$, ** $p<0.05$, * $p<0.1$.

plaintiff and defendant, and minority parties over PAN when being the defendant. Also, justices are less likely to rule unconstitutionally on important cases (which may be an indication that justices prefer to maintain the status quo in sensitive cases) and on cases presented by municipalities. Finally, justices appointed during the PAN administrations are more likely to rule unconstitutionally (contrary to those justices appointed during the PRI administrations) as well as older justices.

Because the coefficients in the table are non-linear, predicted probabilities were computed under different scenarios for a substantive interpretation (see Table 3.4, Column 4.1).[21] These scenarios are basically cases in which, for example, the PAN is challenging a norm enacted by the PRI or vice versa. When all independent variables are at their mean, the probability of a justice ruling unconstitutionally is extremely low: 0.1, i.e. one out of ten decisions, but that probability increases to more than double when the PAN is challenging the PRI. Table 3.4 also shows that, on average, justices are more likely to favor the demand presented by the PAN rather than the PRI when the ruling party is on either the plaintiff (0.24 probability) or defendant (0.12 probability) side of the docket. However, those probabilities increase or reduce according to the political proximity of the justices. Justices appointed during the PAN administrations will rule unconstitutionally on more than half of their decisions when the ruling party is claiming against the PRI and will not support the PAN when being attacked by the PRI on only one out of four decisions. On the other hand, justices appointed during the PRI administrations will only rule unconstitutionally in one out of five times when the ruling party is challenging a norm enacted by their party, and one out of ten times when their party is attacking the ruling party.[22] These results reveal two important aspects of judicial behavior. First, justices appointed during the PAN administrations have a higher probability of voting unconstitutionally than those appointed during the PRI administrations. Second, the results illustrate that the ruling party will have more support from the justices when challenging or defending against the PRI.

TABLE 3.4 Predicted probabilities for unconstitutional rulings on controversies and actions

	Average	*4.1 Controversies*		*Average*	*4.2 Actions*	
		PAN justices	*PRI justices*		*PAN justices*	*PRI justices*
PAN vs. PRI	0.26	0.51	0.19	0.27	0.33	0.24
PRI vs. PAN	0.12	0.29	0.08	0.02	0.02	0.02

Source: Authors' own data.

Note: all other independent variables are at their mean.

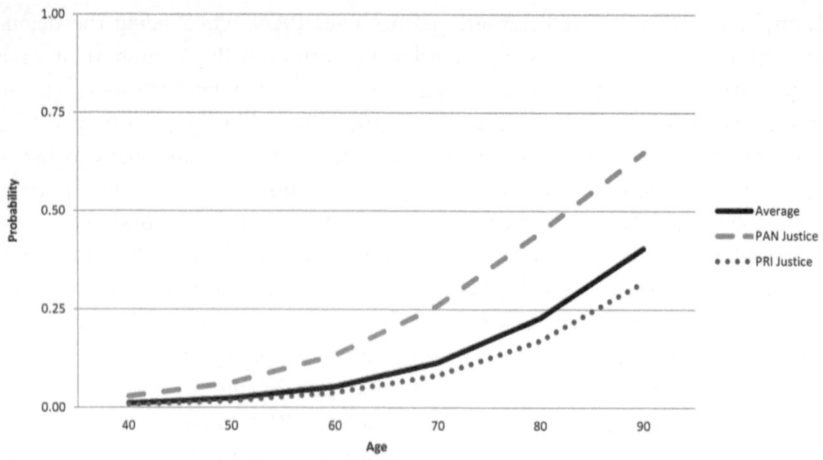

FIGURE 3.4 Probability of unconstitutional rulings on actrions by political affiliation and justice's age

Finally, Figure 3.4 displays how age matters for both PAN and PRI justices ruling unconstitutionally in controversies. On average, older justices are more likely to rule unconstitutionally than younger ones, but justices appointed during the PAN administration will do it more frequently than those of the PRI. It may be the case that older justices (who are nearer their retirement age) do not fear the political consequences of potential reprisals from politicians.

IV.II Judicial behavior on constitutional actions

As in the case of controversies, the results of the regression coefficients for actions (see Column 3.2, Table 3.3) also reveal the logic of power redistribution, but in this case a different logic from the previous model. The ruling party would have greater probabilities of obtaining a favorable outcome when confronting minority parties (either as a plaintiff or defendant) while minority parties will have a favorable ruling when challenging a law enacted by the PRI. The result of the interaction variables reveals that when the two biggest political parties challenge a law enacted by the other party, justices will behave in the same way: not to rule as unconstitutional. What this finding means is that justices would prefer to maintain the status quo rather than be responsible for changing the rules of the game.

The results of the model also reveal that justices are less likely to rule unconstitutionally on electoral cases but more likely on decisions that challenge a norm enacted by the current administration. This happens because of timing restrictions for challenging a norm with constitutional actions. Also, justices are less likely to rule against the federal government, while the opposite is true for other lower levels of government. Finally, it is important to point out that none of the personal attributes of the justices is statistically significant, which suggests that there is no relationship between these variables and the voting behavior of justices.

For a more substantive interpretation, predicted probabilities were computed (see Table 3.4, Column 4.2). Contrary to controversies, justices are more likely to rule an action unconstitutional, as when all independent variables are at their mean, the probability of unconstitutional rulings is 0.25, i.e. one in four; but that probability increases to 0.27 when the PAN is challenging a law enacted by the PRI and decreases to 0.02 when the PRI is challenging a law enacted by the ruling party. If the political proximity of the justices is taken into account, the probabilities change, but not significantly, as happened with constitutional controversies in which justices appointed during the PRI administrations clearly differed from the voting pattern from those appointed during the PAN administrations. Overall, these findings highlight the previous results: justices are not willing to rule against the ruling party, especially the ones appointed during another administration.

V Conclusions

Are Mexican justices true mediators of conflicts between political powers? To answer this question it is important to notice that the type of constitutional control—constitutional action or constitutional controversy—largely conditions justices' judicial behavior. Indeed, according to findings in Section IV justices vote differently depending on whether they are voting on a controversy or an action. On average, justices are more likely to vote unconstitutionally on actions than on controversies. This finding suggests that the institutional context in which justices operate plays a significant role. More precisely, as previously argued, the institutional design of each mean of constitutional control has an effect on the type of justices' argument, the effect of judgments, and the type of actors entitled to use each of these forms of constitutional control.

The econometric analysis of Supreme Court rulings reveals that under a context of institutional stability and divided government Mexican justices behave differently, as the literature would suggest.[23] Some authors (Chávez 2004a; Helmke 2005; Iaryczower et al. 2002; Larkins 1996; Magaloni and Sánchez 2006; Ríos-Figueroa 2007; Sánchez et al. 2011) argue that in new democracies with insecure institutional contexts, justices would vote strategically by ruling in favor of the government as a way to circumvent reprisals. The Mexican case shows that in the opposite political scenario justices would also vote in favor of the ruling government. The chapter shows that the probability of a justice voting against the PAN, both in actions and controversies, is reduced when that party is either the plaintiff or the defendant. How can we explain this finding? Or in other words, why in the first two presidential administrations of the PAN have justices been so deferential to that political party at the moment of resolving conflicts between powers?

One explanation is that justices did not have enough time to assimilate the new political scenario of the country. Even though since 2000 justices have enjoyed more independence and autonomy than during the PRI era, they still remain cautious of their relationship with the ruling party (especially justices appointed during the PRI administration). The legacy of the PRI's conception about the executive–court relations is still fresh among the members of the judiciary power. Even though scholars like Casar (2013) would argue that such fears have no fundamental basis under this new fragmented political scenario (because the president would need the support of Congress to effect justices' independence, such as limiting the power of judicial review or reducing the number of sitting justices), the experience of other Latin American countries of strong manipulation of the judiciary (as in the cases of Bolivia and El Salvador) can make justices doubt their new independence.

A second explanation is the persistence of an unbalanced power culture within the political actors. Evidently, the hegemony of the PRI during more than seven decades cannot be dismantled from one day to another, especially if the country has very similar institutional settings and actors. Even though the Supreme Court gained independence after 1994, this did not correspond with a change in the conception of the other political actors. The long-lasting way of doing politics under the PRI hegemony persisted in the minds of politicians as well as in the members of the judiciary. That is why, at the beginning of Mexican democracy, Octavio Paz said: "the PRI must go to school of democracy. The opposition parties must also enroll in that school" (Paz 2001: 252), which applies to each of the players in public life. We must learn how to live in a democracy.

A third explanation can also be attributed to the lack of transparency in the Supreme Court's spending, since it generates, in the long run, dependency on the executive power. In the 1995 constitutional amendment the Council of the Federal Judicature was created as a depositary for the judicial branch in charge of its administration, surveillance, and discipline. In 1999, there was a "counter-reform" which subordinated the council to the court by converting it into an administrative body while giving power back to the court to be controlled by itself. So in practice, the court is responsible for auditing its own spending, but in the case of accusations of misspending the executive and legislative (*Auditoria Superior de la Federación*) branches are the ultimate institutions responsible for revising the account. This is a very sensitive issue because politicians as well as society are aware of the scandalous discretional spending of the court, to which the executive has paid no attention.[24] Nevertheless, this situation could be a trade-off: the justices lose independence in order to keep the way they manage their budget in the dark.

A final explanation for the favorable behavior of the justices toward the ruling party is the redistribution of political power. Even though in 2000 the PRI lost the presidency that did not mean that it became an irrelevant actor in the political life of the country since it remained a dominant force in the national legislative arena as well as in state and municipality administrations. The other political parties were unable to defeat the PRI in these other political arenas, and turned to the use of controversies and actions as institutional mechanisms to obtain a more favorable distribution of political power. The strategy of power redistribution consisted mainly in supporting the ruling party, the second largest party in the country: the PAN.

Even though each justice can have a different reason for his\her behavior (either a genuine conviction to defend the principles of separation of power or a loyalty toward the parties that appointed him\her) the truth is that, in practice, justices have used the legal arena to redistribute power between the country's two main political forces, at least during the first decade of democracy. So, going back to the initial question, does this mean justices have been true mediators of the conflicts between powers? We believe that the answer is "no". Ideally, a referee is someone who solves conflicts impartially, someone who evaluates the performance of the political forces from a common legal and institutional ground. In Mexico, we have a court with a clear political aim: to redistribute political power in the political arena taking all the benefits and risks that it may involve. Therefore, we believe that these types of empirical studies are relevant for the future research agenda since they can allow us to examine the judicial behavior of the justices on the return of the PRI to the presidency in 2012.

Notes

1 A detailed and comprehensive study by Pilar Domingo (2000) clearly evidences how the Supreme Court was politically subordinated to the logic of the political system.
2 For a comprehensive historical account about the origins of each approach see Nancy Maveety (ed.) (2003) *The Pioneers of Judicial Behavior.*
3 A recent study on the Constitutional Court of Ecuador represents an exception to this consensus (Basabe-Serrano and Polga-Hecimovich 2012).
4 Mexico is an interesting case, since until the democratization period presidential strength did not come from the constitutional text but rather from meta-constitutional powers, i.e. the political machinery (Carpizo 1978). With the arrival of political pluralism, the Mexican executive turned out to be a less powerful branch since the institutional design placed it in a less advantageous scenario (Lujambio 1996, 2000; Marván 1997).
5 There is incipient research about the Argentine and Ecuadorian judiciary that challenges the fragmentation assumption (Castagnola 2010, 2012; Grijalva 2010; Leiras et al. 2015).
6 Between 1994 and 1997 the probability of the court ruling against the PRI was 0.07, while between 1997 and 2000 it was 0.44, and between 2000 and 2002 it was 0.52 (Ríos-Figueroa 2007).
7 Roberto Madrazo, the candidate from the PRI at the gubernatorial election in Tabasco in 1994 refused to accept the solution of the ruling president, Ernesto Zedillo, to step down from office and let the candidate from the PRD step in office. The rebellion of the PRI in Tabasco clearly illustrates the decay of party discipline.
8 This explanation comes from a strategic perspective, what Tom Ginsburg (2003) called the *insurance policy*. The general idea is that reforms are likely to take place when the elite can foresee a future loss of its hegemony in the political arena.
9 *Erga omnes* effect is possible under four different scenarios: (1) the national government attacks municipal or state general norms; (2) the state attacks municipal general norms; (3) the federal executive attacks the federal legislative; or (4) when a state branch attacks acts or norms from another branch of the same state.

10 The authors are very grateful for the research assistance of Gustavo Marín Hernández, Daniel Murillo, and Franz Oberarzbacher in the compilation and codification of the Supreme Court rulings.

11 The case involved five rounds of votes: (1) whether the president can make observations about the budget approved by Congress; (2) if the majority of 6 votes from the previous session could be enough to declare the nullity of the impugned acts; (3) whether a two-thirds majority is required in the lower house to dismiss the president's observations on the budget; (4) whether Congress has to call for an extraordinary session; and (5) whether justices have to vote on other issues unrelated to the main issue and raised in the controversies.

12 The analysis corresponds to cases against the political party itself as well as cases presented by that party in coalition with other parties excluding the cases in which the PAN or the PRI were present in that coalition.

13 The states with the highest percentage of unconstitutional rulings in those years were: Aguascalientes (61 percent) and Michoacán (16 percent) in 2006, and Yucatán (43 percent) and Coahuila (30 percent) in 2007.

14 The docket was divided into the following topics: electoral, tax, administrative, labor, and criminal laws.

15 Only 11 out of 1,834 unconstitutional rulings were on labor issues, a similar situation to actions, since none of those was ruled unconstitutional.

16 This solution can have problems in some cases since some justices appointed during the PRI or PAN administrations did not have an ideological proximity to the ruling party but rather to others; for example, Justice Castro y Castro who was appointed during the PRI government but politically close to the PRD. Nevertheless, it's a good measure of accounting for ideological differences because justices appointed during the PAN administration have a different conception of the role of the Supreme Court and of justice than do those appointed during the PRI administration in which, overall, the high court had a more deferential role in politics.

17 It is important to mention that Justices Zaldívar and Aguilar were more recently appointed, in December 2009, so that they voted a fewer number of times than the other justices.

18 Even though this hypothesis may be in conflict with the political fragmentation hypothesis, the particularities of the time frame for presenting constitutional actions would reduce the number of cases challenging a norm enacted by the previous government. We thank one of the anonymous reviewers for this comment.

19 The PRD does not receive special treatment in the coding system because even though it is the third party in Congress it does not have an active role in the constitutional justice sphere either initiating claims or as the defendant.

20 It is important to point out that federal laws are not necessarily associated with laws enacted by the PAN since they often require support from other parties.

21 Predicted probabilities were computed using margins that the Stata software commands.

22 Similar results were obtained when computing the probabilities of a PAN municipality attacking the PRI and a PRI municipality attacking the PAN.

23 We are not directly testing the divided government hypothesis because during the time frame of the analysis there is no variation in this feature and our data set, so far, does not include earlier years in which the PRI had control over both houses of Congress.

24 A recent report presented by Ana Laura Magaloni Kerpel and Carlos Elizondo Mayer-Serra (2010) publicly denounced the misspending of the court by presenting detailed evidence of the discretional spending of the justices on food, health, trips, etc. This report goes in line with the previous wrongdoing accusations of local newspapers.

References

Bailey, M.A. and F. Maltzman (2011) *The Constrained Court: Law, Politics and the Decisions Justices Make*. Princeton, NJ: Princeton University Press.

Basabe-Serrano, S. (2012) "Judges without Robes and Judicial Voting in Contexts of Institutional Instability: The Case of Ecuador's Constitutional Court, 1999–2007." *Journal of Latin American Studies* 44: 127–161.

Basabe-Serrano, S. and J. Polga-Hecimovich (2013) "Legislative Coalitions and Judicial Turnover under Political Uncertainty: The Case of Ecuador." *Political Research Quarterly* 66(1): 154–166.

Baum, L. (1997) *The Puzzle of Judicial Behavior*. Ann Arbor, MI: University of Michigan Press.

Cabrera Acevedo, L. (1998) *La Suprema Corte de Justicia durante los gobiernos de Portes Gil, Ortiz Rubio y Abelardo L. Rodriguez (1929–1934)*. Mexico City: Suprema Corte de Justicia de la Nación.

Carpizo, Jorge (1978) *El presidencialismo mexicano* (1st ed.) Mexico City: Siglo Veintiuno.

Casar, M.A. (1999) "Executive-Legislative Relations: The Case of Mexico (1946–1997)." In S. Morgenstern and B. Nacif (eds) *Legislative Politics in Latin America*. Cambridge: Cambridge University Press, pp. 114–146.

Casar, María A (2013) "Quince años de gobiernos sin mayoría en el Congreso mexicano." *Política y gobierno* XX(2): 219–263.

Castagnola, A. (2010) *Rethinking Judicial Instability in Developing Democracies: A National and Subnational Analysis of Supreme Courts in Argentina*. Political Science Ph.D. thesis, University of Pittsburgh.

Castagnola, A. (2012) "'*I Want It All, and I Want It Now*': The Political Manipulation of Argentina's Provincial High Courts." *Journal of Politics in Latin America* 2: 39–62.

Chávez, R.B. (2004a) "The Evolution of Judicial Autonomy in Argentina: Establishing the Rule of Law in Ultrapresidential System." *Journal of Latin American Studies* 36: 451–478.

Chávez, R.B. (2004b) *The Rule of Law in Nascent Democracies: Judicial Politics in Argentina*. Stanford, CA: Stanford University Press.

Clark, T.S. (2009) *The Limits of Judicial Independence*. Cambridge: Cambridge University Press.

Cossío, J.R. (1998) *Artículo 105. La Constitución política de los Estados Unidos Mexicanos comentada. I. d. I. Jurídicas*. Distrito Federal, Mexico: Editorial Porrúa. II.

Cossío, J.R. (2001) "La Suprema Corte y la teoría Constitucional." *Política y Gobierno* VIII(1): 61–115.

Dahl, R. (1957) "Decision-Making in a Democracy: The Supreme Court as a National Policy-Maker." *Journal of Public Law* 6(Fall): 279–295.

Domingo, P. (2000) "Judicial Independence: The Politics of Supreme Court Judge in Mexico." *Journal of Latin American Studies* 32: 705–735.

Dworkin, R. (1978) *Taking Rights Seriously*. Cambridge, MA: Harvard University Press.

Epstein, L. and J. Knight (1998) *The Choices Justices Make*. Washington, DC: CQ Press.

Ferejohn, J. (2002) "Judicializing Politics, Politicizing Law." *Law and Contemporary Problems* 65(3): 41–68.

Ferejohn, J. and B. Weingast (1992) "A Positive Theory of Statutory Interpretation." *International Review of Law and Economics* 12: 263–279.

Finkel, J. (2008) *Judicial Reform as Political Insurance: Argentina, Peru, and Mexico in the 1990s*. Notre Dame, IN: Universtiy of Notre Dame Press.

Gibson, J. (1978) "Judges' Role Orientations, Attitudes, and Decisions: An Interactive Model." *American Political Science Review* 72(3): 911–924.

Ginsburg, T. (2003) *Judicial Review in New Democracies: Constitutional Courts in Asian Cases*. Cambridge: Cambridge University Press.

Gillman, H. and C.W. Clayton (1999) "Beyond Judicial Attitudes: Institutional Approaches to Supreme Court Decision-Making. " In C.W. Clayton and H. Gillman (eds) *Supreme Court Decision-Making: New Institutionalist Approaches*. Chicago, IL: University of Chicago Press, pp. 1–12.

Grijalva, A. (2010) "Courts and Political Parties: The Politics of Constitutional Review in Ecuador, " Political Science doctoral dissertation. Pittsburgh, PA: University of Pittsburgh.

Hagle, T.M. (1993) "Strategic Retirements: A Political Model of Turnover on the United States Supreme Court." *Political Behavior* 15(1): 25–48.

Helmke, G. (2005) *Courts under Constraints: Judges, Generals, and Presidents in Argentina*. New York: Cambridge University Press.

Helmke, G. and J. Ríos-Figueroa (eds) (2011) *Courts in Latin America*. Cambridge: Cambridge University Press.

Iaryczower, M., P. Spiller, and M. Tommasi (2002) "Judicial Independence in Unstable Environments, Argentina 1935–1998." *American Journal of Political Science* 46(4): 699–716.

Jackson, Vicky C. and Tushnet, Mark (2006) *Comparative Constitutional Law*, 2nd edn. New York: Foundation Press.

Kahn, R. (1999) "Institutionalized Norms and Supreme Court Decision-Making: The Rehnquist Court on Privacy and Religion." In C.W. Clayton and H. Guillman (eds) *Supreme Court Decision-Making: New Institutionalist Approaches*. Chicago, IL: University of Chicago Press, pp. 175–200.

Kommers, Donal P. (1997) *The Constitutional Jurisprudence of the Federal Republic of Germany*. Durham, NC: Duke University Press.

Larkins, C. (1996) "Judicial Independence and Democratization: A Theoretical and Conceptualization Analysis." *American Journal of Comparative Law* 44(4): 605–626.

Leiras, M., A. Giraudy, and T. Guadelupe (2015) "Who Wants an Independent Court? Political Competition and Supreme Court Instability in the Argentine Provinces (1984–2008)." *Journal of Politics* 77(1): 175–187.

Lujambio, Alonso (1996) *Federalismo y congreso en el cambio político de México*. Mexico City: UNAM.

Lujambio, Alonso (2000) *El poder compartido: Un ensayo sobre la democratización mexicana*. Mexico City: Océano de México.

Magaloni, B. (2003) "Authoritarianism, Democracy and the Supreme Court: Horizontal Exchange and the Rule of Law in Mexico." In S. Mainwaring and C. Welna (eds) *Democratic Accountability in Latin America*. Oxford: Oxford University Press, pp. 266–306.

Magaloni, B. (2008) "Enforcing the Autocratic Political Order and the Role of Courts: The Case of Mexico." In T. Ginsburg and T. Moustafa (eds) *Rule by Law: The Politics of Courts an Authoritarian Regimes*. Cambridge: Cambridge University Press, pp. 180–206.

Magaloni, B. and A. Sánchez (2006) *An Authoritarian Enclave? The Supreme Court in Mexico's Emerging Democracy*. Paper presented to the Annual Meeting of the American Political Science Association, Philadelphia, PA, Aug.–Sept.

Magaloni Kerpel, A.L. and C. Elizondo Mayer-Serra (2010) "¿Por qué nos cuesta tanto dinero la Suprema Corte?" Serie El Uso y Abuso de los Recursos Públicos Cuaderno de debate No. 6.

Maltzman, F., J. Spriggs II, and P. Wahlbeck (2000) *Crafting Law on the Supreme Court: The Collegial Game*. New York: Cambridge University Press.

Marván, Ignacio (1997) *¿Y después del presidencialismo?: Reflexiones para la formación de un nuevo régimen*. Mexico City: Océano de México.

Maveety, N. (ed.) (2003) *The Pioneers of Judicial Behavior*. Ann Arbor, MI: Univeristy of Michigan Press.

Ostberg, C.L. and M.E. Wetstein (2007) *Attitudinal Decision Making in the Supreme Court of Canada*. Vancouver, BC: University of British Columbia Press.

Paz, O (2001) *Sueño en libertad. Escritos políticos*. Mexico City: Seix Barral.

Pérez Liñán, A. and A. Castagnola (2009) "Presidential Control of High Courts in Latin America: A Long Term View (1904–2006)." *Journal of Politics in Latin America* 2: 87–114.

Posner, R.A. (2008) *How Judges Think*. Cambridge, MA: Harvard University Press.

Ramseyer, J.M. and E.B. Rasmusen (2003) *Measuring Judicial Independence: The Political Economy of Judging in Japan*. Chicago, IL: University of Chicago Press.

Raudenbush, S.W. and A.S. Bryk (1992) *Hierarchical Linear Models in Social and Behavioral Research: Applications and Data Analysis Methods*. Newbury Park, CA: Sage Publications.

Ríos-Figueroa, J. (2006) "Judicial Independence: Definition, Measurement, and Its Effects on Corruption. An Analysis of Latin America." Political Science doctoral dissertation. New York City, NY: New York University, p. 203.

Ríos-Figueroa, J. (2007) "Fragmentation of Power and the Emergence of an Effective Judiciary in Mexico, 1994–2002." *Latin American Politics and Society* 49(1): 31–57.

Rodríguez-Raga, J.C. (2011) "Strategic Deference in the Colombian Constitutional Court." In G. Helmke and J. Ríos-Figueroa (eds) *Courts in Latin America*. Cambridge: Cambridge University Press, pp. 81–98.

Rohde, D.W. and H.J. Spaeth (1976) *Supreme Court Decision Making*. San Francisco, CA: W. H. Freeman.

Sánchez, A., B. Magaloni, and E. Magar (2011) "Legalist versus Interpretativist: The Supreme Court and the Democratic Transition in Mexico." In G. Helmke and J. Ríos-Figueroa (eds) *Courts in Latin America*, . Cambridge: Cambridge University Press, pp. 187–218.

Segal, J.A. and H.J. Spaeth (2002) *The Supreme Court and the Attitudinal Model Revisted*. Cambridge: Cambridge University Press.

Segal, J.A. and L. Epstein (1995) "Ideological Values and the Votes of U.S. Supreme Court Justices Revisited." *Journal of Politics* 57(August): 812–823.

Selee, A. (2012) "Municipalities and Policymaking." In R.A. Camp (ed.) *The Oxford Handbook of Mexican Politics*. Oxford: Oxford University Press, pp. 101–118.

Shapiro, M. (1964) "Political Jurisprudence." *Kentucky Law Journal* 52: 294–345.

Spaeth, H.J. (1961) "An Approach to the Study of Attitudinal Differences as an Aspect of Judicial Behavior." *Midwest Journal of Political Science* 5(2): 165–180.

Spaeth, H.J. (1964) "The Judicial Restraint of Mr. Justice Frankfuter: Myth or Reality." *American Journal of Political Science* 8(1): 22–38.

Spiller, P. and R. Gely (1990) "Congressional Control or Judicial Independence: The Determinants of U.S. Supreme Court Labor-Relations Decisions, 1949–1988." *The RAND Corporation* 23(4): 463–492.

Spriggs, J.F.I. and P.J. Wahlbeck (1995) "Calling It Quits: Strategic Retirement on the Federal Courts of Appeals, 1893–1991." *Political Research Quarterly* 48(3): 573–597.

Staton, J.K. (2010) *Judicial Power and Strategic Communication in Mexico*. Cambridge: Cambridge University Press.

Trochev, A. (2008) *Judging Russia: Constitutional Court in Russian Politics 1990–2006*. Cambridge: Cambridge University Press.

Ulmer, S.S. (1973) "Social Background as an Indicator to the Votes of Supreme Court Justices in Criminal Cases: 1947–1956." *American Journal of Political Science* 17(3): 622–630.
Vanberg, G. (2005) *The Politics of Constitutional Review in Germany*. Cambridge: Cambridge University Press.
Verner, J.G. (1984) "The Independence of Supreme Courts in Latin America: A Review of the Literature." *Journal of Latin American Studies* 16(2): 463–506.
Wahlbeck, P.J., J. Spriggs II, and F. Maltzman (1998) "Marshalling the Court: Bargaining and Accommodation on the United States Supreme Court." *American Journal of Political Science* 42: 294–315.
Weldon, J. (1997) "The Political Sources of Presidencialismo in Mexico". In S. Mainwaring and M.S. Shugart (eds) *Presidentialism and Democracy in Latin America*. Cambridge: Cambridge University Press.
Widner, J. and D. Scher (2008) "Building Judicial Independence in Semi-Democracies: Uganda and Zimbabwe." In T. Ginsburg and T. Moustafa (eds) *Rule by Law: The Politics of Courts in Authoritarian Regimes*. Cambridge: Cambridge University Press, pp. 235–260.
Zorn, C.J. and S.R. Van Winkle (2000) "A Competing Risks Model of Supreme Court Vacancies, 1789–1992." *Political Behavior* 22(2): 145–166.

4

THE SUPREME COURT AND THE (NO) RIGHTS REVOLUTION

An empirical analysis of the court's rulings 2000–2011

Andrea Castagnola and Saúl López Noriega

This chapter analyzes the way Supreme Court Justices voted on the protection of fundamental rights between 2000 and 2011. The main idea is that although the constitutional and legal frameworks have a significant impact in ensuring rights in a legal system, there are also other factors that influence how judges define the meaning of their votes, mainly the political ones. So the research question is: which factors influence the way a justice votes on fundamental rights? Even though this concern has been raised in other latitudes, in the Mexican context there is no study that systematically analyzes Supreme Court rulings on fundamental rights, mainly because of a lack of data and because of the traditional way of studying judicial behavior (mainly by analyzing specific sentences). We answer this question by analyzing all individual justices' decisions from 2000 to 2011 on *suit of amparos* and constitutional actions on fundamental rights.

Therefore, our goal in this chapter is twofold. First, from this unpublished database, there is an attempt to study the degree of protection of fundamental rights by the Mexican Supreme Court based on a novel concept of judicial behavior within the academy in the country. That is, the vote of justices while adjudicating cases involving fundamental rights depends on a variety of factors that are beyond the normative design of fundamental rights in the constitution. Hence, it is important to open up new versatile paths that may explain more precisely the Mexican Supreme Court. In addition, this chapter also aims to evaluate the Mexican Court Justices when protecting fundamental rights in a context of democratic transition. In fact, this is a scenario never seen before in the country, where political alternation and pluralism, together with a much more organized civil society and means of communication with greater autonomy, certainly affect the behavior of justices. The not inconsiderable questions that attempt to be answered in this text are: How? And in what way?

So, this chapter is organized as follows: in Section I, we briefly explain the evolution of the court and the *suit of amparo*, which for decades was the only way to demand the protection of rights against the political system. We will show that even when the justices were acting in an undemocratic context and the *suit of amparo* had a poor constitutional design, they were not entirely ineffective in their duty of protection. Their performance during those years ranged between an authoritarian constitutional discourse and special decisions protecting certain rights. In Section II, we analyze the main legal and political features of the two quintessential Mexican constitutional controls for protecting rights: the *suit of amparo* and the constitutional action. We consider that their constitutional design is relevant because it influences the behavior of the actors (i.e., justices, persons entitled to use them, defendants, organisms, etc.) involved in the judicial process. The institutional design of the *suit of amparo* and constitutional action (for example, whether the process is abstract or concrete, or whether the effects of the decisions are *erga omnes* or *inter partes*) has important features to take into account when analyzing the differences of judicial behavior between these two means of constitutional control. Because this chapter shares the same theoretical background as Chapter 3, it is not fully replicated to avoid duplication. In Section III we use an original data set with more than 1,800 cases in both *amparos* and actions to explain the judicial behavior of the justices. Section IV tries to answer to what extent Mexican Supreme Court justices have been true protectors and guarantors of fundamental rights in amparos and constitutional actions. The last section, Section V discusses the main contribution of our findings to the existing literature.

I The Supreme Court and the *suit of amparo* during the PRI hegemony

For much of the twentieth century, the Supreme Court and its responsibility to protect constitutional rights through the *suit of amparo* coexisted in a framework characterized by two important factors: (1) an undemocratic political system, which meant that the constitution could not be read as a legal rule responsible for restraining political power; and (2) a *suit of amparo* whose long-standing design was not suitable to protect constitutional rights.

The *suit of amparo* was created in 1841 in Yucatán. Six years later it became the primary way of constitutional defense in the entire nation because of the Reforms Act, which amended certain aspects of the Constitution of 1824, and which was finally consolidated in 1857. Throughout these years, the *suit of amparo* received significant adjustments to its structure (especially from constitutional and legal reforms) that ended up creating a very complex legal instrument with multiple objectives: to protect personal freedom, fight against unconstitutional laws, challenge court judgments, claim acts and rulings of the government, as well as to protect farmers' social rights submitted to the land reform system (Ferrer Mac-Gregor 2000; Fix-Zamudio 1964, 1993; Fix-Zamudio and Cossío Díaz 1996).

It is important to recall that the changes in the *suit of amparo* also coexisted with numerous reforms that began in the 1960s whose main objectives were to solve the problem of excessive workload in the Supreme Court and the problem of a weak constitutional justice. This process culminated in the judicial reform of 1995 in which the court was empowered with: more institutional capacity to overcome the challenge of enforcing its judgments; a stronger role in unifying normative criteria; more power to set the agenda (and thus less workload); and the creation of a fully constitutional justice by strengthening constitutional controversies and creating the constitutional action. This set of reforms consolidated the Supreme Court as a constitutional court, but it did not necessarily help to transform the *suit of amparo* into an instrument for defending fundamental rights. As shown in Table 1, col. 1.1, the *amparo* has served instead to protect the commercial and fiscal interests of people with great financial resources rather than the citizens and their individual rights.

The *suit of amparo* persisted as a tool with very strict procedural requirements in formal terms, leaving no possibility for analyzing the core of several laws related to collective and diffuse rights. It also maintained its effects only for those involved in the trial, without the possibility of an *erga omnes* effect on its declaration of the unconstitutionality of a certain rule. So, even when a rule is declared unconstitutional, this only applies to those who won the trial, but not to the rest of the citizenry, i.e., it has only *inter partes* effects. In addition, the *amparo* remained a useless instrument for individuals to defend themselves against the omissions of state institutions since it is not clearly established whether a citizen can also present an *amparo* on a right that is included in an international treaty which was signed and ratified by Mexico.

These and other necessary adjustments to redesign the *amparo* were not driven by interpretative exercises in Supreme Court judgments, as have other countries' courts with consolidated democracies (Restrepo Saldarriaga 2002). The dominant consensus was to maintain the *amparo* rigidly, highly technical, and with a limited range of protection (mainly focused on tax issues), contrary to the worldwide dynamics of constitutional justice (Elizondo Mayer-Serra and Pérez de Acha 2006).

During the summer of 2011, Congress passed major constitutional reforms on fundamental rights and *suit of amparo*, which eventually overcame several structural problems of *amparo* and established as mandatory certain principles of constitutional interpretation in terms of rights (Carbonell and Salazar 2011; Zaldívar Lelo de Larrea 2002). Today, there is a more appropriate constitutional design, such as the strategic litigation support structure and the profiles of the justices who have reached court capable of triggering a fundamental rights revolution (Cossío Díaz and Orozco y Villa 2012; Epp 1998; Ríos-Figueroa 2010). Nevertheless, it is necessary to wait for a while until it is possible to determine how this new scenario will operate. In the meantime, a clear announcement about the justices' behavior in the protection of rights is needed so as to understand the rulings of the court on these issues.

On the other hand, as previously mentioned, the presence of a hegemonic political party and its corresponding lack of real electoral competition yielded a constitution that was unsuitable for processing conflicts between political powers and society (García de Enterría 1981). On the contrary, the constitution was used more as a discourse to legitimize the regime and the undemocratic conditions in which power was exercised. For decades, constitutional justice was nothing but dead print (Cossío Díaz 1998; Silva-Herzog Márquez 2002). The constitution was not what it ought to be: the institutional framework that defines the channels of sociopolitical life in society. This does not mean that during the Institutional Revolutionary Party's (PRI) hegemonic regime the Supreme Court completely failed in its task of fulfilling rights; indeed, justices had the chance to build a record of certain rights protections. A review of the court's performance during those years reveals that in many cases certain constitutional rights were protected. However, the main problem with this kind of rights protection—with their interpretative differences over time (Cossío Díaz 2002)—a strong formalist tendency became rooted in the idea that judges do not create law nor promote social change but merely apply general laws. That conception of protection was supported by a conservative view about the relationship between society, the state, and the individual, and thus legitimized certain abuses of criminal and military power.

The court only protected certain types of rights, but was never able to build a narrative capable of guaranteeing the constitutional rights. If verdicts and precedents of that time are reviewed, it is possible to find that some of them did protect some rights, even when they did not develop their content. It is unfortunate because they could have helped understand and challenge the sociopolitical relations from a different perspective. This content development, which is essential to the building of a rights language, was impossible for the justices to do because the court did not have enough autonomy from the other branches and thus could not guarantee constitutional rights. Combined with other factors, such as a political conception of the constitution, and based on authors like Carl Schmitt and Ferdinand Lassalle, it greatly baulked at efforts to promote effective regulation of the constitution from the legal arena.

The ambiguity in the protection of constitutional rights and the role of the Supreme Court is not at all surprising. The political regime was characterized by a series of contrasts that do not easily match the usual definition of authoritarianism or totalitarianism (Paz 1993, 2001). In the taxonomy of political systems, this political regime was a weird bug whose portrait, as political scientist Jesus Silva-Herzog states, requires a description full of *buts*: "Authoritarian *but* civil, not competitive in the electoral arena *but* with regular elections; hyper-presidential *but* with a long institutional continuity; a hegemonic party of revolutionary origin *but* without a closed ideology; corporate *but* inclusive" (Silva-Herzog Márquez 1999: 18).

Summing up, we can then see that during much of the twentieth century the Supreme Court was a weak player within the Mexican institutional framework.

This is due to two key factors. On the one hand, the political system of the hegemonic political party resulted in a president who accumulated too much power and thus could exert meta-constitutional powers that in principle, according to constitutional design, belonged rather to alternative powers among others, the Supreme Court. To the extent that the party who had the monopoly of the constitutional narrative was the president and his political party (PRI), constitutional justice lacked the opportunity to participate in this conversation. On the other hand, beyond the political context, the Supreme Court's institutional arsenal's ability to take on ambitious constitutional justice was very limited. Do not forget that it was not until 1995 that the Supreme Court took the opportunity to exercise unconstitutionality claims and constitutional controversies—for although they already existed—it was in this year they were redesigned so that they could have really powerful institutional scope. That is, for almost eighty years the Supreme Court had only the *suit of amparo* as its weapon, which—as we have seen—during this period had several technical and procedural deficiencies. Hence the *suit of amparo* is the key institution for keeping track of the political and legal developments in the court since the entry into force of the 1917 Constitution, because the way the court resolved the *suit of amparo* throughout its history reflects the restraints it endured during the hegemonic PRI regime and—no less important—the new context it now enjoys and which entails scenarios much more committed to the protection of fundamental rights.

Having said that, this fundamental contradiction of the former regime affected the way constitutional rights were protected for several decades, and influenced the perspectives from which the academy studied the relationship between the Supreme Court, the *suit of amparo*, and constitutional rights. Over those years, academic production focused on studying these topics from chronological accounts of constitutional and legal reforms, and eventually produced descriptions of legal precedents of the Supreme Court and lower courts, and dissections of their formal and technical aspects (Burgoa, 1968; Tena Ramírez, 1958). In addition, these works were very often filled with nationalist feelings and uncritically celebrated Mexican exceptional cases in the constitutional world, due to the invention of the *suit of amparo* and social rights (Cossío Díaz 2001; López Ayllón 1997).

This way of studying these issues is not only explained from the particularities of the former Mexican political system as there are at least two other important reasons. First, the Mexican legal world was based on the Roman legal tradition that focused on formal aspects, to the detriment of sociological, economic, and political aspects. Second, the elite of the legal profession was formed in the main center of study in the country, the Universidad Nacional Autónoma de México (UNAM). At that time, the UNAM was the hotbed of specialized bureaucracy in the dominant political party's (PRI) legal tasks, Needless to say, this hampered the existence of a critical attitude toward the constitutional rights' protection system. The norm, with notable exceptions, was justifying the system (Cossío Díaz 2001; Fix-Fierro 2006; Fix-Fierro 1995).

This introduces uncertainties, derived from the fact that certain important questions were not even raised: How do constitutional judges decide? Based on what criteria do they define their votes? What are the factors that affect the protection of fundamental rights? Which justices tend to be more protectionist? Which rights have greater prominence in the Supreme Court agenda? Why is it so? Does the vote of a constitutional judge change depending on the level of government attacked?

When any of these questions was considered, the traditional answer was: the judges solve cases according to law, i.e., they just contrast the factual aspects of a case with the legal rules. So their votes come from this reasoning, which is rooted in the idea that the law is a coherent, logical, and complete system. Then, the task of the justice is only to apply the law. He/she is an operator of the legal machinery and is isolated from the dynamics of social media, political context, the inner strategies between other justices, etc. However, after the constitutional reform of 1995—which consolidated the constitutional character of the court—and a political pluralism evident in an alternation of government at different levels, it is essential to study the Supreme Court from new perspectives. That is, given the enormous importance and prominence acquired by this institution in recent years in protecting rights and in conflict resolution, it is necessary to create new academic paths in order to answer questions related to justices' behavior.

In this regard, there are positive signs that point to a shift in the study of the Supreme Court, the judicial protection of rights, and judicial behavior. Some examples are: studies that seek to understand the relationship between the court and its members against social media and its possible influence in judicial performance (Staton 2010); analysis of institutional mechanisms that have hindered the efficiency of constitutional justice as well as factors that are helping to gradually push for change in these matters (Elizondo Mayer-Serra 2009; Magaloni 2008; Suárez Ávila 2012); reflections about its political role in a presidential system whose first appearance in democratic life is in conditions of divided government, that is, without the political party of the president having a majority in Congress for over fifteen years (Magaloni 2003; Ríos-Figueroa 2007).

This chapter seeks to join this new academic trend in order to initiate new research directions that will allow understanding the Supreme Court in its full complexity.

II A model of judicial behavior for protecting fundamental rights in the Mexican Supreme Court

As indicated in Chapter 3, analysis of the justices' rulings takes place in a context of political fragmentation and low institutional instability. According to the literature, these two characteristics of the political context create a favorable setting for the judiciary's independence since justices cannot be punished because of their decisions. Therefore, the default hypothesis to test would predict that the probability of a justice finding against the ruler increases because they cannot be punished for their decisions.

It is also important to consider the particularities of the institutional design of each legal instrument since it can shape the way justices vote on each of them. On the one hand, the *amparo* can challenge the constitutionality of a norm when an individual right has been violated either by a law or by an act of an authority (i.e., it is a concrete and *a posteriori* means of control). Basically, it is an individual complaint against a state authority. The *amparo* can reach the Supreme Court when a plaintiff, whose case deals with constitutional issues, appeals the decision of lower courts (Navia and Ríos-Figueroa 2005). The effect of the judgment is always *inter partes*. In this sense, the *suit of amparo* has certain similarities with judicial review as a means of constitutional control which is concrete and subjective; that is, it requires a real dispute and the presence of two antagonistic parties in confrontation with the goal of overruling the applied law in that particular case. However, it is also worth mentioning that unlike judicial review, the *suit of amparo* is part of a concentrated constitutional justice model, so that only the Federal Judicial Power can hear and rule on it.

On the other hand, the constitutional action is an abstract control that reviews *a posteriori* the constitutionality of laws passed by the federal Congress or state legislatures, and international treaties. Unlike the *amparo*, individuals cannot use constitutional actions; the only actors entitled to present them are governmental ones.[1] The effect of the decision can be *erga omnes* if eight or more justices vote for the unconstitutionality of the norm. However, if that super-majority is not reached, the case is dismissed, meaning that the plaintiff would only have a favorable result with a super-majority of votes, since there is no *inter partes* effect with a simple majority. Hence unconstitutional claims are very similar to the abstract German judicial review, which has the following main features: concentrated, abstract, and objective; very similar to the model of constitutional justice as a negative legislator conceived by Hans Kelsen (Kelsen 2001).

Even though both instruments are designed to protect the rights of citizens, we argue that the particularities of the institutional design make the *amparo* more likely to become a stronger instrument for defending individual rights vis-à-vis constitutional actions. The reasons are twofold. First, the *amparo* suit does not present the same level of political confrontation as actions since it involves citizens against a political authority, while in actions the case involves two different political authorities against each other. It is because of this difference that we argue that justices would behave differently because the decisions on constitutional actions become more politically sensitive than the ones on *amparos*. Moreover, we predict that justices are more likely to rule in favor of the plaintiff on salient cases on *amparos*, while on actions the opposite will be true. Along these lines, we would also expect that justices would vote more often against the political authority when legal entities, rather than citizens, are the plaintiff, and on tax cases rather than on other issues. This is because the *amparo* suit, instead of being a legal weapon for citizens to guarantee that their rights are not violated by political authority, has become more like a blank check to compensate big companies for their favors.[2]

Second, the effect of decisions on actions differs from *amparos*. The *suit of amparo*, by having a concrete and *inter partes* effect, allows justices to vote more easily against political authority. This is because, in principle, it does not entail a drastic change in public policy or of the legal system, which in the end reduces the potential political cost for the justices against other branches of the system. Constitutional actions are more politically costly for them, since when a majority of eight votes is reached, the law is definitively eliminated from the legal system. Consequently, when ruling actions as unconstitutional, justices have to be more prudent since they could encounter two important problems: first, if a law is thrown out, there is a greater probability that there will be unplanned or uncalculated normative consequences, such as changes in other legislation; and second, political conflict could arise against the legislative parties that enacted that particular law. Hence, the court can be more deferential with the legislative bodies that are attacked via constitutional actions than with the political authorities attacked in the *amparos*.

III A description of the justices' rulings during the PAN administration

We use an original data set with all Supreme Court individual rulings on constitutional actions on violations to fundamental rights and on *amparos* from 2000 to 2011.[3] During those twelve years there were 1,818 cases, being 94 percent *amparos* and 6 percent actions, and more than 2,600 rounds of votes, as in some cases there was more than one topic involved in the discussion. The dependent variable for *amparos* is coded 1 for those decisions in which justices voted against the political authorities, and 0 otherwise, while the dependent variable for actions is coded 1 for those decisions in which the justice voted for unconstitutionality, and 0 otherwise.

III.I Voting behavior by political actors

Figure 4.1 plots the percentage of unfavorable rulings[4] per year against the National Action Party (PAN) and the PRI, for both *amparos* and actions. On average, justices have been more aggressive in their rulings on *amparos* than on actions, since, overall, on *the former*, one out of two individual decisions or votes were against the political authority while on the latter there was one out of four. Unfavorable rulings against the PAN (see Figure 4.1a) start in a more systematic way in 2006, since prior to that year there were only two occasions in which the ruling party received unfavorable rulings on *amparos* (in 2000 and 2003). On the other hand, unfavorable rulings against the PRI have fluctuated during the whole period, reaching its maximum in 2003 and 2007 (see Figure 4.1b).

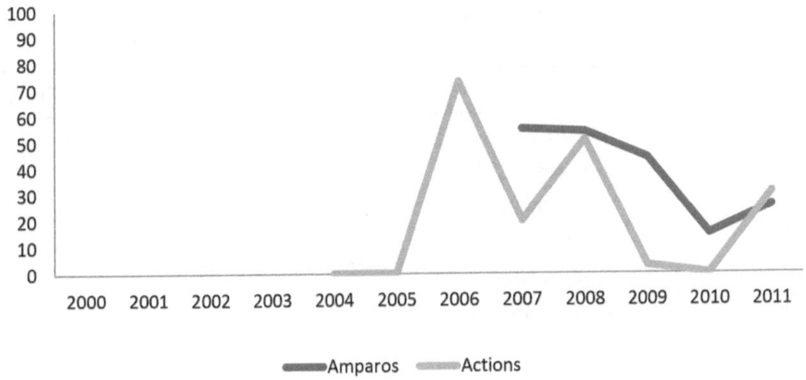

FIGURE 4.1A Unfavorable rulings against the PAN (%)

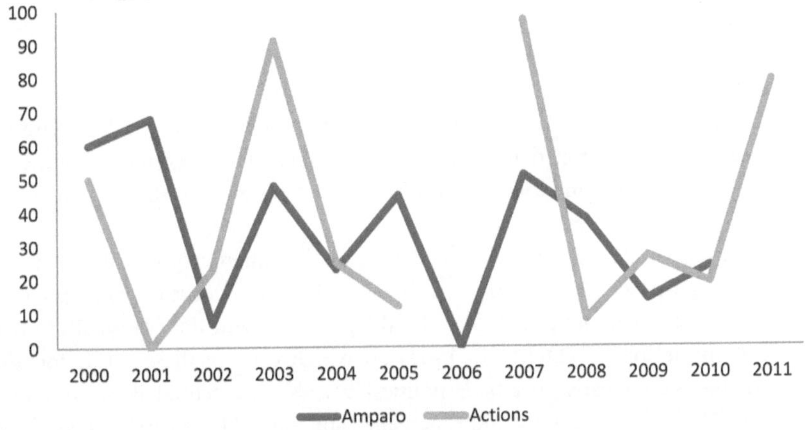

FIGURE 4.1B Unfavorable rulings against the PRI (%)

Regardless of the political parties involved in the cases, overall, the *amparos* that reached court were primarily presented by legal entities to resolve disputes about tax issues. On more than half of the time justices ruled on tax issues[5] and 75 percent of the total unconstitutional rulings against the authorities were on that issue. As Table 4.1 shows, legal entities were the most active actors on tax cases, since they were for the plaintiffs 78 percent of the time and obtained the greatest number of favorable rulings, 82 percent. These results provide evidence for what Carlos Elizondo Mayer-Serra (2009) called *the industry of the suit of amparo* (for example, between 1996 and 2001 there were 48,813 *amparos* against some tax rules; in the next six years there were 134,323). Justices have also ruled on *amparos* presented by citizens but of course less frequently. Regarding non-tax actions, Table 4.1 shows that in this case citizens were the most active actors as

TABLE 4.1 Supreme Court docket according to the political actors involved for the plaintiff in *amparos* and constitutional actions from 2000 to 2011

	Political Actors	*Docket*	*Favorable Rulings*
Amparos on tax issues	Legal entities	78%	82%
	Citizens	22%	18%
Amparos on non-tax issues	Legal entities	45%	30%
	Citizens	51%	65%
	N/A	4%	5%
Actions	Political parties	31%	16%
	Attorney General	30%	54%
	Local legislatures	15%	8%
	National Human Rights Commission	13%	9%
	Others	11%	13%

Source: Authors' own data.

well as the actors that received the most favorable rulings. However, legal entities have been by far the actors that received the most favorable outcomes, since the 82 percent of favorable ruling for legal entities on tax cases exceeds the 65 percent of citizens on non-tax cases.

Constitutional actions, overall, had been used by different political actors and for diverse purposes. According to Table 4.1, the busiest actors were political parties, the Attorney General (PGR), local legislatures, and the National Human Rights Commission (CNDH). The issues on which each of these actors focused their claims were clearly specified: political parties on electoral laws (100 percent); PGR on administrative (39 percent) and tax (34 percent) issues; local legislatures on administrative (42 percent) and criminal laws (37 percent); and the CNDH on administrative laws (77 percent). However, the PGR, directly appointed by the president, received the most favorable rulings, 54 percent of the time, while political parties, the CNDH, and local legislatures rarely did (see Table 4.1).

III.II Voting behavior by justices' political appointing party

Figure 4.2 captures the percentage of unconstitutional rulings by justices, regardless of the political parties involved in the docket. The justices with a grey bar are those appointed during the PRI administrations, while the black are those from the PAN administrations. An interesting result is that PRI justices have been more aggressive in their rulings on *amparo* and not on actions, while the opposite is true for the justices appointed during the PAN administrations.

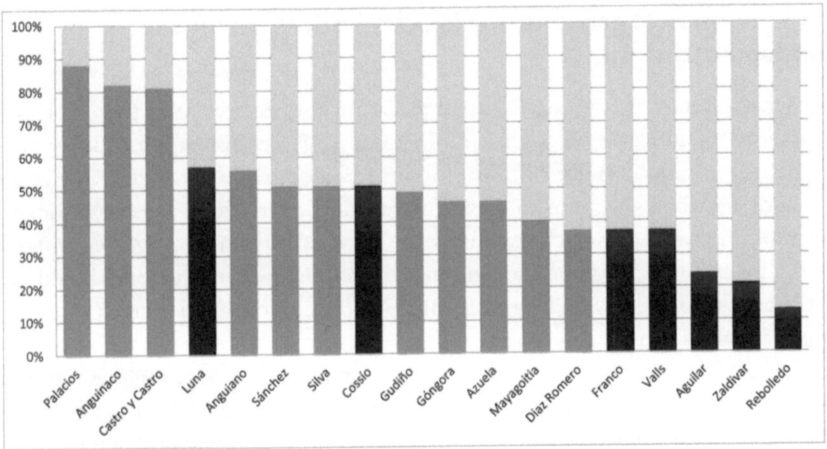

FIGURE 4.2A Unfavorable rulings per justice on amponos (%)
Note: Grey bars correspond to justices appointed by the PRI and black bars to justices appointed by the PAN.
Source: Authors' own data.

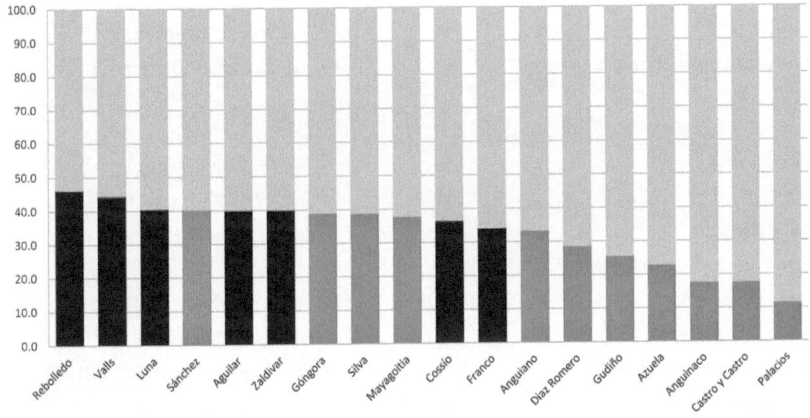

FIGURE 4.2B Unfavorable rulings per justice on actions (%)
Note: Grey bars correspond to justices appointed by the PRI and black bars to justices appointed by the PAN.
Source: Authors' own data.

IV An empirical account of Mexican justices' rulings on fundamental rights

To what extent have Mexican Supreme Court justices been true protectors and guarantors of fundamental rights? As in Chapter 3, to answer this question we model the voting behavior of justices using a random intercept logistic regression for both *amparos* and actions rulings. Our dependent variable in *amparos* is coded 1 for those decisions in which the justices ruled against the authority (i.e., in favor of the plaintiff) and 0 otherwise; and in actions the dependent variable is coded 1 for those decisions in which justices ruled unconstitutional and 0 otherwise. The unit of analysis is justice decision.

Table 4.2 presents the list of independent variables that were included in both models. These variables can be grouped into four categories: (1) characteristics of the cases; (2) attributes of the plaintiff side; (3) attributes of the defendant side; and (4) attributes of the justices. Regarding the first group of variables, in both models we included a dummy variable that captures the relevance of the decision

TABLE 4.2 List of independent variables included in the regression models

Independent Variables	*Model*	*Coding Scheme*
Characteristics of the case		
Salience cases	Am, Ac	1=Salience, 0=otherwise
Tax cases	Am	1=Tax, 0=non-tax
Electoral laws	Ac	1=Electoral, 0=otherwise
Unconstitutional ruling on current norm	Ac	1=Current norm, 0=previous norm
Characteristics of the plaintiff side		
PRI claiming	Ac	1=PRI, 0=Other parties
PAN claiming	Ac	1=PAN, 0=Other parties
Legal entities	Am	1=Legal entities, 0=Otherwise
Characteristics of the defendant side		
Cases against PRI	Am	1=PRI, 0=PAN and PRI
Cases against PAN	Am	1=PAN, 0=PAN and PRI
Cases against other parties	Am	1=Other parties, 0=PAN and PRI
Cases against PRI	Ac	1=PRI, 0=Other parties
Cases against PAN	Ac	1=PAN, 0=Other parties
Cases against federal government	Am, Ac	1=Federal, 0=State and Municipality
Characteristics of the justices		
PAN justices	Ac, Am	1=PAN, 0=PRI
Judicial background	Ac, Am	1=Judicial, 0=Political
Age	Ac, Am	Number

Source: Authors' own data.
Note: Am=Amparo and Ac=Actions.

because not all of the cases that reach court have the same importance. Decisions were coded as salient when they: (1) focus on an issue that strongly polarized society (for example, gay marriage and abortion); or (2) attract strong attention from the public and the media (for example, the "*intellectuals' amparo*")[6]. An additional dummy variable was included in the *amparo* model to capture whether the case was related to a tax issue or not. As previously mentioned, existing literature argues that justices have been more active on granting *amparos* on tax issues than on other topics. For the action model we included two additional dummy variables; one explores whether there is a change in the voting behavior of justices on electoral cases, while the second considers whether the action was against a law enacted by the current administration or the previous one. It is expected that justices would more easily declare a norm unconstitutional if it was enacted by the previous administration rather than by the current one, because the current government can impose threats on unsympathetic judges.[7]

Due to the particularities of each mean of rights protection we included different variables on each model. In the *amparo* model we included one dummy variable to capture whether the case was presented by a legal entity, having as a baseline category cases presented by citizens. In the actions model we included two dummy variables. The dummy variable "PRI claiming" codes 1 for those decisions in which the PRI initiated the demand either by themselves or in coalition with other parties excluding the PAN, while the "PAN claiming" variable captures 1 when the PAN initiated the demand either by themselves or in coalition with other parties. The reference category is when other parties like the Party of the Democratic Revolution (PRD) or the Partido del Trabajo (PT) initiated the demand.[8]

Regarding the third group of variables, the political identity of the defendant, each model included a different set of variables to capture that effect. For the *amparo* model we included three dummy variables to identify whether the *amparo* was against a norm passed by the PAN or the PRI or other parties, the baseline category is cases against both the PAN and PRI. For the actions model we followed the same coding scheme as in Chapter 3, to include two dummy variables to capture whether the action was against a law enacted by the PAN or PRI (having as a baseline category a law enacted by other parties). Both models include a variable that identifies whether the decision is against the federal government (the baseline category is the state and municipality), so as to explore whether a justice behaves differently in that case. Two interaction variables were included in the model to predict the voting behavior of the justices on cases when the PAN tries to invalidate a norm enacted by the PRI and vice versa.

Finally we included three variables in both models to capture the effect of justices' special attributes: political proximity, background, and age. The proximity of a justice to political parties can be determined by the political party of the appointing executive, since the idea is that he/she reflects the political preferences of the party of that executive (Hagle 1993; Spriggs and Wahlbeck 1995; Zorn and Van Winkle 2000). Therefore, PAN justices are those appointed during both

Fox and Calderon administrations while the others are PRI justices. The judicial background variable identifies whether that justice comes from the judicial family, and the age variable captures the age of the justice.

IV.I Judicial behavior on amparo

Table 4.3 presents the results of a random intercept logistic regression for the Supreme Court justices' rulings between 2000 and 2011 on *amparos* (Column 3.1) and actions (Column 3.2). The coefficients for *amparos* suggest that justices behave differently according to the sides on the docket. On the plaintiff side, legal entities have fewer probabilities of obtaining a favorable ruling than do citizens. This finding suggests that, contrary to expectations, justices are more sensitive to claims presented by citizens than by big companies. The coefficients for cases against the PAN and other parties are positive and statistically significant, which reveals that justices are more likely to rule against a norm enacted by the PAN and other parties rather than a norm enacted by the PAN and PRI together. These results suggest that justices are not willing to confront the two biggest parties at the same time. Likewise, justices are also less likely to rule against the authority when the norm questioned comes from the federal government. On important cases as well as on tax cases, justices are more likely to rule in favor of the plaintiff, that is, against the political authority. Finally, both older justices and justices appointed by the PAN are more likely to rule in favor of the defendant, i.e., the political authority. These results stand in contrast with those in Chapter 3.

Because the coefficients in Table 4.3 are non-linear, predicted probabilities for a substantive interpretation were computed under different scenarios. When all the independent variables are at their mean, the probability of a justice ruling in favor of the plaintiff is considerably high: 0.63, i.e., more than half of the time justices ruled against the political authority. But that probability changes when computed under different scenarios. For example, even though the econometric model reveals that justices will be less likely to grant an *amparo* to legal entities vis-à-vis citizens, there is no significant difference in the predicted probabilities, since they will grant an *amparo* to a citizen 65 percent of the time, while to an enterprise 63 percent. In fact, what matters in predicting a favorable outcome for the plaintiff is not necessarily the particularities of the parties involved in the case or the special characteristics of it, but rather the political proximity of the justices. On average, those appointed during the PRI administrations will grant an *amparo* eight out of ten times while a justice appointed during the PAN administration one out of ten. Figure 4.3 plots the predicted probabilities of granting an *amparo* based on the political identity of the justice and their age, because older justices are less likely to challenge political authority. Even though older judges will tend to be less likely than young justices to grant an *amparo*, justices appointed during the PRI administration will be more likely to do it than a justice appointed during the PAN administration. Future research should address this concern.

TABLE 4.3 Random intercept logistic regression for judicial behavior of Mexican Supreme Court Justices from 2000 to 2011

	3.1 Amparos	*3.2 Actions*
Characteristics of the cases		
Salience cases	0.942*** (0.049)	-2.263*** (0.190)
Tax cases	0.745*** (0.034)	–
Electoral cases	–	-0.752*** (0.131)
Unconstitutional ruling on current norm	–	1.345*** (0.184)
Attributes of the plaintiff side		
PRI claiming	–	-17.188 (2634)
PAN claiming	–	1.674*** (0.141)
Legal entity	-0.086*** (0.031)	–
Attributes of the defendant side		
Cases against PAN	1.112*** (0.052)	-.0234* (0.128)
Cases against PRI	0.036 (0.047)	-0.568** (0.246)
Cases against other parties	0.743*** (0.065)	–
PAN vs. PRI		0.338 (0.289)
PRI vs. PAN		17.119 (2634)
Cases against the federal government	-1.016*** (0.123)	-0.725*** (0.184)
Attributes of the justices		
PAN justices	-4.214*** (1.166)	0.447* (0.264)
Judicial background	0.843 (1.198)	-0.024 (0.201)
Age	-0.226*** (0.008)	0.014 (0.014)
Constant	13.566*** (1.300)	-2.799** (0.998)
Sigma_u	1.565*** (0.340)	-2.510*** (0.605)
Number of observations	26,858	2241

Source: Author's own data.

Note: ***$p<0.01$, **$p<0.05$, *$p<0.1$.

IV.I.1 Judicial behavior on constitutional actions

Column 3.2 presents results for explaining judicial behavior on constitutional actions on fundamental rights (see Table 4.3). The judicial behavior of justices reveals an interesting pattern of low-risk power distribution. The PAN would have greater probabilities of obtaining a favorable outcome (either as a plaintiff or

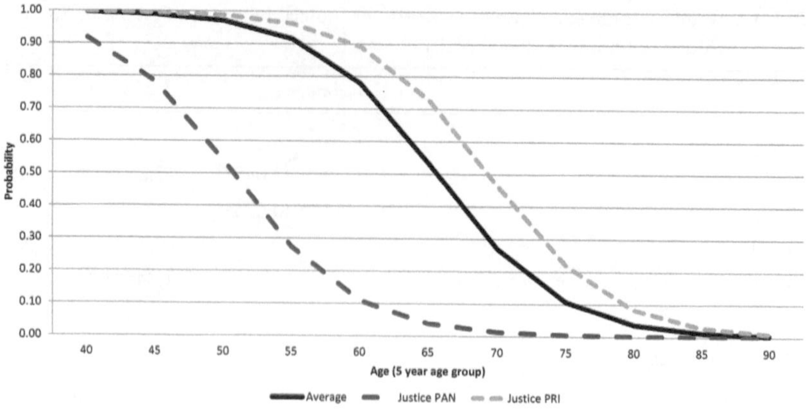

FIGURE 4.3 Probability of granting an *amparo* according to the age of the justice and the administration in which he/she was appointed

defendant) when confronting minority parties, while the PRI would have greater probabilities of a favorable outcome only when minority parties challenge a law enacted by them. The lack of significance of the coefficient suggests that justices are not willing to favor any of the two biggest parties when confronting each other. Regarding the other variables, justices are less likely to rule as unconstitutional salient and electoral decisions, while more likely in cases attacking a current norm. Also justices are less likely to rule against the federal government than on cases against the state or municipal governments. Finally, PAN justices are more likely to rule a norm as unconstitutional than are those appointed during the PRI administration.

Predicted probabilities were computed for substantive interpretation (see Table 4.4). When all independent variables are at their mean, the probability of a justice ruling as unconstitutional is very low: 0.3 (i.e., three out of ten decisions), but the probability increases or reduces depending on the particularities of the case. For example, as Table 4.4 shows, when the ruling party challenges a norm enacted by the PRI the probability increases to 0.50 but when the opposite scenario takes place it reduces to 0.15. In both cases justices are more willing to rule unconstitutional on non-salient cases. The predicted probabilities reveal two important

TABLE 4.4 Predicted probabilities for unconstitutional rulings on constitutional actions

	Average	*Salient cases*	*Non-salient cases*
PAN vs. PRI	0.50	0.14	0.60
PRI vs. PAN	0.15	0.03	0.21

Source: Authors' own data.

Note: all the other independent variables are at their means.

aspects of judicial behavior. First, justices have been ruling favorably on the preferences of the ruling party, as pointed out in Chapter 3; and second, they would prefer to maintain the status quo on relevant cases.

V Conclusions

Did Mexican society experience, during the first decade of democracy, a rights revolution? The answer to this question largely depends on the type of legal instruments employed, that is, whether fundamental rights are being defended via *amparo* or constitutional action. The particularities of each of these means, both the scope and the parties involved, have an important effect on judicial behavior and on the rights of citizens.

A key fact is that, overall, justices have voted more times against the political authority in *amparos* (50 percent) than unconstitutional in constitutional actions (25 percent) irrespective of the particularities of the case, i.e., whether it was or was not important, who were the involved parties, what was the topic, etc. How can we explain this difference? First of all, it is important to remember the distinctive features of each of the means of control. The *amparo* was designed to settle concrete (not abstract) conflicts between a citizen and the state, the justices' decision affects only the parties involved in the conflict (not *erga omnes*), and the judges have to present specific and concrete argumentations. On the other hand, the constitutional action was designed to settle abstract conflicts between political elites, and the decisions have *erga omnes* effects only if there is a super-majority of votes in that direction (at least eight out of eleven).

Why are these differences between constitutional action and *amparo* relevant? In terms of legitimacy, it is necessary to consider that in *amparos* a decision in favor of the plaintiff allows the court to present itself to the public as a guarantor tribunal, even when the *amparo* does not have greater legal impact due to an *inter partes* effect. In the other case, that is, when justices rule in favor of the citizen despite unfavorable public opinion, there is virtually no legal effect, which allows justices to act strategically. Voting in favor of the plaintiff is almost costless because of the material effect of the decision, while in voting against the plaintiff the justice can calculate the cost to popularity relative to the benefit of that decision—one that has a minor impact on the legal system.

On the other hand, in constitutional actions justices tend to suffer media pressures more systematically, thus risking social polarization because of the possible legal effects of the decision—expelling a norm from the system. In intra-elite conflicts, it is not so easy to individualize failures of the rights system or unfinished issues. The legal consequences for expelling a law from the system are more unpredictable. This cocktail of faults makes it more attractive for justices not to vote for unconstitutionality on actions.

Overall, an *amparo* solved by the Supreme Court gets to its docket after years of bouncing around in lower courts, so the legislative body attacked, and even the federal executive, are probably no longer acting by the time there is a final decision. Then, if the unconstitutionality is granted, the legislature under scrutiny will hardly see that decision as a political attack or judicial interference. On the other hand, in actions, the case must be filed directly to the court within a maximum of thirty days of publication of the law, so the political game can change. While the dispute is being resolved in the court, the legislature whose law is under scrutiny is often still in the House. That is why a decision for unconstitutionality can be understood by justices as a political affront, as well as an alleged invasion of powers.[9]

Nevertheless, it is true that, like controversies, *amparos* are a solid and *inter partes* control means (although controversies could have general effects), but the plaintiff is a member of civil society and not a state body. This makes a huge difference, because when civil society is on stage it is easier and more likely for the media and public opinion to pay attention to the court. Thus, justices have to be more careful in order to keep their legitimacy safe. When they solve *amparos* they only have to consider the cost of a parallel trial. Of course, they consider this too when they solve controversies, but the interest of the media and other actors is quite different when the Mexican Court solves an *amparo* rather than a controversy (Staton 2010).

At the same time, because *amparos*' effects are *inter partes*, justices can vote for unconstitutionality and strengthen their legitimacy in sight of public opinion, but consequences in the legal system will not be so important. For them, this is a win-win situation. The justices keep their image safe and avoid conflict with state bodies. Using the same logic, the probability that justices will vote for unconstitutionality is thus lower in actions for protecting rights because their legitimacy card is not at risk, at least not in the same way as in *amparos*. More significantly, justices avoid a real risk, that of dramatically changing the legal system because of the general effect that actions can have. So, it is actually very coherent behavior for the justices of a conservative court, like that of Mexico, to vote more often for unconstitutionality when they are solving conflicts between state bodies in constitutional actions, and less often in constitutional controversies. And, at the same time, when the same justices are protecting rights, they vote more often than in actions for unconstitutionality in *amparos*.

Another key aspect to understand is the profile of the plaintiffs in each means of control. Constitutional justice in the rights field is largely defined by the type of litigants that usually use this method of resolving their conflicts, and, of course, the justices' institutional answers. In this context, one of the most relevant hypotheses mentioned at the beginning of this study was that justices would vote more often against state authority when the plaintiff was a legal entity rather than an individual and, above all, if the discussion topic was taxes. This is because most *amparos* solved by the court have been presented by legal entities, and on tax disputes. Here is an overview of the *suit of amparo*: 75 percent of all rulings against political authority were on tax matters, legal entities being the plaintiff in 82 percent of them.

However, contrary to expectations, legal entities are less likely to get a favorable resolution to their interests, as opposed to citizens, i.e., justices do vote more often for unconstitutionality when a legal entity is the plaintiff, but this is due to the enormous volume of *suits of amparo* brought by them (besides, we must not forget corporations do not usually need more than one important case in order to change the legal system to satisfy their interests). Does this mean that we have a really protective court, whose main concern is the rights of *common* individuals? Not necessarily, because the difference of probability in justices' votes in favor of unconstitutionality between individuals and legal entities is not significant. More importantly, the court continues to maintain broad acceptance criteria for *amparos* in tax issues, allowing them to dominate its docket and judicial agenda.

In the constitutional actions universe, the most active body was the PGR, an institution subordinate to the president. The PGR is not only a frequent litigant at the court through actions, but is also quite successful: more than half (54 percent) of the rulings were favorable to the PGR and most of those rulings were on tax issues. Unfortunately, the CNDH and the analogous state bodies that can present actions have not been activists in the protection of fundamental rights, which allow us to conclude that these institutions have not prioritized fundamental rights in their agenda. Ultimately, the two most important institutions for the protection of fundamental rights have not worked in that direction, either because the interests of the PGR were only on tax issues or because the CNDH neglected to take advantage of this legal instrument. It is important to point out that both the PGR and the CNDH are institutions authorized to present actions, so if there are no committed litigants to trigger these legal remedies at their disposal or to pursue issues other than human rights, then the chances for justices to enhance the protection of fundamental rights decrease.

Now, analyzing the *amparo* from a partisan perspective, we find that political party affiliation does matter in accounting for judicial behavior. Overall, the justices appointed by the PAN, except for Luna and Cossío, have voted fewer times against the PRI–PAN "coalition" (the PRI being the majority in Congress and the PAN on the ruling executive), while justices appointed by the PRI vote more often against the ruling executive. In actions, political factors also affected judicial behavior.

Political affiliation of the parties involved in an action does matter. In a context of low institutional instability and divided government, we found that, contrary to what the literature is inclined to predict, PAN-appointed justices have most of the time voted in favor of the ruling party. This may mean that even in democratic periods, like that analyzed in this chapter, there is still excessive deference by the justices to other branches of government, mainly to the executive branch, because it also takes part in the law-crafting process.

So, are we or are we not having a rights revolution in Mexico during these years of democratic government? Justices have certainly voted more times in favor of the plaintiffs in *amparos* than in actions. At first sight, this could make us think that at least we have a court prone to protect citizen's rights—and, by the way, we should recall that sometimes when justices vote in favor of the plaintiff this does not necessarily mean that they are protecting rights; we all know that some conservative plaintiffs attack laws that protect, for example, gay and abortion rights. However, during the period analyzed, the number of *amparos* related to legal entities' rather than citizens' interest increased. It is true: the type of litigants and cases that the court has received are not precisely suited to promoting a rights revolution. It is also necessary to strengthen private strategic litigation and learn how to use the public route—mainly that related to the CNDH. This, needless to say, is not a responsibility of the justices.

However, there are certain issues on which the court can start being more proactive than previously; for example, agenda setting. The court has allowed the tax issue to dominate its agenda. as it has not reinterpreted the role of a constitutional court (Elizondo Mayer-Serra and Pérez de Acha 2006). It also has the power to take over *amparos* from federal courts, similar to a *writ of certiorari*. This allows the court to assert its jurisdiction over important cases that are being solved in the federal courts. Since 2000, only 5.6 percent of the total *amparos* that reached the court have arrived this way (Cossío Díaz and Orozco y Villa 2012). Or it could be more proactive on the quasi-legislative power enacted in the constitution. There is the possibility of elaborating general agreements to redefine its powers and delegate more tax issues to the collegiate circuit courts, thus focusing on more important fundamental rights cases. But none of these examples have taken place so far, at least not in the way to be expected of a constitutional court.

A rights revolution, at least as understood by Charles Epp (1998), depends indeed on a number of factors that go beyond the justices' scope of action. There is nothing worse than a constitutional court wasting its institutional resources to protect fundamental rights. And this is, precisely, the case of the Mexican Supreme Court during the first decade of democracy: it is a court whose clumsy handling of its institutional potential has been detrimental to the protection of citizens' rights.

Notes

1 These are: legislative minorities—only on laws passed by their corresponding local congress or federal congress; the Attorney General (PGR)—on local, federal, and international treaties on any subject; political parties—only on local or federal laws relating to elections and electioneering—and, from 2006, the National Human Rights Commission (CNDH) and analogous bodies at the local level—on the constitutionality of federal or local laws or international treaties only on fundamental rights.

2 Bear in mind that the effect of the decision is only *interpartes* and not *erga omnes*.

3 The authors are very grateful for the research assistance of Gustavo Marín Hernandez, Daniel Murillo, and Franz Oberarzbacher in the compilation and codification of Supreme Court rulings.

4 Unfavorable rulings means that the justices ruled as unconstitutional the *amparo* or the action, which in practice means that justices ruled against the political authority at which the claim was directed.

5 The rest of the votes were distributed in the following way: 20 percent administrative, 9 percent labor, 3 percent criminal, 2 percent civil, and 1 percent electoral issues.
6 A case in which the main topic was whether it is or is not possible to attack a constitutional amendment through *amparo*.
7 Even though this hypothesis may be in contradiction with the political fragmentation hypothesis, the particularities of the time frame for presenting constitutional actions would reduce the number of cases challenging a norm enacted by the previous government. We thank one of the anonymous reviewers for this comment.
8 As in Chapter 3, the PRD does not receive special treatment in the coding system because even though it is the third party in Congress it does not have an active role.
9 This conclusion, at first sight, appears to be contradictory with one of our earlier results. In Chapter 3 we found that in the period analyzed, it was more likely that the justices would vote for the unconstitutionality in a constitutional action rather than in constitutional controversy. For this we presented three arguments: first, the abstract review of actions can be less politically sensitive to conflict since justices are solving constitutional contradictions between a law and the constitution, while on controversies they are solving specific political conflicts.Second, even though on both actions and controversies there is an *erga omnes* effect when eight or more justices vote against the constitutionality of the norm, in the case of controversies there is still an *inter partes* effect when six or seven justices vote in that direction, while on actions this is not possible. Third, the number of entitled actors is significantly more limited in an action than in a controversy, and the number of topics that each actor can challenge is also fewer. So how do we resolve this apparent contradiction? Why do we conclude in this chapter that, due to the different characteristics of the control means, the probability for justices to vote for unconstitutionality is higher in *amparos* than in actions? Because *amparos* are very different from controversies and actions for protecting rights and have a dufferent, as they are used to solve conflicts between state bodies.

References

Burgoa, I. (1968) *El juicio de amparo*. Mexico City: Porrúa.

Carbonell, M. and P. Salazar (eds) 2011) *La reforma constitucional de derechos humanos: Un nuevo paradigma*. Mexico City: UNAM.

Cossío Díaz, J.R. (1998) *Dogmática constitucional y régimen autoritario*. Mexico City: Fontamara.

Cossío Díaz, J.R. (2001) *Cambio social y cambio jurídico*. Mexico City: ITAM-Miguel Ángel Porrúa.

Cossío Díaz, J.R. (2002) *La teoría constitucional de la Suprema Corte de Justicia*. Mexico City: Fontamara.

Cossío Díaz, J.R. and L.H. Orozco y Villa (2012) "La activa Suprema Corte." *Nexos* 409 (January): 17–19.

Elizondo Mayer-Serra, C. (2009) "La industria del amparo fiscal." *Política y Gobierno* XVI(2): 349–383.

Elizondo Mayer-Serra, C. and L.M. Pérez de Acha (2006) "Separación de poderes y garantías individuales: la Suprema Corte y los derechos de los contribuyentes." *Cuestiones Constitucionales* 14 (Enero–Junio): 91–130.

Epp, C. R. (1998) *The Rights Revolution: Lawyers, Activists, and Supreme Courts in Comparative Perspective*. Chicago, IL: University of Chicago Press.

Ferrer Mac-Gregor, E. (2000) *La acción constitucional de amparo en México y España. Estudio de derecho comparado*. Mexico City: Porrúa.

Fix-Fierro, H. (ed.) (2006) *Del gobierno de los abogados al imperio de las leyes. Estudios socio-jurídicos sobre educación y profesión jurídicas en el México contemporáneo*. Mexico City: UNAM.

Fix-Zamudio, H. (1964) *El juicio de amparo*. Mexico City: Porrúa.

Fix-Zamudio, H. (1993) *Ensayos sobre el juicio de amparo*. Mexico City: UNAM.

Fix-Zamudio, H. and J.R. Cossío Díaz (1996) *El poder judicial en el ordenamiento mexicano*. Mexico City: Fondo Económico de Cultura.

García de Enterría, E. (1981) *La Constitución como norma y el tribunal constitucional*. Madrid: Civitas.

Hagle, T.M. (1993) "Strategic Retirements: A Political Model of Turnover on the United States Supreme Court." *Political Behavior* 15(1): 25–48.

Kelsen, Hans (2001) *La garantía jurisdiccional de la Constitución (La justicia constitucional)*. Mexico City: IIJ-UNAM.

López Ayllón, S. (1997) *Las transformaciones del sistema jurídico y los significados sociales del derecho en México. La encrucijada entre tradición y modernidad*. Mexico City: UNAM.

Magaloni, A.L. (2008) "¿Por qué la Corte no ha sido un instrumento para la defensa de derechos fundamentales?" In F. Mac-Gregor and A. Zaldívar Lelo de Larrea (eds) *La ciencia del derecho procesal constitucional. Estudios en homenaje a Héctor Fix-Zamudio*. Mexico City: IIJ-UNAM, pp. 271–290.

Magaloni, B. (2003) "Authoritarianism, Democracy and the Supreme Court: Horizontal Exchange and the Rule of Law in Mexico." In S. Mainwaring and C. Welna (eds) *Democratic Accountability in Latin America*. Oxford: Oxford University Press, pp. 266–306.

Navia, P. and J. Ríos-Figueroa (2005) "The Constitutional Adjudication Mosaic of Latin America." *Comparative Political Studies* 38(2): 189–217.

Paz, O. (1993) *Itinerario*. Mexico City: Fondo Económico de Cultura.

Paz, O. (2001) *Sueño en libertad. Escritos políticos*. Mexico City: Seix Barral.

Restrepo Saldarriaga, E. (2002) "Reforma constitucional y progreso social: la constitucionalización de la vida cotidiana en Colombia." In R. Saba (ed.) *El derecho como objeto e instrumento de transformación*. Buenos Aires: Editores del Puerto, pp. 73–88.

Ríos-Figueroa, J. (2007) "Fragmentation of Power and the Emergence of an Effective Judiciary in Mexico, 1994–2002." *Latin American Politics and Society* 49(1): 31–57.

Ríos-Figueroa, J. (2010) "Justicia constitucional y derechos humanos en América Latina." *Revista Latinoamericana de Política Comparada* 3 (Enero): 53–68.

Silva-Herzog Márquez, J. (1999) *El antiguo régimen y la transición en México*. Mexico City: Planeta-Joaquín Mortiz.

Silva-Herzog Márquez, J. (2002) "El fin de la siesta constitucional." In M.A. Casar and I. Marván (eds) *Gobernar sin mayoría*. Mexico City: CIDE-Taurus, pp. 369–387.

Spriggs, J.F.I. and P.J. Wahlbeck (1995) "Calling It Quits: Strategic Retirement on the Federal Courts of Appeals, 1893–1991." *Political Research Quarterly* 48(3): 573–597.

Staton, J. K. (2010) *Judicial Power and Strategic Communication in Mexico*. Cambridge: Cambridge University Press.

Suárez Ávila, A. (2012) "The Mexican Supreme Court as a Protector of Human Rights." *Mexican Law Review* IV(2): 239–260.

Tena Ramírez, Felipe (1958) *Derecho constitucional mexicano*. Mexico City: Porrúa.

Tenorio, M. (1995) "Una profesión perdida en el pasado. La Barra." *Revista de la Barra Mexicana* 7(March): 12–13.

Zaldívar Lelo de Larrea, A. (2002) *Hacia una nueva Ley de amparo*. Mexico City: UNAM.

Zorn, C. J. and S. R. Van Winkle (2000) "A Competing Risks Model of Supreme Court Vacancies, 1789–1992." *Political Behavior* 22(2): 145–166.

5

CONSTITUTIONAL CHANGE AND THE SUPREME COURT INSTITUTIONAL ARCHITECTURE

Decisional indeterminacy as an obstacle to legitimacy

Francisca Pou Giménez[1]

I Introduction

Both lawyers and political scientists have recently made extensive contributions to the study of constitutional change.[2] It is usual in these debates to distinguish among three main modalities of change: replacement, amendment, and interpretation of constitutions.[3] These modalities—isolated or in their mutual interrelation—can be analyzed from the perspective of the causal dynamics that could explain the occurrence of change, or from the perspective of the effects, i.e., with an interest in clarifying the relation between alterations at the level of basic constitutional arrangements and wider change in social realities. In addition, we can approach them from a predominantly descriptive or normative viewpoint, depending on whether our central interest lies in quantifying, depicting, or explaining what has been happening, or in assessing the process or its results from one or another evaluative standpoint.

Mexico's transition to democracy, in contrast to the typical Latin American pattern, has not included a constitutional *replacement*; while over the last three decades almost every country in the region enacted a new constitution,[4] Mexico retains its 1917 text. Constitutional *amendment* and constitutional *interpretation* are, then, what needs to be tracked down to reconstruct what has been going on in the country.

Amendment dynamics make indeed for a distinctive story. According to available data, the 1917 Mexican text has borne the effects of more than 200 amendment decrees,[5] which have translated into more than 500 "section" reforms of variable reach.[6] And this is only the tip of the iceberg formed by the astonishing amount of amendment bills registered for discussion.[7] The significant rigidity of the Mexican amendment formula did not, quite predictably, inhibit a dynamics of unremitting reform during the decades of Institutional Revolutionary Party (PRI) hegemony. But more surprisingly, in the 1997–2012 period, when the PRI had already lost the capacity to amend the basic text without the concurrence of other political parties, far from abating, amendments proliferated even more.[8] To analyze why Mexican political life has felt the necessity of permanent constitutional expression, or to explore the relationship between permanent legal change and law enforcement—or un-enforcement—are only two of the many lines of inquiry invited by Mexican amendment dynamics.

What about constitutional interpretation? Which role has it played in the Mexican political and legal transition? Which features are most prominent and what do they suggest about broader patterns of legal, social, and political change? Which has been, in particular, the Mexican Supreme Court (MxSC) interpretive contribution to recent change and—perhaps more importantly—what can we expect for the future, especially if constitutional change through amendment starts to shrink and interpretation progressively acquires more comparative significance? How does the court's interpretive job look, from one or another perspective of evaluation?

Though the role of the MxSC in recent political evolution has not yet been fully reconstructed,[9] no doubt it has participated in trends that have marked the judiciary worldwide. Thus, in Latin America and elsewhere, judges have seen their powers extraordinarily strengthened,[10] in part as an effect of a market-reinforcing agenda that viewed judicial independence as the keystone to the rule of law,[11] and in part as an effect of the progressive consolidation of rights-based, substantivist constitutionalism, which puts limits on political majorities and entrusts their enforcement to courts.[12] From other standpoints, however, the MxSC performance has hardly been standard. As has often been noted, the court's track record in policing federalism and the horizontal division of powers has been good—it has successfully undertaken an arbitral role that the president can no longer fulfill—but it has performed poorly its other main constitutional responsibility: to protect individual rights against public (or private) encroachment.[13] While the apex courts of other regional countries were shaping some of the more interesting developments in contemporary constitutional law,[14] the MxSC retained formalistic and old-fashioned styles of adjudication[15] and continued to devote most of its time to cases filed by corporations brandishing their "fundamental right" not to pay taxes.[16]

Some things changed notably from 2005 onwards. The court understands differently its relation to other sociopolitical actors;[17] it has opened itself to public scrutiny: the plenary deliberations are TV and internet broadcasted, the drafts of high-profile opinions are posted on the web, and the court twitters out its activities; there are changes in the language of some rulings; Chief Justice Silva publicly committed the institution to the active promotion of human rights on every possible occasion;[18] and, most important of all, the court has started to protect people's rights.[19] Thus, after decades of complete regional invisibility, the MxSC rulings on abortion, the rights of transgender persons, same sex marriage, free speech, or conventionality review have received commentary and praise.[20]

No doubt there is much to celebrate about these incipient trends. But as Mexico prepares itself to enter adult democratic life, it is time to engage in a more fine-grained analysis. In this chapter, I will underline features of the court's performance over these past years which I believe may harm in the middle- and long term—as constitutional interpretation gains more systemic weight—its capacity to fulfill its functions properly, while being very problematic from a perspective sensitive to the normative conditions under which judicial review is compatible with democratic rule. I will collectively call these features "decisional fuzziness" or "decisional indeterminacy." an expression meant to broadly cover problems of decisional identification and information management but also of decisional ambiguity, avoidance, and inconsistency. All of these are adding to a single result: the absence of a clear, unified, identifiable, institutional voice for the court, backed by identifiable reasons—something that constitutes, in my view, a sort of very basic precondition for courts to be functional and legitimate in contemporary democracies. While there are many normative theories about the precise conditions under which judicial review is best, consistent with the idea of people's rule, they all presuppose that there is such a thing as "the voice of the Court"; a controversial voice, or a divided voice, at times, perhaps; but a clearly perceptible voice, accompanied by the expression of written reasons which may be object of comment, criticism, or response—by the people, by the other branches, by the press, or by the constitution's amending power. These theories strongly associate courts' democratic legitimacy to the contribution their reasoning does in obtaining a fuller, more inclusive and less biased political debate over matters of constitutional relevance—as compared to the situation in a system without judicial review.[21]

In my view, the identifiability of MxSC's institutional voice and its quality in terms of reasons are damaged by various factors, some of which this chapter will succinctly map out. As I will argue, a first group of factors are associated with features of *external* institutional design—determining the court's position within the Mexican judiciary. This position forces the court to decide too many cases, instead of focusing in a limited number more easily amenable to social and political scrutiny, and to deal with too heterogeneous a range of concerns, in the many jurisdictional and non-jurisdictional areas of responsibility it must attend. Quite expectedly, Mexican Justices have limited time and energy to deal with each case, something that weakens the "deliberative texture" of the rulings.[22] Other problematic factors are associated with features of *internal* institutional design that distract justices from the careful study of the docket, foster personalist dynamics, and do not incentivize them to merge their voices into a more unified conversation. Among these internal features I will single out the defective articulation between the courts' administrative and jurisdictional apparatuses—which forces justices to dedicate to myriad administrative decisions; the practice of having informal audiences with litigants—which is time-consuming and undermines due process; the extant rules to elect the President of the Court—which have perverse distorting and divisive effects over jurisdictional dynamics; and the otherwise highly celebrated system of public debates—which "parlamentarizes" the court and does not force the justices to come to terms with each other's positions with a view to reaching a coherent collective decision.

In my view, in sum, the absence of a clear, reason-backed, MxSC institutional voice can be related—though not exclusively to be sure—to features of institutional design that will be identified and discussed: in the external dimension, to the position occupied by the court within an excessively centralized judiciary, and in the internal dimension, to organic and procedural options that distract the justices from their core responsibilities and promote personalistic dynamics which hinder the emergence of a coherent institutional voice expressed in written rulings.

The paper will explore these external and internal features in turn (Subsections II.I and II.II) after having briefly illustrated the sort of problems I associate to the idea of "decisional fuzziness" (Section II). I will then suggest that fuzziness will turn increasingly troubling as Mexico gets more concerned about constitutional interpretation and the democratic acceptability of judicial review (Section III). While an important body of research has analyzed judicial institutional designs from the perspective of their effects on, among others, independence, power-diffusion, or access to the judiciary—all instrumental to important normative goals—this chapter suggests the need to complementarily undertake evaluations from normative standpoints that have always particularly worried constitutional lawyers. A brief conclusion (Section IV) will close.

II Decisional fuzziness: A few illustrations

When the MxSC issued its August 2008 abortion ruling, reactions inside the country were mixed. Outside, they were not: the ruling was generally celebrated, and emphasis was placed on the fact that the declaration of validity made of Mexico the first Latin American country to legalize abortion during the first trimester.[23] The problem emerged when these people outside inquired more specifically about the reasoning of the Mexican ruling. How had it conceptualized women's rights? Which legal treatment had been accorded to the fetus? Which space had the court given to conscientious objection claims? Was the ruling *Roe*-style, *German*-style, or *Colombian*-style?

Unfortunately, no answer for these questions was readily available. The justices had publicly discussed a draft prepared by their most conservative colleague, whose main tenets were soon rejected, and then the debate ensued without following the initial outline. Justices expressed their varied opinions over many sessions and, finally, on August 27/28, 2008, cast their final votes. Eight of them said the Mexico City statute under charge did not violate the constitution but added to their votes a great amount of caveats, comments, and qualifications. Then, following ordinary rules, they commissioned one of them to write a majority ruling. This document (called *engrose* in Mexico) was issued on February 26, 2009, almost six months later, and caused spirited controversy among the justices who had been in the majority because they thought it did not reflect "the result of the discussion."[24] Although some negotiation was pursued to harmonize their views into the ruling, the attempt ultimately failed and they wrote seven separate, concurring opinions expressing the highly different substantive views they had endorsed in the debate. To those, three dissenting opinions were added. As a result, the content of the ruling remained utterly undetermined.[25] So much so that, in an entirely abnormal turn, no *tesis* of the ruling were composed and published—i.e., the court did not craft the "excerpts" of ruling that are published in the Federal Judicial Gazette, enjoy value as precedents, and disseminate higher courts' rulings down to the wider judiciary.

When in 2011 the court had to return to the abortion issue following an abstract review challenge against two state constitutions newly amended to protect life from conception, the situation was just as expected: the justices started to discuss everything all over again. And as the eight votes necessary under Mexican law to declare a statute void in the abstract were not obtained, this time there was no "opinion of the Court" not even in the formal sense: the ruling was a "dismissal," i.e., a document that, following ordinary procedural rules, stated that the action against the statute had failed.[26] The technical absence of a real ruling did not prevent justices from adding to the dismissal several concurrent and dissenting opinions—whose legal status remains, of course, elusive.

It could be certainly be argued that an extremely fuzzy or confusing judicial experience around an abortion ruling should hardly be taken as a signal of generalized patterns, since abortion is always extremely divisive, in Mexico and everywhere. But divided as abortion rulings ordinarily are, they also mark in my view a terrain where the voice of an apex court can be most crucially valuable: these rulings sit right in the middle of the kind of ground where the constitution paradigmatically calls for a necessary coming to terms of majoritarian legislative decisions with anti-majoritarian rights—privacy, health, autonomy, life, etc.—and where Constitutional Courts' voices merge into a sophisticated and extended conversation frequently involving repeated rounds among legislatures, judges, and, sometimes, even constitutional amending powers. No surprise that analysis of abortion judicial doctrines and their evolution is a staple of legal analysis and scholarship worldwide.

The fact, in any case, is that decision identification in the MxSC is troublesome and costly on every occasion, both in routine cases and in politically salient ones, both where unanimity obtains and when the vote is divided and the interplay among justices' views defies the notion of an identifiable "single conversation." Starting with routine litigation, a first problem is that the myriad cases decided in the chambers—more than 5,000 in 2012 (see Figures 5.4, 5.5, 5.6 and 5.7 in the

Appendix)[27]—are not tracked directly but through the already mentioned system of *tesis*, which are one-page summaries of abstract reasoning emerging from a ruling, drafted by the clerks or by a special unit,[28] favorably voted upon by the justices at some point,[29] published in the Federal Judiciary Gazette, and included in a data base—the Indiana University Southeast (IUS)—where legal clerks and practitioners research what "existing law" apparently holds. Unfortunately, *tesis* are not issued in every case, their relation to the actual decision is sometimes debatable, and, because they lack any reference to the facts of the case, they are intrinsically unable to convey the holding—the *ratio decidendi*—of decisions.[30]

While *tesis* are increasingly supplemented by the availability of full rulings on the website, the latter are not summarized in well-organized subject-matter categories that could facilitate research. Mexican rulings are published without the summaries one finds, for instance, in Colombian, American, or Canadian rulings, which greatly facilitate the tracking of precedent. The crafting of *tesis* was traditionally thought to fulfill this summarizing function but today, in view of the *tesis* system's evident shortcomings, the absence of good informational organization seriously hinders the traceability of the doctrines that govern many neighborhoods of the law.[31]

As regards politically salient cases, both in the plenary and in the chambers and particularly after the court decided a few years ago to discuss all plenary cases in public,[32] grasping what the court is really deciding is even more complex, because of the systemic separation—sometimes divergence—between what is expressed by the justices in the public debate, the actual wording of the final ruling (the *engrose*), and the content of the *tesis* sent out to the world as signal and summary of the binding case law. Moreover, it is quite common, in plenary opinions, to find the directive part of the ruling (*puntos resolutivos*) followed by three of four pages of explanations in which the Court's Proceedings Secretary states how many votes support one or various of the different *puntos* and the reasons why every justice does so. These paragraphs are long, dense, obscure, full of *caveats*, partial endorsements, and quick references to notions and concepts discussed in the ruling or only in the broadcasted debate. They completely dilute the idea of a ruling as an articulated expression of reasons that coalesce around directive points marking out the immediate changes it purports to make in the world.

The most conspicuous effects of massive opinion making, complexity, and segmentation are well known by most observers of Mexican constitutional life. To start with and most visibly, newspapers, legal blogs, academic columnists, and even university professors comment, discuss, and evaluate "what the Court doe,s" relying heavily on the written literal transcription of the justices' expression of position in the public broadcasted debate, available on the web—positions that, strictly speaking, are not yet decisions: not yet the law.[33] While the final written rulings eventually come out, checking whether they reflect what the justices said in public is hard and time-consuming, and in a way pointless—since what really counts as law is the written ruling. But because of this, insufficient attention is paid to the actual language, terms, and reasons for the rulings which come out without much notice), and a sort of pollution hinders the perception of the voice of a court that speaks twice: on the TV and in the rulings. The justices themselves struggle a lot to reconstruct "what they said" on past occasions. Outside, supervision of the court's consistency and coherence weakens.

The challenges posed by this systemic decisional complexity and fuzziness were again paradigmatically reflected in the landmark *Radilla* case and its military jurisdiction offspring. In this case,[34] signaled as a watershed in Mexican legal history, the court intended to clarify, in the abstract, what obligations the federal judiciary had under the Inter-American Court's *Radilla* ruling, which had condemned Mexico for, among other things, the wide boundaries of the military courts' jurisdiction.[35] The MxSC decided to tackle and clarify at the same time the main implications of the June 2011 constitutional amendment impinging on the relations among national and international sources of law and, in an unexpected turn, it also embarked in a full redefinition of the Mexican judicial review model.[36] But justices, ferociously divided, voted and expressed their views as qualifiedly and piecemeal as always. And as the big questions were answered in the abstract, in a non-standard proceeding, when concrete controversies touching on the same matters came up through the ordinary procedural channels, the court had to discuss everything again, from the beginning and with every detail, over the following months, in an extremely dense chain of cases whose discussion includes a "rebellion" by the Second Chamber, which qualified or abandoned some of the criteria approved by the plenary.[37] The discussion of the military jurisdiction-related *amparos,* for instance, took an unbelievable month-and-a-half long series of plenary sessions, in whose context the justices discussed before the TV the procedural and substantive particulars of each and every case.[38] When they eventually wrapped up the exhausting debate, the process of opinion drafting started, and took more than eight months.

The same topic—relations between internal and international sources of law in the rights area—was visited again by the court some time later, in an attempt to soften or fix the situation created by the harsh divisions among justices that, once again, gained the stage during the discussion of the Action of Unconstitutionality 155/2007 and the Second Chamber decisions mentioned above. The court very consciously tried to come up with a unified majority opinion when deciding the Thesis Contradiction 293/2011 in 2013.[39] Confirming its decision-making patterns, however, the majority ruling crafts a very complex criterion, with open internal contradictions, and comes accompanied by two dissenting opinions, five concurring opinions, one "partially explanatory and partially concurrent opinion" and one "partially dissenting and partially concurring" where justices make explicit their conditioned understanding of what they are supposed to be jointly deciding by majority opinion. The end result was again that, on a field of great systemic consequence, and despite the explicitly stated desire of unification, it was the segmentation of the reasoning that prevailed. And, as a consequence, insufficient capacity on the part of the court to give orientation to citizens and lower judges about the contours of the system of legal sources in the country, and insufficient capacity to break a dynamics of never-ending reopening of debates—as demonstrated by the return to the same issues when deciding the home-arrest case and when debating the means of implementation of the inter-American Court *Fernández Ortega* and *Rosendo Cantú* rulings in 2015.[40]

II.I The external design of the court: Too many jobs in too centralized a system

One reason why it is so difficult to identify the MxSC's distinctive voice is arguably that it decides too many cases within too heterogeneous areas of jurisdiction. As will immediately be seen, these features are associated with the functions the court performs in the context of the Mexican judiciary and the wider political system.

The number of cases decided by the MxSC has steadily grown in recent years, despite the many efforts made from the late 1980s to discharge it of non-directly constitutional matters and transform it into a "truly constitutional tribunal."[41] Figures 5.1 and 5.2 show the evolution and composition of the caseload over the last seven years.[42]

These cases fall under several areas of jurisdiction. The main ones are the following: *acciones de inconstitucionalidad* (abstract, *erga omnes* review of general norms); *controversias constitucionales* (horizontal or vertical conflicts of jurisdiction among the federation, states, municipalities and its internal branches, involving abstract or concrete review and general or *inter partes* effects depending on the case); *amparos directos o indirectos en revisión* (appeals of semi-diffuse, *inter partes* legal and constitutional review of acts, norms, and judicial rulings); *contradicciónes de tesis* (unification jurisdiction when the Collegiate Circuit Courts hold conflicting criteria on a particular matter); *recursos de reclamación, inconformidad, queja*, and *incidentes de inejecución* (ancillary or incidental questions within major proceedings and non-compliance proceedings); *modificación o sustitución de jurisprudencia* (formal, *ad hoc* changes of precedent); *incumplimientos graves del Sistema de Coordinación Fiscal* (proceedings examining whether a state has or has not met its duties under the National Tax Coordination System); *revisiones administrativas* (review of Federal Judiciary Council decisions on the organization and discipline of the federal judiciary), and conflicts of jurisdiction among federal judges.[43] In addition, the court can grab cases from the lower courts' docket if they can lead to setting "important and significant" criteria. Finally, the court has appointment powers: it elevates to the Senate candidates to become magistrate of the Electoral Tribunal[44] and appoints three of the seven members of the Federal Judiciary Council.[45] The President of the Judiciary Council is the Chief Justice of the Supreme Court—i.e., the two institutions share "heads" (see Figures 5.1 and 5.2).[46]

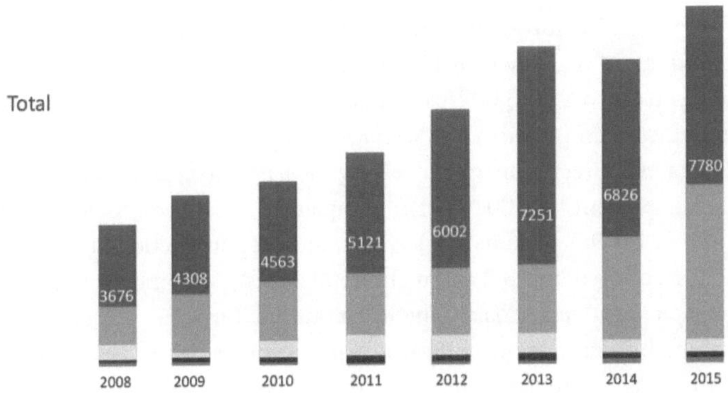

	2008	2009	2010	2011	2012	2013	2014	2015
Other cases	2088	2453	2442	2874	3691	4911	3914	3784
Writ of Amparo*	990	1519	1542	1514	1634	1648	2403	3483
Thesis Contradiction	423	159	430	528	500	481	304	347
Constitutional Controversy	69	105	92	174	119	152	102	76
Action of Unconstitutionality	106	72	57	31	58	59	103	90

FIGURE 5.1 Number of cases decided by the Mexican Supreme Court (2008–2015)
Note: Includes data corresponding to indirect amparo on review, direct amparo on review, and direct amparo.

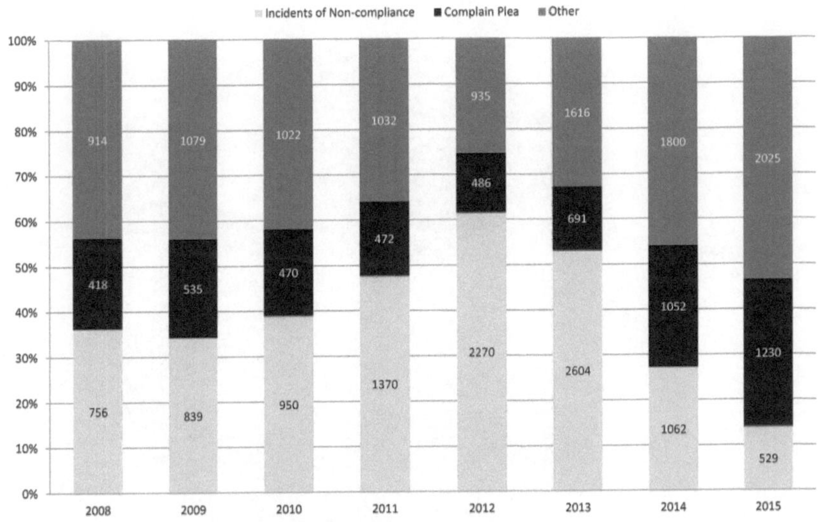

FIGURE 5.2 Composition of "other cases" in Figure 5.1 (2008–2015)

These areas of jurisdiction represent, however, highly disparate shares in the overall docket. As shown in Figure 5.3, in 2012 only five areas were responsible for 81 percent of the 6,002 cases decided by the court: non-compliance *amparo*-related proceedings (*incidentes de inejecución*) which accounted for 37.8 percent (2,270 cases); direct amparo on review (*amparo directo en revisión)* which accounted for 18.3 percent (1,100 cases); complaint pleas (*recurso de reclamación)* which accounted for 9.3 percent (564 cases); thesis contradictions (*contradicciónes de tesis)* which accounted for 8.3 percent (500 cases); and indirect amparo on review (*amparo indirecto en revisión)* which accounted for 8.2 percent (494 cases).[47] In 2015, the burden of non-compliance proceedings had substantially decreased but, taken together, complaint pleas, incidents of non-compliance, and the miscellaneous "other cases" rubric still represented half of the docket.

Caseload size is therefore not so much associated with the number of functions the court performs—which is only slightly above regional standards[48]—as with the extraordinarily heavy take *amparo*-related proceedings (main and ancillary) have on the court. And this take is in turn explained, in my view, by the contours of the Mexican model of judicial review and by deep institutional path-dependencies. Though we cannot attempt here a full-scale description of historical trajectories—and we will therefore fall short from providing the theoretical argument and the empirical evidence necessary to actually make a well-founded

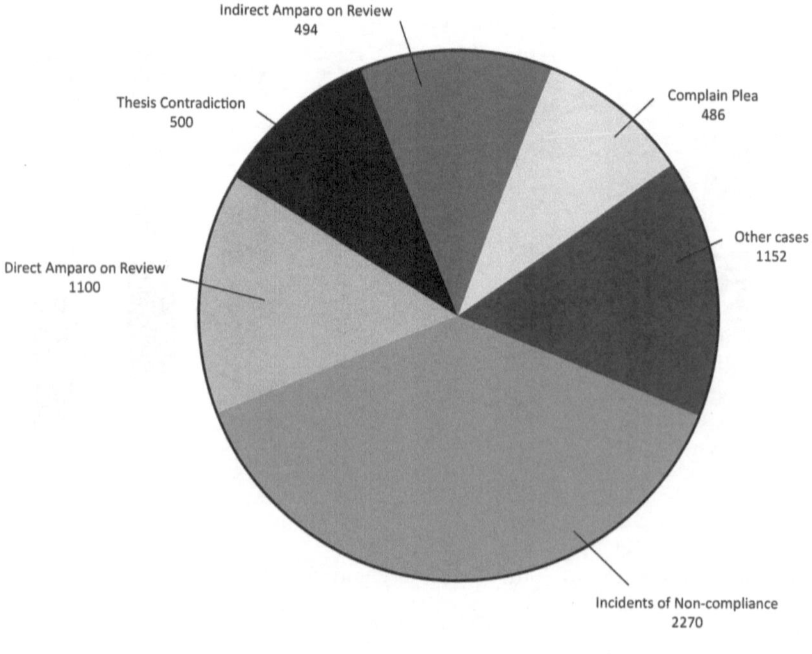

FIGURE 5.3 Cases decided by the Mexican Supreme Court by area of jurisdiction (2012)

claim of path-dependence—two main features, prominent among the conditioning elements of the court's current performance, must be underlined.

The first one concerns the functions the *amparo* performs within the legal system. The Mexican *amparo* is an ancient institution with multiple functions. In the middle of the nineteenth century, it was pioneeringly created to allow citizens to demand before federal judges protection against constitutional rights violations on the part of any kind of authority. It operated as the exclusive channel of constitutional guarantee for more than 150 years.[49] Judicial rulings from both federal and state courts were after some hesitation admitted as objects of review and, in a pretty strange turn, violation of ordinary statutes were equated to a violation of the constitution.[50] As a result, *amparo* became a greatly over-dimensioned institution with highly heterogeneous functions: habeas corpus, protection against unconstitutional regulations, resolution of agrarian conflicts—*and* review of judicial rulings on both legal and constitutional grounds—i.e., *amparo* became a sort of additional appeal. In the meantime and because of this huge scope, it became a jungle of procedural complexity, full of technicalities, grounds for dismissal, and ancillary questions. To this day, it is extremely time-consuming for judges, who devote most of their efforts to procedural, not substantive, analysis.[51] Although the court has issued General Agreements delegating entire categories of cases to the Collegiate Circuit Courts to keep its docket manageable, the constitution does not include a *certiorari* system and the court remains heavily burdened.

The second one concerns more broadly the model of judicial review the country has more recently embraced. When in 1994 the constitution was amended to make room for new channels of review imported from European, Kelsen-inspired models, the country did not create a Constitutional Court, but simply added the new functions—abstract review of norms (*acciones*) and conflicts of territorial jurisdiction (*controversias*)—to the Supreme Court's existing spheres of responsibility. Mexico had from that moment a hybrid system of judicial review combining a semi-centralized framework[52] with a centralized, abstract review one; with the further singularity that, while most Latin American hybrids have created a new Constitutional Court or a specialized Constitutional Chamber within preexisting Supreme Courts,[53] in Mexico the Supreme Court remained alone and concentrated on everything.[54]

These two features help us see that, as Julio Ríos-Figueroa has emphasized, the Mexican is an extraordinarily concentrated judicial model.[55] In countries like Peru, he notes, there are four different apex institutions to do what the MxSC does all alone.[56] And though excessive decentralization can also be harmful, excessive centralization may give judges insufficient time to accurately study the docket:

> A judge that participates in the construction of the Constitution's meaning, and therefore in the eventual nullification or modification of statutes, public

> policy and governmental acts needs time to analyze all in the complex constitutional issues she faces. On the other hand, tasks related to the administration of the judiciary are also very important and very demanding and very different from constitutional interpretation. If a Court concentrates both tasks, its performance as an interpreter and as an administrator may be damaged.[57]

While Ríos-Figueroa refers here to the mix of jurisdictional activity and the tasks associated with the administration of the judiciary—which the court mainly performs through the pivotal figure of the Chief Justice[58]—his remarks are equally apposite to describe the effects of having such a concentration of multiple jurisdictional tasks.

Beyond the question of time, there is the question of needing a profile of justice—and a profile of court—good at doing highly disparate things at the same time. Studies on comparative institutional analysis suggest it can often be difficult. In discussing the pros and cons of different judicial review models from a perspective bound on creating a forum of principle where fundamental rights are taken seriously, and assuming that judges need a degree of peace and quiet to reflect on fundamental values, Víctor Ferreres remarks that not all systems work equally well.[59] While courts of appeals in common law countries have the means to control the litigation flood, higher courts in civil law countries, habitually overwhelmed with work, do not have discretional jurisdiction.[60] In these countries there exist therefore problems in installing the sort of "division of labor" that facilitates a proper exercise of constitutional functions. Even in common law countries:

> [i]f the supreme court focuses too much on cases that give rise to constitutional issues, it leaves other fields of the law unattended. This is detrimental to its other function as the supreme interpreter of *ordinary* law. The more the Supreme Court acts as a "constitutional tribunal" the more it abandons its role as the supreme court in ordinary matters, especially troublesome in modern times, when ordinary law is increasingly complex.[61]

For quite the same reasons, there can be potential problems if a centralized Kelsenian court has to handle many matters besides examining the constitutionality of legislation.[62]

The MxSC's current scheme of attributions, in sum, does not seem to facilitate focus and congruence in daily judicial performance. The court handles many cases and a too heterogeneous package of tasks. Its functional menu is baroque and full of path-dependencies. The MxSC sits at the common apex of several tiers of highly disparate jurisdictional responsibilities which must be deployed in great numbers, under time-consuming procedures. It would be quite heroic if justices had the time and expertise—let alone the "leisure" and "insulation" famously treasured by Alexander Bickel[63]—to perform well all their institutional responsibilities.

II.II The internal design of the court: Verticality, distraction, and personalism

A second source of burdens preventing the MxSC from engaging in fluid and properly institutionalized, constitution-centered reasoning is found in its internal practices and regulations.

In an interesting contribution to the literature on judicialization, Diana Kapiszewski has stressed the importance of carefully inspecting how the courts' internal institutions and culture affect their behavior and performance.[64] While, she notes, there is much to learn from study of the courts' *external* institutions—designed by the elected branches and governing the composition, independence, access to and powers of high courts (size, appointment mechanisms, tenure rules, scope of jurisdiction)[65]—it is equally necessary to pay attention to the way they impact internal organizational practices and cultural patterns, which must be in turn considered important factors of the way to explain how courts make decisions.[66] This scholar then turns to the Brazilian Supreme Federal Tribunal and inquires into aspects such as the sense of security of the justices; their professional profile; their perceptions regarding their separation or non-separation from the court as an institution; articulation of leaderships at the court; forms of organization and attitudes among the law clerks assisting the justices; practices developed in handling the caseload and crafting the rulings; the dynamics articulating deliberations and opinion-drafting; or the attitudes and practices on transparency and the opening up of the court to outside actors.[67]

Kapiszewski's exercise joins a tradition of comparative work on courts that has long been interested in describing how a mixture of ideas, institutions, practices, and formal or informal rules help understand how courts distinctively operate in different countries. Mirjan Damaška's classic study on the "faces" of justice and state authority, for instance, contrasts what he terms "coordinated" and "hierarchical" ideals and shows how each of them encapsulate pretty identifiable correlations between typical ways of accessing the judiciary, patterns of internal organization, attitudes toward supra and subordinated personnel, ways of understanding the nature and identity of law, perceptions about the role of judges in society, different conceptions about the kind of activity required to decide a case under law, and, consequently, different sorts of decisions.[68]

The influence of internal dynamics (in Kapiszewski's terms) over the general performance of the MxSC is in my opinion immense. Though there is no space here for a full examination of this dimension, I will identify in what follows a few salient traits of internal organization that I associate with behavioral patterns with considerable consequences for the court's systemic performance. They all illustrate to what extent the MxSC is permeated by structures and dynamics that rely far too much on the justices as persons, distracting them, and discouraging styles of action and decision that would ease the merging of their acts and voices into something worth being called a collegiate emanation of "the Court."

One of the first features to be mentioned reveals strong hierarchical fingerprints and points to something that compounds the highly problematic functional overload we analyzed in the previous section: the court's massive internal administrative apparatus, its feeble articulation with the units discharging jurisdictional tasks, and the way it "monarchically" relies on the justices for its daily operation, imposing many obligations on them—a pretty bizarre "support" apparatus, then. The MxSC is a huge administrative structure with a small jurisdictional arm. The administrative apparatus employs around 2,700 people, while the jurisdictional apparatus—law clerking teams and proceedings secretaries and sub-secretaries—employs around 400, with only around 125 actually doing clerking work.[69] Justices are *alfa* and *omega* of both: they take all the important decisions at the apex of both substructures and mediate most communication between the two. According to the organization chart,[70] the court has today, together with a few other adjacent administrative units, twelve General Direction (GD) offices organically subordinated at the formal level to a unit titled *Secretaría de la Presidencia* or to the *Oficial mayor* (chief clerk): GD of Legal Affairs, GD of Social Communication and Links with Civil Society, GD of the Judicial Channel, GD of Attention and Services, GD of Human Resources and Administrative Innovation, GD of the Treasury, DG of Physical Infrastructure, GD of Security, GD of Budget and Accounting, GD of Material Resources, GD of Information Technologies, GD of Houses of Legal Culture, GD of Auditing, and GD of Administrative Liability and Patrimony Registry (these two latter ones dependent on the Courts *Contraloría*—the Audits Office).

Despite the formal subordination of these bodies to the *Secretario de la Presidencia*, the *Oficial Mayor*, and the auditor, justices personally take the most important administrative decisions through their participation in committees. According to Section 107 of the court's *Reglamento interior*,[71] in order to better deal with administrative issues under its responsibility or that of the Chief Justice, the plenary chamber can designate ordinary or extraordinary committees formed by the Chief Justice and two justices, preferably coming from one of the two chambers each, for a period of two years. Ordinary committees are now five: Government and Administration; Regulations, Agreements, and Docket Planning; Archives, Libraries, and Informatics; Human Development, Health, Social Action, and Educational Promotion; Publications, Social Communication, Diffusion, and Institutional Relations. A quick look at Sections 110–117 of the *Reglamento Interior* illustrates the heavy list of functions assigned to each of these ordinary committees, to which the extraordinary ones can be added if necessary.[72] Committees therefore expend much time and energy within the court's internal schedules. Justices must reserve a considerable amount of time for meeting in committees to decide the most disparate array of non-jurisdictional questions.

Justices are further distracted from the quiet study of the docket by a practice that, while clearly evincing the heavy persistence of the past, is incompatible with the court's institutional position in contemporary Mexican democracy. During the week, typically in the mornings before and after the sessions and on Friday more flexibly, justices employ a notable amount of their time receiving people in their offices. If they are successful in obtaining a space in the appointment book, citizens or groups of attorneys interested in a particular case—big law firms, non-governmental organizations (NGOs), high government officials, etc.—can have a few minutes' talk with the justices and a corresponding opportunity to raise what they believe are important points to be considered in the analysis of their cases. Attorneys also sometimes seek, though more rarely, meetings with the law clerks. The practice traces from deep in the past and finds surprisingly little public opposition: traditional attorneys are used to the practice and satisfied with it; the new public interest litigants and NGOs now also meet the justices and are surprised (and flattered) by such an amazing possibility; and within the court, the practice has traditionally been seen as something that is eventually useful for justices in detecting details about the law or facts they were unaware of—not an unusual situation in a court that decides 6,000 cases a year filled with the most disparate legal issues, requiring high levels of expertise and time-investment—and more recently as a sign of affability and openness.

The fact remains, unfortunately, that these are meetings where one of the parties without the presence of the other has a change to spell out, before a Supreme Court Justice sitting in an armchair, his/her vision of the law in the instant case. Informal audiences with the justices, in short, should not be considered a sort of felicitous *avant-la-lettre* sign of openness now fitting comfortably with the strong transparency agenda of the Mexican Court, but a practice that undermines the preconditions of legitimate judicial decision-making.[7374] The visitors moreover bring in fuss and noise,[75] and it all adds to a situation in which the court remains trapped by internal dynamics which do not favor its expected institutional performance.

Another feature that distracts justices from jurisdictional tasks and distorts genuine collegiality is the rule—set in article 97 of the Constitution—according to which the Chief Justice is elected every four years by the plenary among its members. To be Chief Justice of the MxSC is to wield immense power: as we saw, he/she will preside over the Federal Judicial Council, which controls the access, promotion, discipline. and resources of the entire Mexican federal judiciary, and in the Supreme Court he/she will be responsible for a huge structure whose command entails great power. Little wonder the "campaign" to occupy the presidency starts early and distorts countless aspects of the court's daily performance. To have a chance of garnering a majority of the eleven votes necessary to be elected, justices must present a candidacy and build a support coalition among their colleagues. While we would all expect complete separation between taking sides in this matter and taking sides on jurisdictional ones, the system is very divisive on the facts and dilutes the spirit of collegiality—something a simple rotation rule such as the one governing the election of the chambers' presidents would easily prevent.

Last but not least, the weakness of the MxSC's collegiate, institutional voice and the dilution of argument is further buttressed by an aspect of the decisional procedure already mentioned in Section II: the fact that justices now take part in public TV debates without having previously reached a collective decision on the matters under discussion—a collective decision that rarely emerges later in the course of the debate. As is well known, one of the values of deliberation lies precisely in its capacity to change the minds of the people in response and reaction to the remarks of every other, and under the current system at the MxSC plenary deliberation has weakened. The court does not attain a collective, deliberated outcome: justices examine the draft circulated by the justice in charge of the case, discuss with their clerking teams what their position will be, and present this position in public—usually on the basis of pre-elaborated documents read on the spot—rarely changing their minds in view of others' position.[76] The results have been documented in Section II: the plenary debate becomes a collection of unilateral views often impossible to combine into a single coherent document, which has to be produced by the clerks after the casting of votes—at great pains and with intrinsically limited possibilities of success.

True, the newly gained publicity of the debates is linked to a strategy of transparency which often helps Constitutional Courts connect with the people and increase their own legitimacy: it tends to reinforce the confidence of people in an institution in charge of protecting their rights, it can abate suspicion from the other branches and increase the courts' capital to arbitrate among them, it can promote accountability, and provide incentives for consistent decision-making. Moreover, the task of a contemporary Constitutional Court must always be done in dialogue with other branches and society, and publicity may be instrumental in that. We must subtract from these gains, however, in the Mexican case, the costs of non-genuine deliberation and non-convergent decision-making induced by a system which gives justices the incentive to deliver a nice public speech and little else.[77]

The elements analyzed so far pick out quite varied organizational dimensions. Others could have been added and no one of them can be said to be the single causal villain. What the analysis suggests is that they jointly favor the maintenance of patterns which do not seem disconnected from the difficulties the court still confronts when it turns to producing more stable and salient constitution-centered reasoning over time.

III Decisional fuzziness and anti-majoritarian legitimacy

As constitutional lawyers well know debate on the legitimacy of judicial review of legislation—debate on the "anti-majoritarian difficulty"[78]—was for long an obsession in academic constitutional conversation. Why should a few persons sitting in the court be empowered to have a final say on the most serious constitutional matters? Why should unelected—typically male, hetero, x-class—

judges prevail over what elected legislatures decide under a constitutional declaration of rights?

The triumph of judicial review as an institution—now globally widened out, after being an American oddity for more than a century—can be seen as depriving the debate of much of its teeth. Traditional arguments and counter-arguments in its context, however, continue to be relevant in analyzing the pros and cons of particular institutional designs and to gauge the performance of courts within constitutional systems. We do not use those arguments any longer in deciding whether to set a court or not—history has answered the question in the affirmative—but to evaluate its performance, ponder whether it works well, and act as reminders of the reasons that justify its institutional presence: they embody evaluative dimensions we should continue projecting onto apex courts to check whether they make a justifiable contribution to our democratic life.

A core strand of arguments within the debate underlines the institutional advantages of Constitutional Courts in performing the kind of task required for living under the supremacy of a document and recognizing certain rights and principles as foundations of justice in the political community. As Víctor Ferreres aptly summarizes in reconstructing what he calls "a skeletal justification of judicial review" while retrieving arguments of several other scholars,[79] we let courts draw the implications of those principles, even with the opinion of democratic legislatures to the contrary, because we believe that, as Alexander Bickel argued, they have the time and insulation required to perform an intellectual task which calls for the construction of durable and coherent doctrines.[80] And because we believe that, as Larry Sager signals, the institutional design of adjudication makes judges particularly well-trained and well-situated to evaluate political choices against constitutional principle, in the same way that quality-control inspectors are specialized in detecting flaws in the products they supervise.[81] And because we observe that, as Owen Fiss remarks, the fact judges are compelled to answer questions raised by the parties on the basis of reasons, makes them particularly suited to exploring the requirements of public reason using terms that can be defended under a principle of universality.[82] Authors like Barry Friedman, or John Ferejohn and Pascale Pasquino have noted, on their part, that constitutional adjudication can make public deliberation in matters of public policy and rights more inclusive.[83] And participants in the debate on the judicialization of social rights—particularly energetic in contemporary Latin America—have underlined that even in social-policy terrains where political majorities should maintain broad decisional margins, judicial intervention may be essential to take co-opted legislatures out of inaction, correct legislative over- or under-inclusions, force topics into the political agenda, or transform preexisting social meanings.[84]

We could go on and on. The point here is not to discuss these arguments in themselves but to emphasize the perhaps pretty obvious fact they assume at all times that courts engage in identifiable, reason-backed reasoning. It is because of this, within certain restrictions, that the political "whole" is more just, or more genuinely democratic, than a political "whole" in which judicial review does not exist. Even those pressing for strong qualifications to better balance judicial review's costs and gains—defenders of Canadian-style dialogical models in whose context courts may be "responded" by the legislature,[85] for instance, or those that oppose excessive rigidity not to gag the constitutional amending power—argue against the background of this same, very simple idea.

From this perspective, the MxSC current performance is clearly found wanting. It is immersed in a dynamics that makes it very costly to reconstruct an institutional voice that is often simply absent, to supervise its evolution or to praise or criticize its coherence and constitutional wisdom. Because, as classically stated in *the Federalist Papers*, courts lack "the sword" and "the purse."[86] they must counteract their comparative institutional fragility by raising a clear voice that will hopefully resonate in an audience. It is true that there is more than an audience an apex court may possibly target—traditional practitioners, colleagues, the other branches, the public at large, etc.—and that privileging one or the other may lead to different conclusions as to the best way of organizing and transmitting its institutional output.[87] But wherever a modest threshold of clarity and reasons is not met, something crucial for the maintenance of the court's legitimacy before any of them will be missing. Openness, novelty and TV broadcasting may now be enough for the court to fortify its public position. But over time, as its interpretive performance acquires more centrality, the authority that will count will not be charismatic, but the one carried along by the careful reasoning contained in its rulings.

IV Conclusion

The position of the MxSC in the country's political and legal dynamics has dramatically changed in recent times. If the court was traditionally shy, technically inclined, and little prone to alter the status quo—in harmony with its being heir to a long tradition of adjudication in whose context statutes, not the constitution, were the center of the law—it is now a highly visible and consequential player in Mexican political life.

While there are reasons to celebrate the court's current contribution to more effective power sharing and the way it enriches public debate as it adjudicates an increasing number of rights claims, over time it will be necessary to evaluate its performance more stringently from perspectives that are critical to gauging its sustained legitimacy in contemporary democracies.

This chapter has identified one clearly problematic feature in current MxSC performance: the deficit of identifiability of its institutional, authoritative voice—its prominent decisional fuzziness. The immense complexity involved in tracking and reconstructing what the court is deciding and the reasons that support what is decided effectively immunize it from much of public opinion and academic criticism it would otherwise incur. The court's criteria are constantly changing, we monitor changes feebly, and we do it feebly because doing so is exceedingly cumbersome.

We have argued that these "behavioral" patterns are not independent from features of institutional design that speak many things about the historical evolution of judicial review and constitutionalism in Mexico. In an era of normative, rights-based constitutionalism, Mexico is operating with institutions, texts, and procedures that often trace back to the nineteenth century. The pattern of legal change seems to have been more accumulation than substitution, and many organic and procedural components sit uncomfortably with contemporary judicial functions. Thus, in the external dimension, the court accumulates too many responsibilities because it simply added a package of Kelsenian attributions to a preexisting semi-decentralized system based on an *amparo* conceived of as a channel of generalized review. The MxSC does not have *certiorari* powers and says too many things to be carefully listened to. The court cannot focus on constitutional principle because it must attend issues touching on the entire legal system. In the internal dimension, the MxSC is not immune to the problems of weak institutionalization and excessive personalism that Mexico evinces in many other dimensions of its collective life. The court is a huge institution but not necessarily a strong one. Justices take administrative decisions they should be discharged from, and work within a structure pervaded by hierarchical dynamics that exacerbate personalism. The recent move toward publicity in deliberations, as we have noted, has paradoxically fueled personalist dynamics, in contra-distinction to institutional ones.

For sure, some of the institutional features discussed here may fare well from other evaluative perspectives, so that careful balance among gains and losses as well as careful identification of all factors influencing the situation is always in order. Our exercise nonetheless helps to visualize at least a few changes that it is hard to imagine would not be good. It is at least an invitation to energetically reject the idea that we live in an optimal institutional status quo, and to continue looking for possible solutions to situations whose correction, this paper has argued, is important for the MxSC to its making an adequate contribution to democratically valuable social change.

Appendix

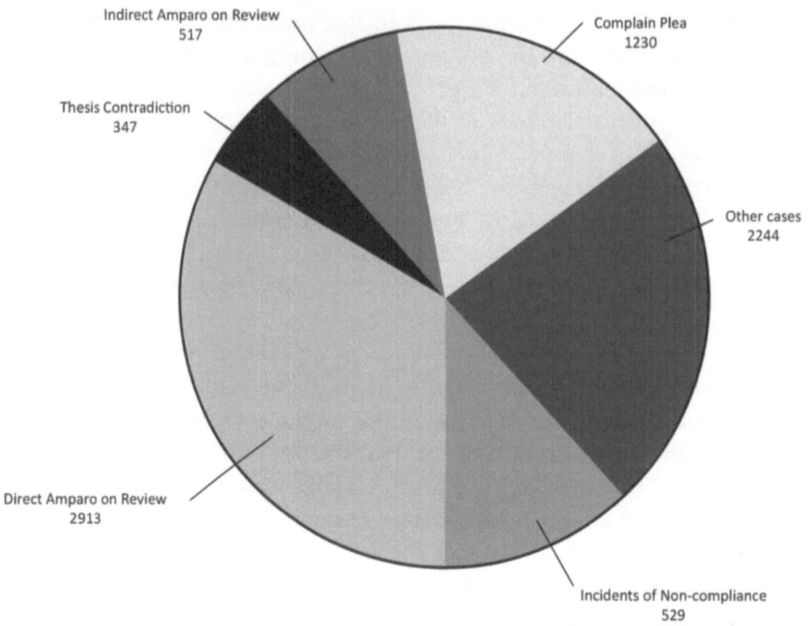

FIGURE 5.4 Cases decided by the Mexican Supreme Court by area of jurisdiction (2015)

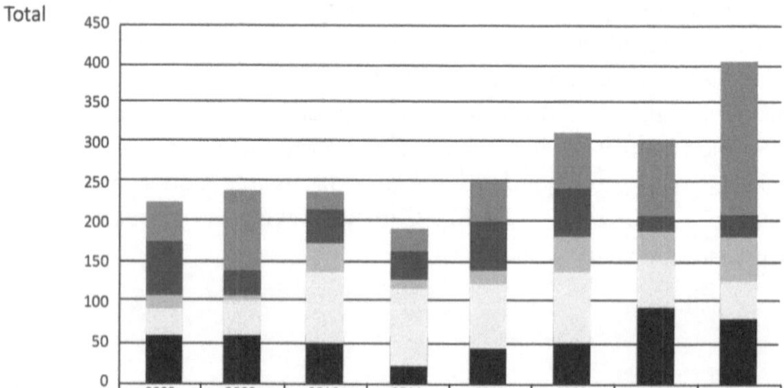

	2008	2009	2010	2011	2012	2013	2014	2015
Other cases	46	98	20	26	49	72	96	195
Writ of Amparo*	66	31	44	35	59	56	13	36
Thesis Contradiction	13	6	29	9	21	44	37	45
Constitutional Controversy	30	43	92	96	75	90	57	51
Action of Unconstitutionality	63	57	49	24	46	50	98	81

FIGURE 5.5 Cases decided by the Plenary Chamber, by area of jurisdiction (2008–2015)
Note: Includes data corresponding to indirect amparo on review, direct amparo on review, and direct amparo.

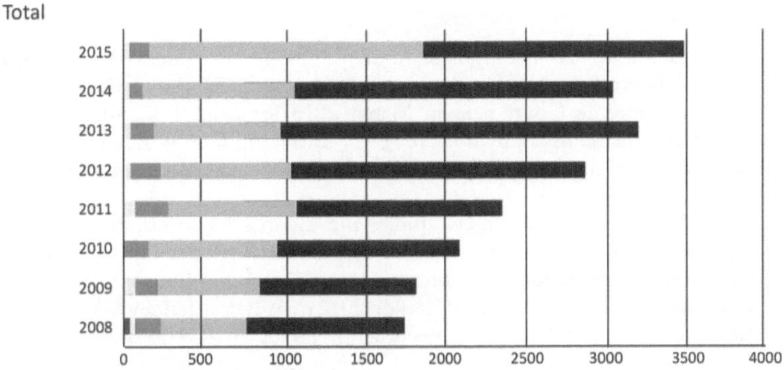

	2008	2009	2010	2011	2012	2013	2014	2015
■ Action of Unconstitutionality	24	11	3	6	9	3	3	4
□ Constitutional Controversy	23	39	0	57	19	25	23	14
■ Thesis Contradiction	181	143	124	198	187	138	75	130
■ Writ of Amparo*	516	676	816	798	828	812	976	1698
■ Other cases	1011	967	1185	1312	1820	2199	1942	1631

FIGURE 5.6 Cases decided by the First Chamber, by area of jurisdiction (2008–2015)
Note: Includes data corresponding to indirect amparo on review, direct amparo on review, and direct amparo.

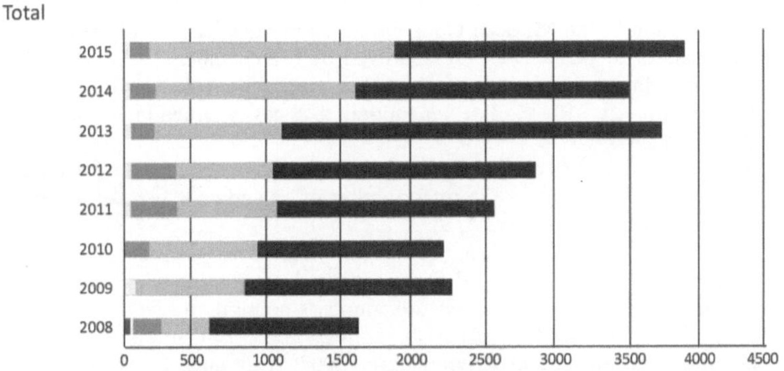

	2008	2009	2010	2011	2012	2013	2014	2015
■ Action of Unconstitutionality	19	4	5	1	3	6	2	5
□ Constitutional Controversy	16	23	0	21	25	37	22	11
■ Thesis Contradiction	229	10	277	321	292	299	192	172
■ Writ of Amparo*	408	812	682	681	747	780	1414	1749
■ Other cases	1031	1388	1237	1536	1822	2640	1876	1958

FIGURE 5.7 Cases decided by the Second Chamber, by area of jurisdiction (2008–2015)
Note: Includes data corresponding to indirect amparo on review, direct amparo on review, and direct amparo.

Notes

1 I am grateful to Tom Ginsburg, Andrea Pozas-Loyo, Alberto Puppo, Saúl López-Noriega, Pedro Salazar, and other participants at the ITAM-FLACSO Seminar on the Mexican Supreme Court held in March 2013 for helpful comments on a previous draft. I also thank an anonymous reviewer for raising several important points, as well as Franz Oberarzbacher and Samuel Cataño for their invaluable assistance in producing the graphics.

2 The field covers, among others, studies and theories on constitution making; amendment, replacement, and endurance of constitutional texts; constitutional design; constitutional interpretation; and borrowings, diffusion, or migration of constitutional ideas. See Nolte and Schilling-Vacaflor 2012a (analytical framework and case studies); Negretto 2012 (replacement, amendment); Elkins 2010; Ginsburget al. 2008 (diffusion); Choudhry 2006; Jackson 2010 migration); Ginsburg et al. 2009a; Uprimny 2011; Uprimny and Sánchez 2012 (constitution making); Gargarella 2011; Loyo and Ríos-Figueroa 2011(amendment); Choudhry 2008; Congleton and Swedenborg 2006; Ginsburg 2012; Ginsburg et al. 2009b (constitutional design, endurance); Michelman 2004 and essays at I-Con 2003 (borrowings); Gargarella 2007 (transplants).

3 Negretto 2012: 749, 751.

4 According to Nolte and Schilling-Vacaflor (2012b: 6), from 1978, sixteen out of eighteen Latin American countries enacted a new constitution. See also Negretto 2012: 753; Uprimny 2011: 111–12.

5 Casar and Marván 2014: 9. The period they consider is 1920–2012. An "amendment decree" is the legal document that includes the constitutional amendments approved as a package at a particular point in time. Each decree may contain reforms to one or several constitutional provisions.

6 Ibid., 9; Carpizo 2011. The constitution has only 136 articles; many of these have since been amended several times.

7 In the 1997–2012 period there were 3,403 amendment bills presented and registered for discussion in the Mexican Congress: 2,470 in the Chamber of Deputies and 933 in the Senate). Of them 294 were approved by the chambers and coalesced into sixty-nine amendment decrees, which were then ratified by state legislatures. See Casar and Marván, op. cit., 13–15. For a counting that covers amendments up to 2014, see Valadés and Fix-Fierro 2015.

8 As seen in n. 7, seventy-nine decrees have been passed in only fifteen years. They represent 33.5 percent of the total number of amendment decrees passed since 1917 (Casar and Marván, op. cit., 1, 9).

9 See in Pozas and Ríos-Figueroa (Chapter 1 in this volume) references to recent literature focusing on the Mexican judiciary—which does not include, however, systematic assessments of the court's role in the country's political and legal transition.

10 Beatty 2004; Ferreres Comella 2009; Comella 2003; Tate and Vallinder 1996.

11 Domingo and Sieder 2001; Hammergren 2007; Rodríguez Garavito 2009.

12 For standard accounts of contemporary normative constitutionalism see Aguiló 2004; Carbonell and García Jaramillo 2010; Salazar 2006; Zagrebelsky 1995.

13 Helmke and Ríos-Figueroa 2011; Helmke and Ríos-Figueroa 2007.

14 Rodríguez-Garavito 2011 (stressing how judicial activism on socioeconomic rights has become prominent in Colombia, Costa Rica, Argentina, and Brazil and how their courts, with those of India and South Africa, have nourished emerging practices of subaltern constitutionalism in the global south).

15 See Zaldívar 2002: 2–4 (underlining the "letrist, rigorist, formalistic and anti-protectionist" styles of interpretation of the Mexican judiciary) and Lara 2011: 77–83 (describing the traditional way of writing opinions, the efforts made by some justices to change their structure and style, and noting that much progress remains to be done).

16 See Elizondo 2009; Elizondo and Pérez de Acha 2006 (documenting the astonishing magnitude of *amparo fiscal* (tax law-centered *amparo*) and the way it dominated the entire dynamics of constitutional review in recent decades).

17 See Staton 2010 (highlighting the relevance of public relations activity for contemporary Supreme and Constitutional Courts—Latin American ones included—exploring relations between power building, transparency, and legitimacy in judicial activity and taking Mexico as a case study).

18 Former Chief Justice Silva (2011–2014) supplemented his staff with a Coordination of Human Rights that closely assisted his daily decision-making and that advanced a powerful institutional human rights agenda. The court's projects and achievements in this domain are carefully reported in the Annual Activity Reports of the Court's Presidency. Current Chief Justice Aguilar has transformed this office into the General Direction of Study, Promotion and Development of Human Rights.

19 See in SCJN 2011 brief pieces analyzing a first wave of still very timid rights-protecting Supreme Court rulings. References to more numerous, recent cases can be found in the articles gathered together in Ferrer Mac-Gregor et al. 2013. Periodic accounts of relevant rulings can be found in the aforementioned Annual Activity Reports produced by the Presidency of the Supreme Court.

20 On sexual and reproductive rights rulings, see Madrazo and Vela 2011; on freedom of speech rulings, Pou Giménez 2011, 2013, 2014a; on same-sex marriage rulings, Alterio forthcoming; Quintana 2015; on non-discrimination doctrines, Alterio forthcoming; Pou Giménez forthcoming; on conventionality review doctrines, Contesse 2014; Pou Giménez forthcoming; Sánchez Gil 2014; Silva García 2014; and, more generally, in pieces gathered together in Caballero Ochoa et al. forthcoming.

21 I will refer to these theories in greater detail in Section III.

22 I mean to refer here to the absence of written, explicit articulation of reasons, independently of whether there is a deliberative exercise behind the decision or not. The idea is, more precisely, that both *ex ante* deliberation and *ex post* articulation of the reasons supporting the decision (not only the former) are important to seeing as legitimate the Supreme Court's participation in the constitutional conversation. In my view, the MxSC lacks time and preconditions to engage adequately in any of them.

23 Women's Link Worldwide granted the 2009 Gold Gavel to the MxSC for that ruling. See http://www2.womenslinkworldwide.org/wlw/new.php?modo=observatorio&id_decision=279 (accessed November 10, 2014).

24 See Actions of Unconstitutionality 146/2007 and 147/2007, decided by the Plenary of the Supreme Court on August 28, 2008.

25 Blogs and public opinion echoed the blatant non-decision. A detailed account of the process and the problems of the ruling, denouncing the non-correspondence between the final text and the debate may be found in Adame 2009.

26 The Mexican Constitution requires an 8-vote majority (out of 11) to strike down a law in an abstract review channel. If a majority is not obtained, the statute remains on the books and, technically, there is no substantive pronouncement from the court on the statute: the decision is a non-decision.

27 See Figures 5.4 and 5.5 in the Appendix.

28 The unit is called *Coordinación de Compilación y Sistematización de Tesis.*

29 That is, justices vote on both the ruling and the *tesis* that emerges from it, at different points in time.

30 The *tesis* are a heavy fingerprint of the traditional image of the law in countries of the continental tradition (as opposed to common-law tradition). In continental law judicial decisions have been seen as abstract norms, as mini-pieces of the law deriving from exercises of adjudication in which the judge only pronounces what the law already says. They need—should—not refer to facts.

31 The only opinions that must be published systematically in the Federal *Diario Oficial* are rulings declaring the unconstitutionality of general statutes or regulations—in this case, the statute or fragment of statute that has been declared unconstitutional disappears from the books; because of this, the *Ley reglamentaria del artículo 105* makes the publication of the ruling in the official legal periodical mandatory. The remaining opinions were not traditionally available; but since the court committed itself to a strong transparency policy many of them are, although not, as I am now an underling, well-organized along content lines.
32 *Canal Judicial* was founded on May 29, 2006.
33 The transcripts, called *versiones taquigráficas,* are available here: http://www.scjn.gob.mx/pleno/Paginas/ver_taquigraficas.aspx (accessed November 10, 2014).
34 See *Varios 912/2010*, decided by the Plenary of the MxSC July 14, 2011 (usually referred to in Mexico as the *caso Radilla*, from the inter-American ruling whose implementation was discussed in its context).
35 Contrary to inter-American case law stating that military courts cannot have jurisdiction over cases that involve civilians. See *Rosendo Radilla Pachecovs. Estados Unidos Mexicanos*, decided November 23, 2009, Serie C, No. 209.
36 The court announced, under the new interpretation, that all Mexican judges, not only federal ones (as was the situation previously) could perform diffuse or decentralized *inter partes* judicial review of legislation.
37 For relevant criteria on the matter after the *Varios 912* see *acción de inconstitucionalidad 155/2007*, *contradicción de tesis 293/2011* (discussed but still not decided), *conflictos competenciales 38/2012 and 60/2012, amparos en revisión 133/2012, 134/2012, 770/2011, 60/2011, 61/2012, 62/2012 y 63/2012, 217/2012, 252/2012, 224/2012*, and *amparo directo 15/2012*. To survey the Second Chamber change of mind on the position of inter-American sources of law see, for instance, *amparos directos en revisión 1511/2012, 1981/2012, 1131/2012*, and *amparo directo 30/2012*.
38 From August 6 to September 13, 2012 (seventeen days of public debate) the court discussed thirteen cases on military jurisdiction which were directly relevant to the implementation of the *Radilla* inter-American ruling and other rulings (*Inés Fernández Ortega, Valentina Rosendo Cantú*, and *Cabrera García y Montiel Flores*) that had similarly condemned Mexico because of the excessive reach of military courts' jurisdiction in the country.
39 Decided in September 2013. The written ruling was issued in April 2014.
40 See ADR 1250/2012 (home-arrest case) and Varios 1396/2011 (judicial compliance of *Fernández Ortega* and *Rosendo Cantú* inter-American rulings).
41 See Cossío 2011: 104.
42 See in the Appendix the composition of the docket distinguishing what the justices decide in chambers and in plenary (Figures 5.4, 5.5, 5.6, and 5.7).
43 Since the 2011 human rights constitutional reform, the court may also review executive decrees issued under emergency powers (article 29 MxSC) and has lost the "*facultad de investigación*" (non-judicial procedure aimed at investigating gross violations of human rights that has now been transferred to the National Human Rights Commission [CNDH]).
44 See article 99 MxSC.
45 See article 100 MxSC.
46 The Chief Justice does not pertain to either of the two chambers of the MxSC. He/she participates and directs the plenary and heads the administrative apparatus of the court—besides presiding over the Judiciary Council.
47 Abstract review *acciones* and federalism conflict-solving *controversias,* core attributions of Kelsenian courts worldwide, amounted in 2012 to only 0.9 percent and 1.9 percent of the total caseload, respectively.
48 See in Frosini and Pegoraro 2008: 50–51 an inventory (typically extensive and varied) of different functions or areas of competence entrusted to Latin American constitutional courts.

49 For a full description of the historical evolution of the system, see Cossío 2011.

50 Pushed by litigation—lawyers wanted local cases to reach the more prestigious federal courts—the Supreme Court issued a doctrine stating that the constitutional principle of legality gave citizens a fundamental right to correct application of the law (i.e., statutory law). This doctrine blurred to a great extent the difference between legality and constitutionality in Mexico and added great size to the *amparo*.

51 See details in Pou Giménez 2012, 2014b.

52 *Amparo* is not a channel of diffuse and incidental review; it is a channel, as we have mentioned, that gives independent access to the federal judiciary (not to any judge, only federal ones).

53 Frosini and Pegoraro 2008: 41–44, 46–47.

54 Following the *Radilla* ruling, the Mexican system still has another framework of review: diffuse, incidental review in the hands of ordinary judges, federal or local. So there are now three different modalities of judicial review: abstract control via *acciones* and sometimes *controversias*, semi-concentrated control via *amparo*, and incidental diffuse control in ordinary proceedings.

55 Ríos-Figueroa 2010: 168. See in Pozas-Loyo and Ríos-Figueroa 2011 an account of the process that led to the creation of the Federal Judiciary Council in Mexico, and the way in which the Supreme Court exerted its influence and contributed to the shaping of the particular centralized design that ensued.

56 Ibid.

57 Ibid., 170; Ferreres 2009.

58 As noted, the Chief Justice of the Supreme Court is both member and President of the Federal Judicial Council and President of the Supreme Court, and has part of his/her administrative staff dedicated to council-related matters.

59 Ferreres 2009: 36.

60 Ibid., 36–37.

61 Ibid., 37.

62 Ibid., 38.

63 Bickel 1962: 25–26.

64 Kapiszewski 2010: 52.

65 Ibid., 55–56.

66 Ibid., 59.

67 Ibid., 60–67. Kapiszewski concludes that internal culture at the *Supremo Tribunal Federal* is pretty eclectic, combining professionalism, collegiality, segmentation, discretion, transparency, and openness.

68 Damaška 1986. See also Guarnieri and Pederzoli 2002.

69 These are approximate figures inferred from the information about personnel (*directorio*) and budget (*remuneración por puesto*) freely available on the MxSC's site. See: http://www.scjn.gob.mx/Transparencia/Paginas/trans_int_rem.aspx (accessed May 30, 2013). In May 2013 the *Colegio de Secretarios de la Suprema Corte* had 187 members, including *secretarios de studio y cuenta* (law clerks) and several *secretarios particulares* (who help to organize the clerking work). Around sixty-three persons working within the category of *secretario de studio y cuenta* are however, ascribed to offices of the administrative apparatus, not in *ponencias*—which are the units that gather together the law clerks working for each of the justices. So around 124 people do direct law-clerking work for the justices (information kindly provided by the *Oficina del Colegio de Secretarios*, telephonic communication, May 30, 2013; membership of the *Colegio* is not compulsory—which is why numbers presented here are only approximate—though in fact this body gathers together in these posts almost everybody).

70 www.scjn.gob.mx/Transparencia/Paginas/estructuraOrganica.aspx (accessed May 30, 2013).

71 *Reglamento Interior de la Suprema Corte de Justicia de la Nación*, published at the *Diario Oficial* on April 1, 2008, amended August 31, 2009. Available at: www.scjn.gob.mx/Transparencia/XIV%20Reglamento%20Interior%20de%20la%20Suprema%20Corte%20de%20Jus/RI_SCJN_Modificado_31AGO09_v2.pCity (accessed May 30, 2013).
72 *Reglamento*, Section 109.
73 See Elizondo Mayer-Serra and Magaloni 2010 for a thorough critique of this practice.
74 The Argentine Court—one of the "old" courts in the Latin American scenario, as is the Mexican Court, also with a huge docket—had the same inveterate practice. Under Chief Justices Petracchi and Lorenzetti, it progressively implemented a determined transparency reform with many measures in common with the ones now taken in Mexico, except that they also included on the agenda the regulation of audiences and forbade all encounters with justices without the presence of the other party. The Argentine Court has created a public information center and makes available registered data of cases (including acting attorneys and intervening lower courts), notifies when important cases will be discussed so that people can raise their views, posts rulings on the web, provides a list with the attorneys that act before the court, and has issued rules on audiences and the presentation of *amicus curiae*.
75 Silence in the corridors of the Colombian Constitutional Court, which welcomes the visitor with a sign displaying an internal regulation according to which private audiences with the magistrates on issues related to cases pending before them (Section 84 of the *Acuerdo 05 de 1992* of the Colombian Constitutional Court) are strictly forbidden, comes contrastingly to mind. I thank Martha Cecilia Paz for useful information and repeated opportunities to learn about internal administrative and jurisdictional dynamics at the Colombian Constitutional Court.
76 Of course, in the context of this chapter, this must be fundamentally taken as a hypothesis that careful empirical research might or might not support. As indicated in Section II, however, this is the general picture that viewers get from seeing the justices' broadcast deliberations, at least in politically salient cases where the court gets the most attention.
77 Maybe a middle way could be found if they were forced to recap and spell out their positions in public having previously sustained a draft discussion in private—i.e., knowing what the alternative arguments are and having a rough vision of what are the majority and the dissenting views. I thank Luz Helena Orozco y Villa for raising this suggestion in a fruitful conversation on publicity matters.
78 Bickel 1962: 16–17.
79 Ferreres 2009: 32–33.
80 Bickel 1962: 25–26.
81 Sager 2004.
82 Fiss 2003: 11–12.
83 Ferejohn and Pasquino 2010; Ferejohn and Pasquino 2009.
84 Abramovich 2007, 2009; Gauri and Brinks 2008; Rodríguez Garavito 2011; Sabel and Simon 2004.
85 Roach 2004.
86 *The Federalist* No. 78.
87 See Baum 2006. I thank Tom Ginsburg for raising the audience point and suggesting its more systematic exploration in the Mexican context. I hope I will be able to do so in future work.

References

Abramovich, Víctor (2007) "Acceso a la justicia y nuevas formas de participación en la esfera política." *Revista de Estudios Socio-Jurídicos* 9 (Special Issue, April): 9–33.

Abramovich, Víctor (2009) "El rol de la justicia en la articulación de políticas y derechos sociales." In Víctor Abramovich and Laura Pautassi (eds) *La revisión judicial de las políticas sociales. Estudio de casos*, 1–89. Buenos Aires: Editores del Puerto.

Adame, Jorge (2009) "Análisis de la sentencia que declara la constitucionalidad de la ley del Distrito Federal, permite a la madre dar muerte al concebido menor de doce semanas." *Boletín mexicano de Derecho comparado* 125(Mayo–Agosto): 1103–1127.

Aguiló Regla, Josep (2004) *La constitución del estado constitucional*. Bogotá and Lima: Temis-Palestra.

Alterio, Micaela (forthcoming) "La Suprema Corte y la justiciabilidad de los mensajes estigmatizantes." *Anuario Iberoamericano de Justicia Constitucional* 20 (in press).

Baum, Lawrence (2006) *Judges and Their Audiences: A Perspective on Judicial Behavior*. Princeton, NJ: Princeton University Press.

Beatty, David (2004) *The Ultimate Rule of Law*. Oxford: Oxford University Press.

Bickel, Alexander (1962) *The Least Dangerous Branch*. New Haven, CT: Yale University Press.

Caballero Ochoa, José Luis, and Rubén Sánchez Gil (eds) forthcoming. *Derechos constitucionales e internacionales. Perspectivas, retos y debates*. Mexico City: Tirant lo Blanch (in press).

Carbonell, Miguel and Leonardo García Jaramillo (eds) (2010) *El canon neoconstitucional*. Madrid: Trotta.

Carpizo, Jorge (2011) "La reforma constitucional en México. Procedimiento y realidad." *Boletín Mexicano de Derecho Comparado* 131: 543–598.

Casar, María Amparo and Ignacio Marván (2014) "Pluralismo y reformas constitucionales en México: 1997-2012." In María Amparo Casar and Ignacio Marván (eds) *Reformar sin mayorías. La dinámica del cambio constitucional en México (1997-2012)*. Mexico City: Taurus, pp. 13–85.

Choudhry, Sujit (ed.) (2006) *The Migration of Constitutional Ideas*. Cambridge: Cambridge University Press.

Choudhry, Sujit (ed.) (2008) *The Migration of Constitutional Ideas*. New York: Cambridge University Press.

Congleton, Roger and Brigitta Swedenborg (eds) (2006) *Democratic Constitutional Design and Public Policy: Analysis and Evidence*. Cambridge, MA: The MIT Press.

Contesse, Jorge (2014) "¿La última palabra? Control de convencionalidad y posibilidades de diálogo con la Corte Interamericana de Derechos Humanos," In Marisa Iglesias et al. (eds) *Derechos Humanos: posibilidades teóricas y desafíos prácticos. SELA 2013*. Buenos Aires: Libraria Ediciones, pp. 106–124.

Cossío Díaz and José Ramón (2011) *Sistemas y modelos de control constitucional en México*. Mexico City: Instituto de Investigaciones Jurídicas de la UNAM.

Damaška, Mirjan (1986) *The Faces of Justice and State Authority. A Comparative Approach to the Legal Process*. New Haven, CT: Yale University Press.

Domingo, Pilar and Rachel Sieder (eds) (2001) *Rule of Law in Latin America: The International Promotion of Judicial Reform*. London: University of London, Institute of Latin American Studies.

Elizondo Mayer-Serra, Carlos (2009) "La industria del amparo fiscal." *Política y Gobierno* 16(2): 349–383.

Elizondo Mayer-Serra, Carlos and Ana Laura Magaloni (2010) "La forma es fondo: cómo se nombran y deciden los Ministros de la Suprema Corte de Justicia." *Cuestiones Constitucionales* 23(July–Sept.): 27–60.

Elizondo Mayer-Serra, Carlos and Luis Manuel Pérez de Acha (2006) "Separación de poderes y garantías individuales: la Suprema Corte y los derechos de los contribuyentes." *Cuestiones Constitucionales* 14(Jan.–June): 91–130.

Elkins, Zachary (2010) "Diffusion and the Constitutionalization of Europe." *Comparative Political Studies* 43: 969–999.

Ferejohn, John and Pasquale Pasquino (2010) "The Countermajoritarian Opportunity." *Journal of Constitutional Law* 13(2, Dec.): 353–395.

Ferrer Mac–Gregor, Eduardo, José Luis Caballero Ochoa, and Christian Steiner (eds) (2013) *Derechos humanos en la Constitución: Comentarios de jurisprudencia constitucional e interamericana.* Mexico City: Fundación Konrad Adenauer Stiftung, Instituto de Investigaciones Jurídicas UNAM, SCJN.

Ferreres Comella, Víctor (2009) *Constitutional Courts and Democratic Values.* New Haven, CT: Yale University Press.

Fiss, Owen (2003) *The Law as it Could Be.* New York: New York University Press.

Friedman, Barry (2009) *The Will of the People: How Public Opinion Has Influenced and Shaped the Meaning of the Constitution.* New York: Farrar, Straus and Giroux.

Frosini, Justin and Lucio Pegoraro (2008) "Constitutional Courts in Latin America: A Testing Ground for New Parameters of Classification?" *Journal of Comparative Law* 3(2): 39–63.

Gargarella, Roberto (2007) "Injertos y rechazo: radicalismo político y trasplantes constitucionales en América Latina." In Efrén Rivera (ed.) *Derecho y cultura. SELA 2007.* San Juan, PR: Editorial Tal Cual, pp. 267–289.

Gargarella, Roberto (2011) "Pensando sobre la reforma constitucional en América Latina." In César Rodríguez Garavito (ed.) *El derecho en América Latina. Un mapa para el pensamiento jurídico del siglo XXI.* Buenos Aires: Siglo XXI.

Gauri, Varun and Daniel Brinks (eds) (2008) *Courting Social Justice: Judicial Enforcement of Social and Economic Rights in the Developing World.* New York: Cambridge University Press.

Ginsburg, Tom (2003) *Judicial Review in New Democracies: Constitutional Courts in Asian Cases.* Cambridge: Cambridge University Press.

Ginsburg, Tom (ed.) (2012) *Comparative Constitutional Design.* Cambridge: Cambridge University Press.

Ginsburg, Tom, Svitlava Chernykh, and Zachary Elkins (2008) "Commitment and Diffusion: How and Why Constitutions Incorporate International Law." *University of Illinois Law Review* 101: 201–238.

Ginsburg, Tom, Zachary Elkins, and Justin Blount (2009a) "Does the Process of Constitution-Making Matter?" *Annual Review of Law and Social Sciences* 5: 201–223.

Ginsburg, Tom, Zachary Elkins, and James Melton (2009b) *The Endurance of National Constitutions.* Cambridge: Cambridge University Press.

Guarnieri, Carlo and Patricia Pederzoli (2002) *The Power of Judges: A Comparative Study of Courts and Democracy.* Oxford: Oxford University Press.

Hammergren, Linn (2007) *Envisioning Reform: Improving Judicial Performance in Latin America.* University Park, PA: Pennsylvania University Press.

Helmke, Gretchen and Julio Ríos-Figueroa (2011) "Introduction: Courts in Latin America." In Gretchen Helmke and Julio Ríos-Figueroa (eds) *Courts in Latin America.* Cambridge: Cambridge University Press.

International Journal of Constitutional Law (I-Con) (2003) "Symposium: Constitutional Borrowing." *I-Con* 177.

Jackson, Vicki C. (2010) *Constitutional Engagement in a Transnational Era*. Oxford: Oxford University Press.

Kapiszewski, Diana (2010) "How Courts Work: Institutions, Culture, and the Brazilian Supremo Tribunal Federal." In Javier Couso, Alexandra Huneeus, and Rachel Sieder (eds) *Cultures of Legality: Judicialization and Political Activism in Latin America*. Cambridge: Cambridge University Press, pp. 51–77.

Lara, Roberto (2011) *Argumentación jurídica. Estudios prácticos*. Mexico City: Porrúa.

Madrazo, Alejandro and Estefanía Vela (2011) "'The Mexican Supreme Court (Sexual) Revolution?' Symposium: Latin American Constitutionalism." *Texas Law Review* 89: 1863–1893.

Magaloni, Ana Laura (2007) *¿Por qué la Suprema Corte no ha sido un instrumento para la defensa de los derechos fundamentales?* Mexico City: Centro de Investigación y Docencia Económica, Estudios Jurídicos, Cuadernos de Trabajo.

Michelman, Frank I. (2004) "'Reflection.' Symposium: Borrowing." *Texas Law Review* 84: 1737–1761.

Negretto, Gabriel L. (2012) "Replacing and Amending Constitutions: The Logic of Constitutional Change in Latin America." *Law and Society Review* 46(4): 749–779.

Nolte, Dietlef and Almut Schilling-Vacaflor (eds) (2012a) *New Latin American Constitutionalism. Promises and Practices*. Farnham: Ashgate Publishing.

Nolte, Dietlef and Almut Schilling-Vacaflor (2012b) "Introduction: The Times are Changin' Constitutional Transformations in Latin America since the 1990s." In Nolte and Schilling-Vacaflor (eds) *New Latin American Constitutionalism. Promises and Practices*. Farnham: Ashgate Publishing, pp. 3–30.

Pou Giménez, Francisca (2011) "Libertad de expresión: Dimensiones y límites. Censura previa e incriminación de ideas." In *Sentencias de la Suprema Corte de Justicia de la Nación desde el análisis de los derechos humanos. Recopilación de ensayos*. Mexico City: Oficina del Alto Comisionado de los Derechos Humanos, Suprema Corte de Justicia de la Nación, pp. 901–948.

Pou Giménez, Francisca (2012) "Judicial Review and Rights Protection in Mexico: Assessing Recent Amparo Constitutional Reforms." Available at http://ssrn.com/author=1474973 (accessed November 10, 2014).

Pou Giménez, Francisca (2013) "La libertad de expresión y sus límites." In Ferrer Mac–Gregor, Caballero Ochoa, and Christian Steiner(eds)*Derechos humanos en la Constitución: Comentarios de jurisprudencia constitucional e interamericana*. Mexico City: Fundación Konrad Adenauer Stiftung, Instituto de Investigaciones Jurídicas UNAM, SCJN.

Pou Giménez, Francisca (2014a) "Libertad de expresión y discurso homofóbico en México ¿Es correcta la teoría constitucional de la Suprema Corte?" *Boletín Mexicano de Derecho Comparado* 140(May–Aug.): 586–616.

Pou Giménez, Francisca (2014b) "El nuevo amparo mexicano y la protección de los derechos ¿Ni tan nuevo ni tan protector?" In *Anuario de Derechos Humanos 2014*. Santiago: Centro de Derechos Humanos, Universidad de Chile.

Pou Giménez, Francisca forthcoming. "Estereotipos, daño dignitario y patrones sistémicos: la discriminación por género y edad en el mercado laboral." *Discusiones* XV (in press).

Pou Giménez, Francisca forthcoming. "Lo que quisiera que la quisiera que la Suprema Corte hiciera por mí: lealtad constitucional y justicia dialógica en la aplicación de la 293/2011." In Rubén Sánchez Gil and José Luis Caballero (eds) *Derechos constitucionales e internacionales. Perspectivas, retos y debates*. Mexico City: Tirant lo Blanch (in press).

Pozas-Loyo, Andrea and Ríos-Figueroa, Julio (2011) "'The Politics of Amendment Processes: Supreme Court Influence in the Design of Judicial Councils.' Symposium: Latin American Constitutionalism." *Texas Law Review* 89: 1807–1833.

Quintana Osuna, Karla (2015) "Matrimonio igualitario en México: Su evolución desde la Judicatura." *Revista del Centro de Estudios Constitucionales* 1(July–Dec.): 229–261.

Ríos-Figueroa, Julio (2010) "El sistema de administración de justicia." In Gabriel L. Negretto (ed.) *Debatiendo la reforma política. Claves del cambio institucional en México*. Mexico DF: CIDE, pp. 159–202.

Roach, Kent (2004) "Dialogic Judicial Review and Its Critics." *Supreme Court Law Review* 23: 49–104.

Rodríguez Garavito, César (2009) *La globalización del Estado de derecho: El neoconstitucionalismo, el neoliberalismo y la transformación constitucional en América Latina*. Bogotá: Uniandes.

Rodríguez Garavito, César (2011) "Beyond the Courtroom: The Impact of Judicial Activism on Socioeconomic Rights in Latin America." *Texas Law Review* 89: 1669–1698.

Sabel, Charles and William Simon (2004) "Destabilization Rights: How Public Litigation Succeeds." *Harvard Law Review* 117: 1015–1101.

Sager, Lawrence G. (2004) *Justice in Plainclothes: A Theory of American Constitutional Practice*. New Haven, CT: Yale University Press.

Salazar, Pedro (2006) *La democracia constitucional. Una radiografía teórica*. Mexico City: Fondo de Cultura Económica.

Sánchez Gil, Rubén (2014) "Notas sobre la Contradicción de tesis 293/2011." *Revista Iberoamericana de Derecho Procesal Constitucional* 21(Jan.–June): 333–344.

Silva García, Fernando (2014) "'Derechos humanos y restricciones constitucionales: ¿reforma constitucional del futuro vs interpretación constitucional del pasado?' (Comentario a la CT 293/2011 del Pleno de la SCJN)." *Cuestiones constitucionales. Revista mexicana de Derecho Constitucional* 30(Jan.–July): 251–272.

Staton, Jeffrey (2010) *Judicial Power and Strategic Communication in Mexico*. Cambridge: Cambridge University Press.

Supreme Court of Justice of the Nation (SCJN) (2011) *Sentencias de la Suprema Corte de Justicia de la Nación desde el análisis de los derechos humanos. Recopilación de ensayos*. Mexico City: Oficina del Alto Comisionado de los Derechos Humanos, SCJN.

Tate, C. Neal and Torbjorn Vallinder (1996) *The Global Expansion of Judicial Power*. New York: New York University Press.

Uprimny, Rodrigo (2011) "Las transformaciones constitucionales recientes en América Latina. Tendencias y desafíos." In Rodríguez Garavito, César (ed.) *El derecho en América Latina: un mapa para el pensamiento jurídico del siglo XXI*. Buenos Aires: Siglo XXI.

Uprimny, Rodrigo and Luz María Sánchez (2012) "Tres décadas de transformaciones constitucionales en América Latina: balance y perspectivas." Long research piece presented at ILADD 2012, unpublished (on file with author).

Valadés, Diego and Héctor Fix-Fierro (2015) "Estudio introductorio." In *Constitución Política de los Estados Unidos Mexicanos. Texto reordenado y consolidado, 11–34*. Mexico City: Instituto de Investigaciones Jurídicas (UNAM).

Zagrebelsky, Gustavo (1995) *El derecho dúctil. Ley, derechos, justicia*. Madrid: Trotta.

Zaldívar Lelo de Larrea, Arturo (2002) *Hacia una nueva ley de amparo*. Mexico City: Instituto de Investigaciones Jurídicas (UNAM).

CONCLUSION

The challenges of courts in democratic consolidation

Matthew C. Ingram

This volume endeavors to understand the role of the Mexican Supreme Court in the consolidation of democracy in Mexico since 2000. In order to achieve that understanding, two points deserve early clarification: (1) what is meant by democratic consolidation; and (2) how the field of public law treats similar efforts to understand the relationship between, on the one hand, law and legal institutions, and on the other hand, politics and political development. This conclusion summarizes the main findings of the preceding chapters, and aims to situate the volume and its contributions within a larger literature on law, development, and democracy.

The chapter proceeds as follows. First, I briefly review concepts of democratic consolidation, highlighting the normative commitments inherent in more satisfying, substantive definitions. This section identifies two normative commitments weaving throughout this volume—the legitimacy of judicial review of state action and the progressive, rights-protective character of democracy—and connects these normative issues to major areas of inquiry in the public law field: empowerment, activation, decision-making, and impact. Emphasizing the normative underpinnings of democratic consolidation and relating these to public law questions charts a path toward evaluating the role of the Supreme Court in the consolidation of democracy in Mexico. Second, I offer an overview of the central political and legal transformations highlighted throughout the chapters in this volume. While the political phenomenon of the transition to democracy is extraordinarily important (and relevant to the volume's overall emphasis on the consolidation of democracy), I focus primarily on sketching a summary of legal transformations, including (a) institutional or procedural changes; and (b) changes in the substantive content of rights and liberties (i.e., what the authors refer to as "organic" and "dogmatic" changes, respectively). Third, a discussion of each chapter's contribution to the four areas of inquiry in public law follows the structure of the field outline above, starting with Chapter 1 situated within a broader discussion of judicial empowerment, and ending with Chapter 5 situated within a broader discussion of judicial impact. Fourth, returning to a central theme of the volume, I consider how the conclusions from each chapter, framed within the broader, comparative literature in public law, help us understand the relationship between the Supreme Court and the deepening or consolidation of democracy in Mexico. There is no shortage of disagreement about how to conceptualize democracy, including maximalist definitions like the one advocated by Salazar in Chapter 2. Indeed, normative debates abound in discussions of what it means for democracy to be "deep" or "consolidated," and these debates draw values into the discussion of law and democracy. In this regard, I return to some observations about the inextricable links among law, democracy, and values. Finally, I conclude with some directions for future research in Mexican public law.

I Democratic consolidation and the public law field

Debates abound regarding the conceptualization of democracy (Coppedge et al. 2011; Munck and Verkuilen 2002). Still, the procedural/substantive dichotomy distinguishes between two main types of democracy. Procedural democracy marks regimes that have elections, voting, and other procedures associated with democratic life, but does not address the real sense or extent to which these procedures are available to all citizens. For instance, the U.S. can achieve the highest marks in standard measures of procedural democracy for more than 100 years despite official racial segregation, the inability of women to vote, and the exclusion of minorities from political participation via a host of formal and informal barriers. Substantive concepts of democracy aim for more satisfying concepts that capture the real ability of ordinary citizens to access and engage with democratic procedures by considering the effectiveness of fundamental rights.[1] Democratic consolidation, then, can mean the consolidation of thin procedural mechanisms that distinguish democracy from authoritarianism, or it can mean the consolidation of thick, full forms of citizenship, inclusion, and egalitarianism that make those procedures more meaningful and consequential.

The authors in this volume advocate a more substantive notion of democracy. Salazar Ugarte (Chapter 2) is perhaps most explicit, limiting his discussion of strategic litigation only to progressive, rights-protective versions of this phenomenon. However, Castagnola and Lopez Noriega ask whether the Supreme Court is a "true protector" of rights, and suggest the human rights ombuds should initiate more cases in order to increase the volume of rights cases on the court's agenda (Chapter 4). Thus, democratic consolidation means the deepening or consolidation of both procedures and fundamental rights associated with more inclusive, democratic societies. Indeed, given that formally democratic procedures coexisted with Mexico's authoritarianism, it makes more sense to speak of democratic consolidation in substantive terms in Mexico.

Crucially, normative commitments inhere in substantive versions of democracy, entangling moral theory with political theory. In the spirit of intellectual honesty, I sympathize with the authors' substantive, progressive, rights-protective version of democracy. Just as values shape my preference for democracy over dictatorship, values shape my preference for one type of democracy over another (see e.g., Murphy et al. 2006: 640). Yet others might not hold the same values regarding either democracy vis-à-vis dictatorship, or substantive vis-à-vis procedural forms of democracy. To be sure, I imagine it would be harder to defend a preference for authoritarianism (these days), but it would be easy for readers to articulate a competing, more conservative, individualistic, or traditional concept of democracy, one that might be less inclusive but still meet many standard definitions of democracy.

Following Shapiro (1972, 1993, 2000), the key is that normative arguments are inseparable from political theory, and political theory inseparable from public law. Even in most empirical exercises, we ought to remain self-aware of what we anticipate results *ought* to look like, or what the goal of research *should* be, and of the normative commitments packaged, implicitly or explicitly, into such judgments.

Two normative commitments are particularly relevant in this volume: (1) the legitimacy of judicial review (and by extension, of judicial empowerment to conduct such reviews); and (2) the rights-protective end of legal mobilization and judicial behavior. These normative commitments and their relation to evaluating the Supreme Court's role in the consolidation of democracy in Mexico are apparent upon closer examination of the classic areas of inquiry in public law.

The public law field can be understood as comprising four general areas of inquiry:[2] (1) *empowerment* of legal institutions, i.e., building, crafting, or constructing justice institutions (Crowe 2012; Finkel 2008; Ginsburg 2003; 2012; Landes and Posner 1975; Tate and Vallinder 1995; Whittington 2007); (2) once empowered, the *activation* of these institutions (e.g., Epp 1998; 1985); (3) once activated, the *decision-making* of actors within these institutions (e.g., Epstein and Knight 1998; Helmke 2005; Kapiszewski 2012; and Spaeth 2002); and (4) once decisions are rendered, the broader social *impact* of these decisions (e.g., Kapiszewski and Taylor 2012; Rosenberg 2008 [1991]). Serendipitously, the five chapters in this volume on the Mexican Supreme Court fit nicely into these four areas. Chapter 1 (Pozas-Loyo and Ríos-Figueroa) examines judicial empowerment via the shifting military jurisdiction of the Supreme Court. Chapter 2's (Salazar Ugarte) examination of strategic litigation addresses a key mechanism by which crucial cases can reach the judiciary, reflecting the object of inquiry that is central to studies of court activation. Chapters 3 and 4 (Castagnola and López Noriega) both examine the determinants of justices' votes on a sample of cases at the Supreme Court from 2000–2011, constituting a study of judicial decision-making that fits into mainstream studies of judicial behavior. Finally, Chapter 5 (Pou Giménez) examines the "fuzziness" or ambiguity of Supreme Court decision-making, which also speaks to the legal instability that such ambiguity generates in society, eroding the court's legitimacy. Thus, this chapter captures an aspect of the court's impact on society.

In this conclusion, I examine each of the chapters' contributions to the relevant main four areas of public law scholarship in which I have situated the chapter. In some cases, a chapter may contribute to more than one area, as is the case with Pozas-Loyo and Ríos-Figueroa (Chapter 1 on empowerment and decision-making), and Pou Giménez (Chapter 5 on decision-making and social impact). In these cases, I discuss the relevant chapters in both areas. The conclusion relates the chapters to each other to generate a systematic picture of the Supreme Court's empowerment, activation, decision-making, and impact, connecting each chapter's treatment of the Mexican Supreme Court and the volume's collective treatment to broader empirical and theoretical currents in comparative work in the field.

II Overview of political and legal transformations, 1977–2013

Following a gradual democratic opening marked by a variety of electoral reforms, including a major relaxation of electoral laws in 1977, the dominant-party system marked by the Institutional Revolutionary Party's (PRI) seventy-one-year reign in the presidency came to an end in 2000 when the former opposition, the National Action Party (PAN), won the presidential race. For this reason, most observers mark 2000 as the moment of Mexico's democratic transition. Notably, opposition parties had been winning governors' offices as early as 1989, mayoral offices even earlier, and the percentage of PRI legislators in the national Congress had been steadily declining from the late 1980s throughout the 1990s (e.g., Mizrahi 2003; Shirk 2005). By 1988, the PRI had lost its super-majority in the lower house (Chamber of Deputies), by 1997 it had lost even a simple majority in the chamber and its super-majority in the Senate, and by 2000 it held only a plurality in both houses (Ríos-Figueroa 2007: 40).

Alongside these political developments, legal developments proceeded apace. These legal changes can be classified into two categories: (1) changes to substantive rights and liberties; and (2) institutional, procedural, or organizational changes. Notably, most of the changes to rights or liberties could not have any real effect or "bite" until the institutional changes took place that made the process of vindicating those rights more accessible.

Mexico's 1917 Constitution formally provided *de jure* protection to numerous rights, including labor and land, but in reality Mexican society was and remains highly unequal and these rights remained effectively out of the reach of ordinary citizens throughout the twentieth century. Further, vindication of any grievances during the authoritarian period was, for all practical purposes, impossible. Despite the addition of multiple other substantive rights in the 1990s and early part of the twenty-first century (e.g., indigenous rights, due process, and information and transparency; see Salazar Ugarte (Chapter 2), the 2011 human rights reform is hailed as a major transformation in the conceptualization of substantive individual rights in Mexico. As emphasized by Salazar Ugarte (Chapter 2) and Pou Giménez (Chapter 5), the 2011 human rights reform explicitly links domestic individual rights protection to international law, making it much more difficult for the state to deny the existence of a wide range of rights, and simultaneously making it more difficult for the state to remain idle or passive when those rights are violated.

Landmark institutional changes at the federal level began in 1994 (taking effect in 1995). On December 31, 1994, a federal judicial reform altered the size, tenure, selection mechanisms, and composition of the Supreme Court, created a federal judicial council to oversee judicial administration (weakened by a 1999 counter-reform; see Chapter 1; Pozas-Loyo and Ríos-Figueroa 2011), and the mechanisms for judicial review were strengthened. Prior to 1994, two avenues of judicial review existed: writ of *amparo* and constitutional controversies (*controversias constitucionales* [CC]). The 1994 reform left *amparo* unchanged, expanded the CC mechanism, and added a third mechanism—actions of unconstitutionality (*acciones de inconstitucionalidad* [AI]).

These mechanisms of review can be evaluated according to three criteria: (a) type of review (abstract or concrete); (b) standing (i.e., who can initiate a case, and when); and (c) legal effects (*inter partes* or *erga omnes*). First, *amparo* is a type of concrete review formally available to individual citizens and legal entities (e.g., corporations) as a mechanism to challenge a wide range of state actions. As noted by authors in this volume; e.g., Pou Giménez (Chapter 5); Castagnola and López Noriega (Chapter 4), however, the *amparo* procedure is highly technical and complex and must be filed in the federal court, making it all but inaccessible to most people. Even if successful, a decision in an *amparo* case only has narrow, *inter partes* effects. CC existed as a type of concrete review, and only government entities (state and federal branches of government) had standing to challenge each other, vertically or horizontally. The CC mechanism was thus a means of managing the horizontal separation of powers at the federal level and state levels, as well as the vertical separation of powers in Mexico's system of federalism. Even CC, though, only had narrow, *inter partes* effects prior to 1994 (Finkel 2005: 93). That year, the reform expanded CC to grant standing to municipalities to challenge state or federal actions, and to allow for general, *erga omnes* effects under very strict conditions: (a) if eight or more (of the eleven) justices vote to invalidate the challenged state action; and (b) if a higher level of government was attacking a lower level (e.g., federal legislature attacked state legislature, or federal executive attacked federal legislature, or a state branch attacked another branch from same state). If a majority only of justices voted to invalidate, or if one of the other conditions was not met, then the ruling would only have *inter partes* effects (see Chapter 4).

Finally, since 1994, the new AI mechanism allows for an abstract review. That is, legislation can be challenged after it is approved but before it goes into effect, empowering the court to nullify laws, thereby having inherent *erga omnes* effects by affecting the entire population. A broad range of actors have standing to trigger this constitutional "filter," including at least one-third of the federal Chamber of Deputies, Senate, or state legislatures, the attorney general (AG), political parties, and the national human rights ombuds (*Comision Nacional de Derechos Humanos* [National Human Rights Commission] [CNDH]). As of 2006, state ombuds offices too can initiate an AI. Notably, while AIs appear to be a broad mechanism of judicial review, two rules restrict its broader impact: (1) AIs must be initiated within thirty days of the approval of the legislation targeted to be challenged; and (2) each actor with standing can only challenge legislation relevant to its sphere of action. For instance, political parties can only challenge electoral laws,[3] ombuds offices can only challenge legislation affecting fundamental rights, etc., and they only have a 30-day window in which to initiate the challenge. Since the exact content and ramifications of laws are not always transparent beyond political insiders, the standing requirements and 30-day statute of limitation present real obstacles to citizen-led constitutional challenges. Further, in order to be successful, an AI must receive at least eight votes. Since there are no *inter partes* effects for abstract review, if the AI receives fewer than eight votes, the case is dismissed.

Beyond these major institutional transformations, the authors in this volume highlight three other recent, high-profile changes: (1) the 2011 human rights reform, which provides new rights-protective legal language, concepts, and exhortations consistent with international law; (2) the 2011 *amparo* reform, which addressed many of the deficiencies identified above, allowing class actions, filings before any court, and the potential for *erga omnes* effects (see in Chapter 2 Salazar Ugarte's discussion of implementing 2013 legislation); and (3) the elimination of special military jurisdiction, the persistence of which was causing increasing tension and contradictions during the recent militarization of the domestic fight against drugs and organized crime (see Chapter 1).

III Empowerment, activation, decision-making, and impact

With this political and legal background in mind, how has the Mexican Supreme Court been empowered, activated, made its decisions, and had an impact? How do the different objects of inquiry of the public law field help us organize the lessons from this volume?

III.I Empowerment

Speaking to the question of judicial empowerment, Pozas-Loyo and Ríos-Figueroa offer in Chapter 1 a socio-legal study of the evolution of military jurisdiction in Mexico from 1917 to the present: starting with narrow jurisdiction in the early post-revolutionary period, broadening through 1994, then narrowing again since 1995. This chapter includes an insightful typology of military jurisdictions, and the authors provide an excellent description of the development of jurisprudential positions on the Supreme Court from 1917 to 2012.

Regarding these jurisprudential positions, the authors relate them to three different roles the court has played in the time span: (1) adjudicators; (2) regime supporters; and (3) constitutional interpreters. These roles are a function of two factors: formal power and the political constraints on exercising that power. Adjudicators have low to moderate formal authority (understood as jurisdiction), including some powers to interpret the constitution, but little power at least in terms of the effect of their decisions, which remained narrowly *inter partes*. However, this low/moderate power is paired with a very broad political space in which to operate, so the Supreme Court is able exercise this power to its full extent. Regime supporters work with the same low level of formal powers but enter a more constrained political space marked by two key changes: (1) judicial selection is more politicized, and therefore weakened; and (2) the single-party regime consolidates. The overall effect is to reduce the political space in which the Supreme Court operates, making it difficult to exercise even low power. Third, constitutional interpreters are defined by two key changes: (1) formal power expands greatly in 1994/1995, as summarized in the legal transformations above; and (2) the political space in which the Supreme Court operates expands in 1997, then again in 2000, and remains broad, as summarized in the political transformation above. In this final role, the court narrows military jurisdiction, constraining the military to provide greater accountability. Justice Cossio's 2009 opinion in this direction anticipates the Inter-American Court of Human Rights's (IACHR) 2010 decision. However, before more progressive Supreme Court decisions in 2012, two intervening factors shaped the debate over military jurisdiction in crucial ways: international pressures in the form of the IACHR decision, and domestic legislative pressures in the shape of the human rights and *amparo* reforms of 2011 (outlined above). Further, public opinion was slowly turning against the military in the context of human rights violations attributed to the military in its prosecution of the "war on drugs."

While the authors restrict themselves to making descriptive propositions regarding the evolution of the judiciary's power to review criminal accusations against the military, several implications of their argument resonate beyond the specifics of military jurisdiction and the Mexican case. For instance, in their analytic emphasis on the "roles" of the Mexican Supreme Court in the evolution of military jurisdiction, Pozas-Loyo and Ríos-Figueroa speak to a deep literature on judicial roles (e.g., Becker 1966; Flango et al. 1975; Helmke and Ríos-Figueroa 2011; Kapiszewski 2011); "role orientations" (Gibson 1977, 1978; Scheb et al. 1989); and "role perceptions" (Hilbink 2012; Jr 1977; Ungs and Baas 1972). More explicitly, "adjudicators" resonates with a more mechanical, bureaucratic approach to decision-making characterized by judicial institutions with a very narrow range of formal powers, legally capable of doing very little even in the absence of political constraints; "regime supporters" speaks to the more politically constrained and patently pro-regime function of a court, resonating with Brinks's (2005) label of the Brazilian Supreme Court as "faithful servants" of the regime, and more broadly with the pro-regime nature of judicial interventions in the pursuit of governance in Whittington (2007) and Nunes (2010); and "constitutional interpreters" resonates with the fuller range of judicial behavior that is possible when the court is both formally empowered and has the political space in which to exercise that power.

The authors also draw attention to the court's own role in expanding its power. Specifically, Cossio's 2010 opinion and the court's 2012 decision created an opening for and then formalized an institutional arrangement respectively, in which the Supreme Court and the judiciary in general would have greater power to hear and decide cases involving allegations of criminal activity on the part of military personnel. As an instance of judicial self-empowerment, the chronicle of events speaks to Staton's (2010) argument about the manner in which judicial institutions can act to empower themselves, rather than waiting for politicians or other outside actors to expand jurisdiction, legal effects, etc. Given the persistence of the military's influence and power throughout the PRI's hegemonic regime, the curbing of the military's special privilege is a substantive sign in the maturation of Mexico's democracy.

Pou Giménez adds to this account in Chapter 5 with a textured, in-depth account of the manner in which the court's decision-making process bolsters or undermines its own institutional standing, and therefore its real power to influence. Convincingly, Pou Giménez argues that multiple features of the court's decision-making process combine to generate vague, ambiguous, or "fuzzy" decisions (see discussion of impact Section III.IV below). Specifically, Pou Giménez is concerned about the divergence between (a) justices' positions during public debate and decision on the case and (b) clerks' summaries of these positions, which contain multiple caveats, legal–technical jargon, partial endorsements, and obscure and dense language that "completely dilute[s] the idea of a ruling as an articulate expression of reasons that coalesce around directive points marking out the immediate changes it purports to make in the world" (see Chapter 2, this volume). The divergence between justices' positions at public debate and jurisprudential positions in the final, official, written decision that appears unceremoniously weeks or months after the debate is critical since it is only the latter that counts for future litigation. The unsettling implication of this fuzziness is that major rulings lack real solidity or substance, so the Supreme Court undermines its own institutional legitimacy, weakening itself. Indeed, speaking directly to the issue of military jurisdiction and entering into a conversation with Chapter 1, while the Supreme Court's early decision in the landmark 2012 Radilla case appeared to narrow military jurisdiction as outlined above, this was after seventeen full days of public, plenary debate (!), and at the time of the author's writing, eight months later, drafting of the written opinion—the real decision that will have jurisprudential weight—had not even begun (see Chapter 2, this volume). Put bluntly, the full evaluation of the court's role in expanding or contracting military jurisdiction—or judicial power in general—

cannot be complete until that official decision is rendered, and given the ambiguity-inducing features of the decision-making process, said expansion or contraction is likely to be unclear. I return to the broader implications of this lack of clarity in the discussion of judicial impact (see Section III.IV).

III.II Activation

In the absence of cases to decide, the formal and political power of courts is not likely to matter much. Scholars of legal mobilization examine the sources of legal movements and the litigation they generate that can shape a court's agenda (Epp 1998; Epp 1985), and Salazar Ugarte's (Chapter 2) study of the landscape of strategic litigation in Mexico fits nicely into this area of research.

To be sure, legal mobilization can be understood as part of the broader phenomenon of social movements or mobilization in general. Following McAdam et al. (1996), the origin or success of mobilizations can be traced to three factors: (1) opportunity structures; (2) mobilizing structures; and (3) cultural framing processes. Opportunity structures consist of political openings for the movement, and these openings can come in many forms, including an economic crisis, an electoral loss, or other social, economic, or political phenomenon that alters the political landscape—broadly construed—in a way that opens a space for the movement and its message. Mobilizing structures consist of existing organizations that can provide fruitful partnerships or alliances for the movement. For instance, an existing and sympathetic civic group, political party, or church organization might provide needed contacts, staff, expertise, or other resources for the movement. Finally, framing processes speak to the non-material, cultural–ideational dynamics that help or hinder the movement. Framing, in a sense, is about how the movement's message is packaged, and how this packaging (conscious or otherwise) appeals or fails to appeal to different audiences. Recent examples in this area include Epp's (1998) emphasis on mobilizing structures in his concept of "support structures for legal mobilization", Teles's (2008) emphasis on openings in his use of "governing coalitions" to explain conservative mobilizations, and Woods's (2008) emphasis on framing in her study of the emergence of a progressive judicial norm consensus in Israel. To be clear, each pillar of social movement theory is analytically distinct, but they can also be interactive. For example, new legal concepts, shifts in legal culture, and other cultural–ideational frames can generate opportunities for legal mobilization, and new civic organizations and institutions can provide openings in that they make more alliances and partnerships possible.

It is in this context of mobilization theory in general and legal mobilization in particularly that Salazar Ugarte's discussion of strategic litigation clarifies how the judicial apparatus can be activated in Mexico to address a particular agenda of legal issues. Openings or opportunities for legal mobilization appear in the reframing of legal rights in the Radilla case, new legal concepts and language in the human rights reform of 2011, and new institutional or procedural openings in the *amparo* reform of 2011. Mobilizing structures appear in the form of the *Centro de Investigación y Docencia Económicas* (CIDE)'s legal clinic in the Acteal case, the legal representation of Castañeda in his litigation of independent candidacies, and local and regional non-governmental organizations (NGOs) in the Mininuma case. Framing takes the form of re-articulating indigenous rights as international rights in the Mininuma case, and in the conceptualization of rights in the IACHR's ruling in the Radilla case.

III.III Decision-making

Castagnola and López Noriega's two chapters (Chapters 3 and 4) on judicial behavior should be read together by anyone interested specifically in the judicial behavior of the Supreme Court in the context of its formal adjudicatory function. In both chapters, a key and valuable contribution is the original data set of Supreme Court cases from 2000–2011 developed by the authors. Pou Giménez's piece should also be read alongside these chapters for a fuller understanding of the factors that contribute to the decision-making process. Indeed, the three chapters (Chapters 3, 4, and 5) complement each other nicely since Castagnola and López Noriega emphasize the explanatory role of judicial profiles (e.g., attitudes, background, age), case-specific stimuli (e.g., tax issues, electoral issues), and external political constraints (e.g., the identity of the plaintiff or defendant, salience of the case), while Pou Giménez considers the effect of the court's internal rules and practices.

Chapter 3 examines 1,000 cases involving either CCs or actions of unconstitutionality (AIs) challenging general norms (see above). Overall, the type of review mechanism employed by plaintiffs matters. The likelihood of a justice ruling state action unconstitutional, invalid, i.e., Pr(y=1), is greater in AIs (0.25) than in CCs (0.10). That is, all else being equal, plaintiffs are less likely to win via the CC mechanism than via an AI. As the authors note, this raises several interesting questions about the dynamics of judicial behavior conditioned by abstract or concrete review, the potential for *erga omnes* or *inter partes* effects, and the nature of interests being affected by each mechanism (e.g., current administration vs. former administration, narrow interests of parties vs. normative architecture of an area of law). Beyond the simple case types, case salience reduces the likelihood of an unconstitutional ruling, and the party identification of the justices matters (but only in CCs). Notably, the authors' more nuanced coding of salience appears to be an improvement over previous measures which equated salience with federal policies (e.g., Staton 2010).

More specifically, PAN justices are more likely to vote for a PAN plaintiff attacking a PRI defendant (while PRI justices are less likely to do so). However, a counterintuitive result appears when PRI plaintiffs attack a PAN defendant, that is, PAN justices are predictably less likely to vote to invalidate the PAN's state action, but PRI justices are also less likely to do so. This may be an artifact of the time period studied, but also signals the possibility of a pro-regime–anti-regime dynamic that may influence PRI justices more than PAN justices (see Ingram 2013 for analysis of pro-regime–anti-regime dynamics in the empowerment of state courts in Mexico). That is, PRI justices may systematically have a different perspective on their judicial role than PAN justices. Thus this finding ties back into the discussion of judicial roles in Chapter 1, though at a more disaggregated level, addressing individual justices rather than the court as a collective actor. Generally, Castagnola and López Noriega find justices are more deferential to the PAN in this period of PAN presidencies (see Chapter 3).

Chapter 4 examines 1,818 rights-related cases filed as either *amparos* or AIs. Of these cases, 94 percent are *amparos* and only 6 percent are AIs, so the *amparo* is clearly the dominant mechanism for seeking redress for violations of substantive rights. Notably, 65 percent of *amparos* involve tax issues, legal entities (i.e., corporations) constitute the plaintiff in 78 percent of these tax cases, and the Supreme Court rules in favor of these legal entities 82 percent of the time (contrast with favorable ruling for individual citizens on tax issues, for only 45 percent of the time, about half as often). Thus, at first glance, it appears the *amparo* mechanism is largely an avenue for economic elites to protect their financial interests (see Chapter 4). A much broader set of actors and issues are active in AIs, including political parties and the human rights ombuds filing cases on electoral laws and fundamental rights, respectively.

Overall, as was the case in Chapter 3, the likelihood of the plaintiff receiving a favorable ruling (i.e., invalid) varies depending on the type of review mechanism; Pr(y=1) for *amparos* is 0.63, while it is 0.30 for AIs. That is, plaintiffs are about twice as likely to be successful when seeking redress via *amparos* than via AIs. The type of actor in the plaintiff's position has a statistically significant relationship with the decision in the case, but does not seem to have meaningful substantive effect. Specifically, holding other variables at their means, the risk of invalidating state action is 65 percent for citizens, while only 63 percent for legal entities. This finding is compelling since early summary statistics indicate that legal entities receive highly favorable treatment in *amparo* litigation, but this favorable treatment seems to disappear when controlling for other explanations. In general, justices are deferential toward the ruling party (PAN), and the party identification of the justice matters. PAN justices are more likely to invalidate. Since *amparos* that reach the Supreme Court are likely very old (see Chapter 4), this suggests voting against actions carried out by non-PAN governments. Indeed, *amparos* provide a kind of "win-win" situation for justices since they can vote for the plaintiff but the decision has only *inter partes* effect. Thus, a justice gets to appear rights protective, but the appearance is also politically safe since the decision does not really challenge political power or broad legal norms.

Across both Chapters 3 and 4, the risk of invalidation appears to be highest with *amparos* (0.63), lower with AIs in rights-related cases (0.30), lower still with

AIs in political conflicts (0.25), and lowest with CCs (0.10). That is, the risk of invalidation might be ordered as follows:

$$\Pr(y=1 \mid \text{Amparo}) > \Pr(y=1 \mid \text{AI[rights]}) > \Pr(y=1 \mid \text{AI[political]}) > \Pr(y=1 \mid \text{CC})$$

The ordering above reflects an interaction among type of review mechanism and the underlying issue area, so the relationship might also be depicted according to a 2x2 table (not reported here) with type of review along one axis and issue area along another. These interactions would be interesting to explore in future research using a single model and including all data points.

Incorporating other arguments from the literature on judicial behavior, Pou Giménez (Chapter 5) examines the causal role of the internal rules and practices of the Supreme Court. Factors contributing to the vague, ambiguous, "fuzzy" voice of the court include: (1) high volume of work; (2) judicial centralization; (3) burden of administrative duties; (4) frequent private, *ex parte* hearings with litigants; (5) selection process of the chief justice; and (6) public debate of cases. According to Pou Giménez, the Supreme Court does not have the organizational capacity to handle the volume of its work, limiting the time that can be dedicated to each case, and undermining the quality of deliberation. The court's decisions are not organized in a way that facilitates access and searchability, so once decided, a case is effectively lost among a morass of other, non-searchable cases. Second, the court centralizes a wide range of jurisdictions and administrative work, reducing its ability to specialize or even focus on a range of highly important cases. Third, the administrative burden of committee work related to the judicial council is especially onerous, defeating one of the main purposes of judicial councils, which is to release judges from administrative duties in order to free up time for judges to concentrate on judging (Garoupa and Ginsburg 2009; Ingram 2012). Fourth, *ex parte* hearings are increasingly outside the norm, even in Latin America. Pou Giménez suggests moving toward the Colombian or Argentine models, where these kinds of hearings are now expressly prohibited. Fifth, the chief selection process is an internal election, generating distracting incentives for campaigning and the development of personal loyalties that undermine the internal independence of judges. Finally, public debates prior to any internal circulation of draft opinions or an internal, private debate about a case generate wide-ranging discussions and contradictory, partial position-taking that clerks later summarize in abbreviated, obscure fashion. As noted above, the divergence between the appearance of one decision in the public debate and the often indecipherable official written decision yields the ambiguousness that Pou Giménez convincingly argues destabilizes the Supreme Court's legitimacy.

Elegantly, Pou Giménez offers a set of specific, concrete reforms that match each of her critiques. Docket control can help the court reduce its volume of work and also focus its attention on a more select agenda of cases that might deserve greater attention, e.g., rights-related cases. Decentralization would also contribute to decongesting the Supreme Court; specifically, delegating some types of cases, e.g., tax cases, to lower federal courts would advance this goal, and delegating administrative duties back to the judicial council would both empower this internal organ of the judiciary and free up justices from the burden of these responsibilities. Indeed, the court could look to some of the council models within Mexico's own thirty-two sub-national units to find a different design that might be more productive (see Ingram 2012). *Ex parte* hearings should also be prohibited, and the selection of chief justice should be done by simple rotation rather than by campaign and election. Finally, at least private debate among the justices over a draft opinion should precede any public debate, helping to structure that debate so that it is both easier for audiences to follow and easier to translate into a written opinion. Much of the ambiguity seems tied to unclear rules on the timing and method for assigning and writing opinions, so perhaps these internal rules could also be adjusted.

III.IV Impact

As noted in subsection III.III, Pou Giménez's (Chapter 5) contribution is centrally concerned with the divergence between justices' positions at public debate and jurisprudential positions documented in the final, official, written decision that appears unceremoniously weeks or months after the debate. This divergence or gap between public debate and final opinion yields what she calls "fuzziness". The fact that major rulings lack real solidity or substance means this fuzziness translates into legal uncertainty.

This uncertainty, in turn, has unsettling implications for the quality of democracy in Mexico. Pou Giménez is primarily concerned about the legitimacy of the Supreme Court as consolidation of democracy continues, and in the weakened potential for the court to enhance the quality of democracy. For instance, in the event that a debate over the counter-majoritarian nature of judicial review arises, a clear, strong, and consistent court helps democracy, but also helps immunize the court against challenges to its legitimacy. If this fuzziness or ambiguity continues, it not only hinders democratic debate, but also fails to immunize the court against future challenges regarding its legitimacy. Situating herself solidly in favor of the legitimacy of judicial review, Pou Giménez summarizes the rationales for judicial review, noting how the institution affords: (1) time and insulation for judges to construct durable and coherent intellectual doctrines; (2) well-trained and well-situated legal professionals to evaluate political choices against the demands of constitutional principles; (3) individuals particularly suited to explore the requirements of public reason using terms that transcend the requirements of the specific parties to a case and that can be defended under more universal principles; and (4) reinforcement of and a more inclusive public deliberation. Further, in Latin America, judicial intervention may be necessary to shake co-opted legislatures out of inaction, correct unfair legislative over- or under-indulgences, force topics onto the political agenda, and transform pre-existing and widely consequential social meanings (Chapter 2). However, if the judiciary has no consistent, institutional voice, then it cannot contribute to monitoring, improving, and oxygenating democratic society in any of these ways. Even in the case that a ruling is issued, enforcement and future reliance on any kind of jurisprudential compass are rendered all but impossible.

Pou Giménez's argument offers a disturbing counterpoint to the systematic evolution of institutional power or patterns of decision-making identified by Pozas-Loyo and Ríos-Figueroa (Chapter 1), or by Castagnola and López Noriega (Chapters 3 and 4). Her points are brought dramatically to life in the examples of the prominent decisions regarding abortion (2008) and military jurisdiction (2012). Upon closer inspection, the abortion ruling, which was heralded domestically and internationally for its progressiveness, lacks any real substance. It would be very difficult to tease a core jurisprudential position from a close reading of all the final, official documents of the decision. Add to this the uncertainties inherent in the Radilla case, for which an opinion was not even being drafted at the time of writing (see above), and a disquieting picture emerges of the Supreme Court's decision-making process and the negative impact that it may have on the democratic practice in Mexico.

III.V Overlap across areas of inquiry

Empowerment, activation, decision-making, and impact are discrete and analytically distinct areas of inquiry, but they are not isolated from each other. As the court becomes more powerful and accessible via different mechanisms of review, it becomes a more appealing forum for resolving conflicts, and thus parties may be moved to bring more cases to its attention. Specifically with regards to social movements and rights-based litigation, the court's increasing power may trigger civil society and civic organizations to file rights-related litigation. For instance, as Castagnola and López Noriega note in Chapter 3, only fifty-five CCs were filed in the seventy-seven years between 1917 and 1994, i.e., fewer than one per year. However, from 2000–2011, after the 1994/1995 reforms and the 2000 PRI-to-PAN transition, more than 600 CCs were filed, i.e., a rate of more than fifty per year! While the political opening following the 2000 transition surely played a role in motivating new legal challenges, the expanded standing and legal effects of CCs were also consequential.

Further, as the decision-making of the courts reflects a more rights-protective orientation, as the court adopts a more consistent role as constitutional interpreter (Chapter 1), or as the court alters its internal rules so that its decisions have greater clarity, certainty, and legitimacy (Chapter 5), then rights-oriented organizations may also find the court a more attractive forum in which to seeks redress for any grievances, and may also be able to draw upon the less ambiguous jurisprudential positions articulated in decisions to frame new arguments and cases. With regard to the history of *amparo*, Chapters 2 and 4 suggest that economic elites have long found the *amparo* mechanism—and the Supreme Court itself—a fruitful avenue via which to seek redress on tax issues. In their own way, these economic elites constitute a segment of civil society, perhaps more closely associated with the market but not necessarily, so the *amparo* reform of 2011 and the expansion of mechanisms by which a broader range of rights claims can reach the Supreme Court promises to generate a new agenda of cases and shape decision-making patterns well into the future. Perhaps most dramatically, if the court reorganizes the jurisdiction of federal courts so that the it can delegate more tax cases to lower federal courts and therefore be able itself to hear a broader range of rights cases, then more rights cases may be filed.

Just as empowerment and decision-making can affect activation, activation can also influence decision-making. As rights-based movements gain both in numbers and in strength, their claims for rights protection should both (a) be a push to the court to reorganize the jurisdictions or dockets of federal courts; and (b) open a political space for the Supreme Court to decide cases in a rights-protective manner. That is, just as the executive and legislative branches can either shrink or expand the political space in which the court can maneuver; social movements and public opinion more generally can also alter the court's room to maneuver. In sum, there is a clear potential for positive synergies and feedback loops between judicial empowerment, activation, decision-making, and impact.

IV Lessons learned and future agenda

What lessons regarding the role of the Supreme Court in the consolidation of democracy in Mexico can be distilled from the foregoing discussion? How do the answers to these questions help chart an agenda for future research?

First, it bears emphasizing that normative commitments inhere in substantive concepts of "deep" and "consolidated" democracy. These commitments include an acceptance of the legitimacy of judicial intervention to examine the constitutionality of state action, and the adoption of a progressive, rights-protectiveness stance that supports a fuller set of social, economic, and cultural rights, and the vision of a more inclusive, egalitarian society. To the extent that readers advocate the exclusion of these values in a concept of democratic consolidation, they are encouraged to do so explicitly in the same manner that adopting this definition explicitly includes them. That is, we should be clarifying why and how legal institutions *ought* to be empowered, why and how these institutions ought to be activated, why and how different forms of judicial review ought to exist and why and how judging ought to be political, and why and how decisions ought to have certain broader social impact. Following early exhortations by Murphy and Tannenhaus (1972) to continue to examine the legitimacy of judicial review, and of Shapiro (1972, 1993) to integrate normative legal theory, political theory, and empirical legal studies, we ought not to isolate political and legal theory from empirical studies in law and politics. If the goal is not just competitive democracy, but also to more closely approximate more egalitarian, inclusive, and participatory societies, then the normative arguments in that direction ought to be more patently connected to the empirical studies of the extent to which institutions help us achieve that goal.

Second, the work in this volume demonstrates that the Supreme Court is active in its own empowerment and, conversely, its own *dis*empowerment. Specifically, the court has expanded its power while narrowing military jurisdiction, but it has also diluted that power by undermining the certainty and clarity of its decisions. Notably, it could empower itself further by adopting practices that endowed its decisions with greater clarity, following the reforms recommended by Pou Giménez. Further, it could empower itself still more by reorganizing jurisdictional rules to hear fewer tax cases, delegating them to other federal courts, and thereby positioning itself to hear cases related to a broader set of rights. Indeed, by pursuing a more rights-protective role and generating less ambiguous decisions, the court could become substantially more powerful and legitimate in the eyes of broader segments of Mexican society, simultaneously contributing to oxygenating public discussions about key issues affecting its citizens.

Third, regarding mobilization, the Supreme Court cannot decide cases unless it has cases to decide, and in many respects, while it could alter the composition of its docket to some extent, it needs litigants to bring cases in order to decide those cases. Echoing similar calls by Pou Giménez (Chapter 5) and Salazar Ugarte (Chapter 2), Castagnola and López Noriega argue (Chapters 3 and 4) that the CNDH should bring more rights cases. In this spirit, systematic research that explains why some types of cases are successful in reaching the court while others are not has much to offer. Recalling the normative commitments above, research that straddles moral theory and legal mobilization could also explore why it is desirable for broader segments of the population to be able to reach the court. These are issues that are often assumed or taken for granted, but deserve systematic attention.

Regarding the prospects for associational life and mobilization more generally, research has found that high crime rates, especially persistently high insecurity, undermines civil society by eroding the bases of public trust and confidence. People alter their schedules to stay at home more often, even skipping work or school, and they are less willing to join civic groups or other cause movements. Over time, substantial missed work or school curtails earnings and educational attainment, further eroding the foundations of informed, critically minded civic engagement (Prillaman 2003). For these reasons, the current security crisis in Mexico undermines the prospects for associational life and legal mobilization. Thus, increasing public safety should be a policy priority not only to reduce the direct costs to crime victims, but also to reduce the indirect costs to society over the longer term. If ordinary citizens are going to have sufficient trust in public institutions and confidence to be active in public life, including litigation and perhaps especially in strategic litigation, crime rates must be brought under control. Still, the court can take steps toward shaping public debates about the balance between liberty and security in modern democracies, and the balance between protecting rights and public safety.

Decision-making studies of the Supreme Court are increasingly sophisticated, as evidenced by the combination of perspectives offered in this volume, which include both quantitative and qualitative assessments of the multiple legal and extra-legal, internal and external factors shaping the court's output. Building on existing work (e.g., Sanchez et al. 2011; Staton 2010), Castagnola and López Noriega contribute original data and sophisticated analysis that should be exciting to anyone interested in the Mexican high court. Further, their original data sets provide the foundation for years of additional research. Future directions for this research agenda include more systematic analysis of pre-2000 data alongside post-2000 data. Also, Chapters 3 and 4 examine only merits decisions, excluding procedural decisions and other judicial behavior on the bench. This raises questions about how best to examine the output of courts. Finally, returning to Pou Giménez's emphasis on the internal dynamics of the Supreme Court, how do the incentives facing justices change as the number of votes required for different legal effects changes? For instance, in an AI, a decision has *erga omnes* effects if there are eight votes, but the case is dismissed if there are seven or fewer. If a judge knows there are not enough votes to achieve general effects, what are the incentives to cast a vote to invalidate in order to appear supportive of a particular party or issue without risking any real consequences in terms of policy change?

From a qualitative perspective, Pou Giménez's legal background and experience as an institutional insider yield unique and fresh insights that are just as exciting for students of law and politics as they might be for legal practitioners. Research that continues to disaggregate the different legal and non-legal determinants of judicial decisions, and especially to consider how these factors interact with each other, will be a welcome addition to the literature.

Finally, as in most other countries, very little is known about the Supreme-Court's broader social impact. Pou Giménez's evaluation of the uncertainty or "fuzziness" of the court's decisions offers a compelling, if disturbing, assessment of this impact. Studies that advance along these lines, especially studies that systematically assess the impact, consequence, enforcement of, compliance with, or reliance upon decisions will have much to offer.

In sum, the research in this volume offers an extraordinary contribution to our understanding of the role of the Supreme Court in Mexico's democratic consolidation. Across several areas of inquiry—empowerment, activation, decision-making, and impact—the volume provides a rich and sophisticated analysis of the Supreme Court in Mexican politics. The end result yields a detailed portrait of the present and establishes a valuable foundation for future evaluations of the role of the judiciary and the justice sector more broadly in the country's ongoing consolidation of democracy.

Notes

1 For a parallel debate between procedural and substantive versions of the rule of law, see Kleinfeld (2006) and Tamanaha (2004).
2 This categorization does not exclude from "public law" actors other than judges, or institutions other than courts. Indeed, I would generally advocate a much broader definition of public law and even blur the boundaries between public and private, following Shapiro (1972, 1993). However, given the volume's focus on the Mexican Supreme Court, I refer primarily to judges and courts, and mainly in the context of a national peak court.
3 Electoral laws could not be challenged via the AI mechanism until a 1996 reform, which also made the Federal Electoral Tribunal part of the judicial apparatus (see Rios-Figueroa 2007: 38).

References

Becker, Theodore L. (1966) "A Survey Study of Hawaiian Judges: The Effect on Decisions of Judicial Role Variations." *American Political Science Review* (Sept.): 677–680.

Brinks, Daniel (2005) "Judicial Reform and Independence in Brazil and Argentina: The Beginning of a New Millennium?" *Texas International Law Journal* 40(3): 595–622.

Coppedge, Michael and John Gerring, with David Altman, Michael Bernhard, Steven Fish, Allen Hicken, Matthew Kroenig, Staffan I. Lindberg, Kelly McMann, Pamela Paxton, Holli A. Semetko, Svend-Erik Skaaning, Jeffrey Staton, and Jan Teorell (2011) "Conceptualizing and Measuring Democracy: A New Approach." *Perspectives on Politics* 9(2): 247–267.

Crowe, Justin (2012) *Building the Judiciary: Law, Courts, and the Politics of Institutional Development.* Princeton, NJ: Princeton University Press.

Epp, Charles (1998) *Rights Revolutions: Lawyers, Activists, and Supreme Courts in Comparative Perspective.* Chicago, IL: University of Chicago Press.

Epstein, Lee (1985) *Conservatives in Court.* Knoxville, TN: University of Tennessee Press.

Epstein, Lee and Jack Knight (1998) *The Choices Justices Make.* Washington, DC: CQ Press.

Finkel, Jodi (2005) "Judicial Reform as Insurance Policy: Mexico in the 1990s." *Latin American Politics & Society* 46(4): 87–113.

Finkel, Jodi (2008) *Judicial Reform as Political Insurance.* South Bend, IN: University of Notre Dame Press.

Flango, Victor Eugene, Lettie McSpadden Wenner and Manfred W. Wenner (1975) "The Concept of Judicial Role: A Methodological Note." *American Journal of Political Science* 19(2): 277–289.

Garoupa, Nuno, and Tom Ginsburg (2009) "Guarding the Guardians: Judicial Councils and Judicial Independence." *American Journal of Comparative Law* 57: 103–134.

Gibson, James L. (1977) "Discriminant Functions, Role Orientations and Judicial Behavior: Theoretical and Methodological Linkages." *Journal of Politics* 39(4): 984–1007.

Gibson, James L. (1978) "Judges' Role Orientations, Attitudes, and Decisions: An Interactive Model." *American Political Science Review* 72(3): 911–924.

Ginsburg, Tom (2003) *Judicial Review in New Democracies.* Cambridge: Cambridge University Press.

Helmke, Gretchen (2005) *Courts under Constraints.* Cambridge: Cambridge University Press.

Helmke, Gretchen and Julio Ríos-Figueroa (eds) (2011) *Courts in Latin America.* Cambridge: Cambridge University Press.

Hilbink, Lisa (2012) "The Origins of Positive Independence." *World Politics* 64(4): 587–621.

Howard, J. Woodford Jr (1977) "Role Perceptions and Behavior in Three U.S. Courts of Appeals." *Journal of Politics* 39(4): 916–938.

Ingram, Matthew C. (2012) "Crafting Courts in New Democracies: Ideology and Judicial Council Reforms in Three Mexican States." *Comparative Politics* 44(4): 439–458.

Ingram, Matthew C. (2013) "Elections, Ideology, or Opposition? Assessing Competing Explanations of Judicial Spending in the Mexican States." *Journal of Law, Economics, and Organization* 29(1): 178–209.

Kapiszewski, Diana (2011) "Tactical Balancing: High Court Decision Making on Politically Crucial Cases." *Law & Society Review* 45(2): 471–506.

Kapiszewski, Diana (2012) *High Courts and Economic Governance in Argentina and Brazil.* New York, NY: Cambridge University Press.

Kapiszewski, Diana, and Matthew T. Taylor (2012) "Compliance: Conceptualizing, Measuring, and Explaining Adherence to Judicial Rulings." *Law & Social Inquiry* 38(4): 803–835.

Kleinfeld, Rachel (2006) "Competing Definitions of the Rule of Law." In Thomas Carothers (ed.) *Promoting the Rule of Law Abroad: In Search of Knowledge.* Washington, DC: Carnegie Endowment of International Peace, p. 31.

Landes, William M., and Richard A. Posner (1975) "The Independent Judiciary in an Interest-Group Perspective." *Journal of Law and Economics* 18: 875–901.

McAdam, Doug, John D. McCarthy, and Mayer N. Zald (1996) "Introduction: Opportunities, Mobilizing Structures, and Framing Processes – Towards A Synthetic, Comparative Perspective on Social Movements." In Doug McAdam, John D. McCarthy, and Mayer N. Zald (eds) *Comparative Perspectives on Social Movements.* Cambridge: Cambridge University Press, pp. 1–20.

Mizrahi, Yemile (2003) *From Martyrdom to Power: The Partido Accion Nacional in Mexico.* South Bend, IN: University of Notre Dame Press.

Munck, Gerardo, and Jay Verkuilen (2002) "Conceptualizing and Measuring Democracy." *Comparative Political Studies* 35(1): 5–34.

Murphy, Walter, and Joseph Tannenhaus (1972) *The Study of Public Law.* New York: Random House.

Murphy, Walter, C. Herman Pritchett, Lee Epstein, and Jack Knight (2006) *Courts, Judges, and Politics*, 6th edn. New York: McGraw Hill.

Nunes, Rodrigo (2010) "Politics without Insurance." *Comparative Politics* 42(3): 313–331.

Pozas-Loyo, Andrea and Julio Ríos-Figueroa (2011) "The Politics of Amendment Processes: Supreme Court Influence in the Design of Judicial Councils." *Texas Law Review* 89: 1807–1833.

Prillaman, William C. (2003) "Crime, Democracy, and Development in Latin America." Policy Papers on the Americas Volume XIV, Study 6. Washington, DC: Center for Strategic and International Studies (CSIS).

Ríos-Figueroa, Julio (2007) "Fragmentation of Power and the Emergence of an Effective Judiciary in Mexico, 1994–2002." *Latin American Politics & Society* 49(1): 31–57.

Rosenberg, Gerald N. (2008 [1991]) *The Hollow Hope: Can Courts Bring about Social Change?* 2nd edn. Chicago, IL: University of Chicago Press.

Sanchez, Beatriz, Beatriz Magaloni, and Eric Magar (2011) "Legalist versus Interpretivist: The Supreme Court and Democratic Transition in Mexico." In Gretchen Helmke and Julio Ríos-Figueroa (eds) *Courts in Latin America.* Cambridge: Cambridge University Press, pp. 187–218.

Scheb, John M., Thomas D. Ungs, and Allison L. Hayes (1989) "Judicial Role Orientations, Attitudes, and Decision Making: A Research Note." *Western Political Quarterly* 42(3): 427–435.

Segal, Jeffrey, and Harold Spaeth (2002) *Supreme Court and the Attitudinal Model Revisited*. Cambridge: Cambridge University Press.

Shapiro, Martin (1972) "From Public Law to Public Policy, or the 'Public' in 'Public Law'" *Political Science and Politics* 5(4): 410–418.

Shapiro, Martin (1993) "Public Law and Judicial Politics." In Ada Finifter (ed.) *Political Science: The State of the Discipline II*. Washington, DC: American Political Science Association.

Shirk, David A (2005) *Mexico's New Politics: The PAN and Democratic Change*. Boulder, CO: Lynne Rienner.

Staton, Jeffrey K (2010) *Judicial Power and Strategic Communication in Mexico*. Cambridge: Cambridge University Press.

Tamanaha, Brian (2004) *On the Rule of Law: History, Politics, Theory*. Cambridge: Cambridge University Press.

Tate, C. Neal and Torbjorn Vallinder (eds) (1995) *The Global Expansion of Judicial Power*. New York: New York University Press.

Teles, Steven (2008) *The Rise of the Conservative Legal Movement*. Princeton, NJ: Princeton University Press.

Ungs, Thomas D. and Larry R. Baas (1972) "Judicial Role Perceptions: A Q-Technique Study of Ohio Judges." *Law & Society Review* 6: 343–366.

Whittington, Keith (2007) *Political Foundations of Judicial Supremacy*. Princeton, NJ: Princeton University Press.

Woods, Patricia (2008) *Judicial Power and National Politics: Courts and Gender in the Religious-Secular Conflict in Israel*. Albany, NY: State University of New York.

INDEX